Austrian Economics: Tensions and New Directions

Recent Economic Thought Series

Editor:
Warren J. Samuels
Michigan State University
East Lansing, Michigan, U.S.A.

Other books in the series:

Austrian Economics: Tensions and New Directions

Edited by
Bruce J. Caldwell
Stephan Boehm

Kluwer Academic Publishers
Boston/Dordrecht/London

Distributors for North America:
Kluwer Academic Publishers
101 Philip Drive
Assinippi Park
Norwell, Massachusetts 02061 USA

Distributors for all other countries:
Kluwer Academic Publishers Group
Distribution Centre
Post Office Box 322
3300 AH Dordrecht, THE NETHERLANDS

Library of Congress Cataloging-in-Publication Data
Austrian economics: tensions and new directions/edited by Bruce J.
  Caldwell and Stephan Boehm.
      p.   cm. — (Recent economic thought series)
      Includes bibliographical references and index.
      ISBN 0-7923-9262-0
      1. Austrian school of economists. I. Caldwell, Bruce J.
  II. Boehm, Stephan. III. Series.
  HB98.A975 1992
  330.15'7—dc20   92-22611
                                                              CIP

Printed on acid-free paper.

Printed in the United States of America

In memoriam
LML

Contents

Contributing Authors

Mark Blaug
Department of Economics
University of Exeter
Amory Building
Rennes Drive
Exeter, Devon EX4 4RJ
UNITED KINGDOM

Stephan Boehm
Faculty of Social and
    Economic Studies
Institute of Economics
Karl-Franzens University of Graz
A-8010 Graz
AUSTRIA

Bruce J. Caldwell
Department of Economics
Joseph M. Bryan School of
    Business and Economics
462 Bryan Building
University of North Carolina at
    Greensboro
Greensboro, NC 27412–5001
USA

Peter E. Earl
Department of Economics
    and Marketing
P.O. Box 84
Lincoln University
Canterbury 8152
NEW ZEALAND

John Foster
Department of Economics
University of Queensland
Brisbane, Queensland 4067
AUSTRALIA

Alan P. Hamlin
Department of Economics
University of Southampton
Southampton SO9 5NH
UNITED KINGDOM

Geoffrey M. Hodgson
The Judge Institute of
    Management Studies
University of Cambridge
Mill Lane
Cambridge CB2 1RX
UNITED KINGDOM

Israel M. Kirzner
Department of Economics
New York University
269 Mercer St.
New York, NY 10003
USA

Richard N. Langlois
Department of Economics
The University of Connecticut
Storrs, CT 06269-1063
USA

Brian J. Loasby
Department of Economics
University of Stirling
Stirling FK9 4LA, Scotland
UNITED KINGDOM

Uskali Mäki
World Institute for Development
    Economics Research
The United Nations University
Annankatu 42 C
SF-00100 Helsinki 10
FINLAND

Martin Ricketts
School of Accounting, Business
    and Economics
University of Buckingham
Hunter Street
Buckingham MK18 1EG
UNITED KINGDOM

Mario J. Rizzo
Department of Economics
New York University
269 Mercer St.
New York, NY 10003
U.S.A.

Jeremy Shearmur
Department of Political Science
Australian National University
P.O. Box 4
Canberra, ACT 2601
AUSTRALIA

Robert Sugden
School of Economic and
    Social Studies
University of East Anglia
Norwich NR4 7TJ
UNITED KINGDOM

Christopher Torr
Department of Economics
University of South Africa
P.O. Box 392
Pretoria 0001
SOUTH AFRICA

Lawrence H. White
Department of Economics
University of Georgia
Athens, GA 30602
U.S.A.

Ulrich Witt
Faculty of Economics
University of Freiburg
Europaplatz 1
W-7800 Freiburg
GERMANY

Preface

When we first invited the group of distinguished scholars represented here to contribute to a new volume on Austrian economics, four themes were stressed: tensions, new directions, selectivity, and criticism. In this brief introduction we will explain why those themes were emphasized and thereby shed light on our intentions and aspirations for the volume.

The subtitle "Tensions and New Directions" indicates clearly the intent of the volume desired. If we take the 1871 publication of Carl Menger's *Principles of Economics* (*Grundsätze der Volkswirthschaftslehre*) as marking its birth, the Austrian tradition is now well over one hundred years old. The origins of the so-called "Austrian Revival" are more difficult to pinpoint precisely, but many would accept two decades as a reasonable estimate of its lifespan. In any case, since the mid-1970s several collections of articles written by Austrians have been published. The intent of these collections appeared to be to educate, persuade, and inspire various audiences. Uninformed readers needed to be told about the specifics of the Austrian position, to be shown how it differed from and improved upon its rivals. The initiated needed to be reassured that their commitment to a novel program was justified. As such, much of the recent Austrian literature has consisted either of exegetical accounts of the views of past figures, or of critical assessments of the positions of alternative research programs in economics from an Austrian perspective.

It seemed to us that it was time to examine the Austrian contribution in a different light. Instead of focusing on the past, we invited participants to consider what the future might hold for the Austrian tradition. What areas, in particular, seem particularly promising for new research? In a like manner, instead of criticizing other positions from the standpoint of Austrian analysis, we asked contributors to turn a critical eye on the

Austrian program itself. Where are its weak points—be they internal inconsistencies, restrictions on the generality or applicability of the analysis, or whatever—and how important are they in an overall assessment of the Austrian position? It is altogether fitting that such questions be asked. Austrians have long emphasized the importance of the future for decision making in the present. It struck us that decisions about the direction that research should take do not constitute exceptions to this rule. And although it is appropriate to allow a certain amount of time to pass before a revived program is subjected to appraisal, to allow too much time to pass is no compliment.

With "tensions and new directions" providing the general theme of the volume, the problem of selecting topics to be considered in individual chapters was at least partially solved. Unfortunately, the general theme was too broad to reduce the field substantially. For example, we agreed that one chapter should focus on methodology. But having made that decision we were immediately confronted by another, since at least three different candidates came to mind: we could investigate the revival of the Misesian approach as trumpeted in recent work by Hans-Hermann Hoppe; we could examine the "interpretive turn" towards hermeneutics that has been defended by Don Lavoie and others at George Mason University; or we could invite Uskali Mäki to expand on his realist account of Austrian theory.

No classroom lecture on opportunity cost could make the point more clearly: we made choices, and we are painfully aware of the opportunities that were forgone. We take some solace in recognizing, though, that not every topic can be addressed in one volume. There is plenty of room for additional collections; ours is (we hope) but a first step.

Some final words on the importance of critical appraisal and its role within this volume. Our invitation to the contributors contained the following invocation: "The editors share the conviction that *criticism* is an essential element in the advance of knowledge. Discussants will be urged to adhere to this general principle." Our directive reflects what might be termed a broadly Popperian, or even an Austrian, approach. We embrace the view that the dynamics of rivalrous competition in the marketplace of ideas helps to eliminate shoddy products and to encourage the spread of sound ones. We believe that a competitive environment provides incentives for both innovation and discovery in the realm of ideas. Finally, we perceive well-informed criticism to be the highest form of praise, for it means that one has taken seriously the ideas that are under scrutiny. Thus we offer no apologies for, and indeed insist on the virtues of, a critical approach to the study of the Austrian tradition.

Of course, the usual procedure is to proclaim loudly the universal benefits of competition while working hard to eliminate it from one's own market. In a conscious effort to overcome this nearly instinctual response, we have asked two prominent Austrian scholars to provide their own appraisals of the contents of the volume in "Afterwords," and invited them to include in their discussions an assessment of our specific approach.

One never knows how a collection of this sort will turn out when it is begun. Suffice it to say in closing that we feel that the participants have executed their charge admirably, and that as such this is a volume with which we are both well pleased.

Austrian Economics: Tensions and New Directions

1 AUSTRIAN ECONOMICS BETWEEN THE WARS: SOME HISTORIOGRAPHICAL PROBLEMS

Stephan Boehm

The initial premise informing this chapter is deliberately cautious. The identity of an enterprise labeled "Austrian economics" during the interwar years cannot be simply considered *a given*, somehow prior to further considerations: it needs to be established by persuasive arguments.

The virtue in opting for such a defensive strategy may be seen to derive from the circumstance that any failure to land the Austrian fish in a prefabricated net may serve a valuable purpose, too. But in rehearsing my doubts as to the prospects of succeeding in uncovering the essential homogeneity of Austrian economic thought in the 1920s and 1930s, the "other" conclusion should not be foregone either — namely, that it would be well-nigh impossible to achieve. All I am arguing at this stage is that in more than one sense we may have to start from scratch. Simply to posit the existence of a well-defined, coherent set of Austrian ideas will not do; the onus of proof decidedly rests with those who raise such claims.

The basic thesis I am putting forward is a fairly simple one: interwar Austrian economic thought is a venture of many dimensions that does not easily lend itself to a reduction to some invariable standard. The label "Austrian economics" is merely a shorthand expression for what is, in fact, an ill-defined body of ideas with many facets. Hence, I do not find it especially helpful at best, and misleading at worst, to talk about *an* Austrian doctrine or research program; rather, it would seem to be more to the point to speak, perhaps, of an (open) set of distinct Austrian themes.

1

Some Background to this Discussion

A mere quarter-century ago, an inquiry such as the present one would hardly have raised an eyebrow; it would most likely have been dismissed as another abortive episode in a well-rehearsed set-piece entitled "The History of Neoclassical Economics." But by the late 1960s and early 1970s, as is well known, a widespread feeling of discontent with the drift of mainstream economics had begun to assert itself, and a general sense that all was not well with the direction in which the discipline was heading had started to ripple through the front ranks of the profession. To be sure, the "cracks in the neoclassical mirror" (apologies to Edward J. Nell) had been detected from a variety of viewpoints. But from the perspective adopted in the following remarks, one important consequence of this exercise in collective soul-searching has been (as we may now say with hindsight) that it paved the way for a greater awareness of, and an increased readiness to accept, the existence of other traditions, or tendencies, in economic thought (which may have been moribund for decades) and the historical reconstructions that it entailed.

With respect to Menger scholarship, in particular, two events taking place in 1971 deserve credit for having rekindled curiosity for the ideas of the "founder" of the Austrian school: the conference held in the University of Vienna commemorating the centenary of the publication of the *Grundsätze* (Hicks and Weber, 1973), and the Bellagio conference on the Marginal Revolution (Black, Coats, and Goodwin, 1973). As a result of these gatherings, the Holy Trinity of Jevons, Menger, and Walras (enshrined in textbook and other treatments of the development of economic thought in the late nineteenth century), which had been taken for granted to such an extent that the problems lurking behind such a presupposition could not even be perceived, came to be disbanded, and the Austrian economist gloriously emerged as "the odd man out" (Blaug, 1985, 306). That judgment, originally enunciated in its strong version by Erich Streissler (1973), has won numerous adherents over the years — not least owing to William Jaffé's oft-cited piece (Jaffé, 1976).[1] The published proceedings of the Menger conference held at Duke University have only reinforced the notion that Austrian economic thought at the turn of the century was a differentiated product (see Caldwell, 1990).

The Modern Austrian Revival

It is knowledge of hindsight that about the time of the growing concern with Menger's work, a modern Austrian revival drawing its inspiration mainly from Mises and Hayek (in that order) has taken off. For many observers the renaissance of Austrian economics in the United States, and its challenge to mainstream economics, must have appeared as an historical puzzle calling for an explanation in terms of the genealogy of the challengers.[2] It is submitted here that it is precisely because of the recent fillip to Austrian economic thought that the vicissitudes besetting Austrian economics (and its representatives) between the wars assume an added dimension.

Ideally, the winning trophy in any endeavor to demonstrate a smooth historical transition from Menger to present-day American Austrians would surely have to be bestowed on a coherent account which succeeds in capturing the interwar episode as the missing link between the early Austrians and their contemporary exponents. But the route may not be quite as straightforward as it appears to be; there are several obstacles that stand in the way. First, the notion of *the* missing link is in itself highly deceptive suggesting as it does an unobstructed highway, whereas, in fact, there are numerous crossroads. Second, there has been a tendency to dismiss everything emanating from Vienna between the wars merely as a stepping-stone toward the main event to be staged elsewhere. In particular, the Austrian achievement has — given Hayek's initial dominating position at the London School of Economics and Political Science — understandably been chronicled and gauged from the vantage point of the Aldwych, in line with the adage that London was merely a suburb of Vienna during the early 1930s.[3] Regarding Vienna exclusively as a breeding ground, or springboard, for future kudos earned elsewhere deflected attention away, however, from her role as an intrinsically vibrant, leading international center of economic learning and research.

Now, it is of course true that in the 1930s Austrian economics, or what was then widely held to be its epitome, suffered from a series of blows it proved rather difficult to recover from. In a way, it was in continuous retreat. It was perceived to have failed several "acid tests," notably in the Hayek-Sraffa exchange, the capital controversies, and the debates with the Keynesians. Among latter-day Austrians, the late Ludwig Lachmann in particular sensed the urgency to grapple with these awkward issues and did not hesitate to concede numerous points to the other side of the fence (Lachmann, 1982, 1983, 1986). But, by and large, it does not seem to be unfair to maintain that concern with these battles long ago does not feature prominently on the Austrian research agenda.

As a somewhat paradoxical result of all this, the interwar period in the history of the Austrian school has somehow been trapped between the Mengerian and the modern Austrian revival. Having said that, I do not in any way wish to call into question the validity of the historical reconstructions which have been offered from a modern Austrian perspective. On the contrary, *as far as they go*, they can only be endorsed. It is proposed, however, that the backward view of reconstructing the history of economic thought, which may be highly useful and is indeed indispensable in many cases, be supplemented with a simple-minded, old-fashioned approach working forward. Since the backward-looking view inevitably encourages the identification of affinities and correspondences, it is prone to be reductive, whereas the forward-looking perspective is indifferent toward incongruities. It is only by combining both approaches that we may hope to attain a reasonably "full" picture of the interwar episode.

Was there an Austrian School During the Interwar Period?

An initial difficulty confronting the historiography of Austrian economics in the period under consideration is the problem to what extent, if at all, Austrian economists thought of themselves as upholding a tradition setting them apart from other neoclassical streams of thought.

As is well known, the teachings of the Austrian school had enjoyed their heyday during the two decades before World War I. Wieser's *Social Economics*, originally published in 1914, represents not only the last compilation forthcoming from the "old" Austrians, but also, with its strong "institutionalist" leanings, a highly personal statement far removed from Menger's concerns with "pure" theory.

We have it on the authority of Ludwig von Mises that by the early 1920s — about the time of Menger's demise — "one no longer distinguished between an Austrian School and other economics. The appellation 'Austrian School' became the name given to an important chapter in the history of economic thought; it was no longer the name of a specific sect with doctrines different from those held by other economists" (Mises, 1969, 41). Mises immediately goes on to concede that even the one apparent exception — the Austrian or Monetary Theory of the Trade Cycle — "is a continuation, enlargement, and generalization of ideas first developed by the British Currency School and of some additions to them made by later economists, among them also the Swede, Knut Wicksell."[4]

Mises's position is shared in several historical accounts of the Austrian school. For example, James Bonar, in his entry on the "Austrian School of Economists" in *Palgrave's Dictionary*, drily observes, "It was stated in reply to enquiries in 1914 that they have practically ceased to exist as a separate School" (Bonar, 1926, 73). That rather cursory remark seems to have prompted the editor, Henry Higgs, to invite Friedrich von Wieser to prepare another article on the same topic. In his concluding considerations, Wieser briefly addresses the strictures leveled by the "younger investigators" against what they took to be "the psychological basis" of the Austrian theory. In an especially murky passage, Wieser defends the "old" theory: "The founders of the school ... never employ principles taken from scientific psychology. The law of satisfaction of wants, which is chiefly in question, they have taken from general economic experience, and the development of their doctrine is purely empirical" (Wieser, 1926, 817). It is noteworthy to observe in this connection that the *Encyclopaedia of the Social Sciences* does not carry a separate entry on the Austrian school, but Frank Knight deals at length with the Austrian theory of value and distribution in his article on "Marginal Utility Economics" (Knight, 1931).

The feelings of the interwar Austrians were succinctly expressed by F. A. Hayek, who, in his entry on the "Viennese School" in the German encyclopedia of the social sciences, maintained that it was indicative of the ultimate success of a school that it ceased to exist after its central tenets had been incorporated into the generally accepted body of thought (Hayek, 1965, 70).[5]

Fritz Machlup, characteristically undaunted, nevertheless furnished a list of "the most typical requirements for a true adherent of the Austrian school," which may be held to be representative of the views of an "interwar Austrian" — namely, the concern with (1) methodological individualism; (2) methodological subjectivism; (3) tastes and preferences; (4) opportunity costs; (5) marginalism; and (6) the time structure of production and consumption (Machlup, 1981, 9). Given the way in which Machlup circumscribes those items, there is nothing specifically Austrian here. Consequently, Israel Kirzner demurred on the grounds that Machlup's list would have to be supplemented by an appreciation of the view of "markets (and competition) as processes of learning and discovery" (Kirzner, 1987, 149).

The emphasis on the discovery aspects of markets to which Kirzner is alluding here gradually materialized in the course and as a result of Hayek's participation in the socialist calculation debate, raging roughly from the mid-1930s to the mid-1940s. For the historiography of modern Austrian economics it assumes a vital meaning for two reasons: (1) far from constituting a "retreat" on the part of the Austrians from the original formulation of the thesis advanced by Mises, it is held to amount to a consistent elaboration of the latter; and (2) it had been the emerging articulation of the Austrian view of the market process during the 1940s (in the works of Hayek and Mises) which prefigured the Austrian revival (Kirzner, 1988, 1990).[6]

What surfaces, then, from the reconsiderations of the Austrian stance

in the controversy over economic calculation under socialism is the conclusion that the Austrian protagonists, or, at any rate, Hayek and Mises,
without having been aware of it at the time, were indeed swimming
outside of the mainstream, as epitomized by the British (Marshallian)
partial equilibrium and the Lausanne general equilibrium traditions.

Interlocking Circles

Any effort to assess the Austrian contribution, however incomprehensive,
should attend to the circumstance that economic research proceeded
decentralized in the sense that it was loosely attached to, or associated
with, some discussion group or circle (see Craver, 1986; Haberler, 1961;
Prendergast, 1986). Leaving aside university affiliations and the Austrian
Institute for Business Cycle Research, there was the group centering on
Mises's *Privatseminar*; the (much) smaller circle gathering around Hans
Mayer; and Karl Menger's Mathematical Colloquium. Furthermore, the
Economic Society served as an important venue for the international
transmission of ideas.

While the role of the Menger Colloquium in the germination of neo-
Walrasian general equilibrium analysis has been documented by Roy
Weintraub (1983) and Lionello Punzo (1989, 1991), considerably less is
known about the activities of the Mises Circle.[7] Apart from the fact that
it existed for a relatively long period, from 1923 to 1934, it is especially
notable for the noneconomists (e.g., Felix Kaufmann, Alfred Schutz, Eric
Voegelin, and Walter Weisskopf) that it numbered among its members,[8]
and the frequent visits from foreign scholars (e.g., Howard Ellis, Hugh
Gaitskell, François Perroux, Alfred Stonier, and Alan Sweezy) that it
attracted. With respect to the topics that figured prominently in the
discussions of the Mises Circle, it's probably easier to say what was *not*
dealt with. Rather surprisingly, the problem of economic calculation
under socialism received scant attention. Apparently, Mises held that he
had contributed the last word on the subject in *Die Gemeinwirtschaft*
(1922). Furthermore, there was hardly any exploration of mathematical
problems in economics although at least two of the regular participants
were highly qualified as mathematicians, viz. Felix Kaufmann and Karl
Schlesinger. According to the available sources, problems in monetary
and capital theory and aspects of the methodology of the social sciences
were the favorite topics of discussion among the members of the
Mises group.

The circle around Hans Mayer included, *inter alios*, Leo Schönfeld-

Illy, Rosenstein-Rodan, and Morgenstern. The two last-mentioned were Mayer's closest collaborators, both in the editorship of the *Zeitschrift für Nationalökonomie*, which began being published in 1929, and in the monumental compilation of the four-volume work *Die Wirtschaftstheorie der Gegenwart* (A Survey of Contemporary Economics, 1927–1932), containing eighty-one survey articles on virtually all aspects of economic theory and policy — arguably the first truly international cooperative venture of its kind.[9]

The most distinctive work emanating from the Mayer Circle related to the theory of imputation (*Zurechnung*) and the "dynamization" of the theory of subjective value.[10] Although the desire to absorb non-Austrian modes of thinking — such as Edgeworth's, Pareto's, or Wicksteed's (who in turn was under strong influence from Austrian writers) — was pronounced among the economists of the Mayer group, they, nevertheless, strove to preserve a niche for their heritage and to identify a role for a "neo-Viennese school" (see Sweezy, 1934, ch.4). Whether they were successful at it is a moot question.

Since several scholars attended the meetings of more than one group, there is a flow of ideas between the various circles which needs to be explored. Alan Sweezy was arguably the first outside observer to urge an appreciation of "the heterogeneity of opinion" among the interwar groups of economists in Vienna (Sweezy, 1933–1934, 176). In a similar vein, Oskar Morgenstern revealingly observed on the then Lionel Robbins's *Essay on the Nature and Significance of Economic Science*, "This essay ... acquaints the English reader with much of the literature of the Viennese economists, although Professor Robbins represents the Viennese authors in certain important points as *being more of a school with uniform views than they really are*" (emphasis added). Morgenstern goes on to say, "What I have said in this book [*Die Grenzen der Wirtschaftspolitik*] contains so many implicit divergences of opinion between myself and Professor Robbins as to render any further statement of my disagreement with his interesting book unnecessary" (Morgenstern, 1937/1934, 154–155).

Some Distinctive Themes and Individual Contributions

Shackle's The Years of High Theory *as a Foil*

In order to shed further light on the home scene, it would thus seem to be entirely appropriate for historians of economic thought to jettison cherished modes and to lift their sights across the Channel. It may be instructive to use George Shackle's history of the interwar years as a backdrop against which to gauge the Austrian record.[11]

Judging from Shackle's riveting account in *The Years of High Theory* (Shackle, 1967), which considers six major theoretical innovations making their appearance during the years from 1926 to 1939, it seems that Vienna was a quiet backwater hardly noteworthy for theoretical fertility and ingenuity. As the narrative unfolds, Cambridge (U.K.) and Stockholm — and, to a lesser extent, London, Oxford, and Cambridge (Mass.) — emerge as the major venues on the economist's map of the world, with Keynes, Sraffa, Joan Robinson, Myrdal (Shackle's special hero), Hicks, Harrod, Chamberlin, and Leontief serving as the *dramatis personae*. Save for a passing reference to Böhm-Bawerkian capital theory in a chapter dealing with Myrdal's *Monetary Equilibrium*, Shackle does not expatiate on Austrian theories. Moreover, considering that Shackle's is a highly personal account,[12] it is all the more remarkable that he elects not to elaborate on Hayek's role in the 1930s. Indeed, in the one place where Shackle considers Hayek's work at all, he briefly takes issue with the latter's conception of equilibrium (1967, 92) for failing to provide a scheme of how such a state could ever be attained, thus enunciating a criticism that he has advanced on other occasions.[13]

For Shackle, the abyss separating the *old* Economics of Tranquility germane to the Victorian era (with the "old" Austrians figuring among its foremost representatives) from the *new* Economics of Disquietude emerging from the late 1920s onward (with Myrdal and Keynes as its chief protagonists) was "the discarding of the assumption . . . of *universal perfect knowledge*" (Shackle, 1967, 6; emphasis added). On this reading of the history of economic thought, Keynes's 1937 *Quarterly Journal of Economics* article, "The General Theory of Employment," is accorded the status of an apotheosis of the novel strand in economics, and the Austrian contribution to the budding economics of ignorance and uncertainty would appear to be negligible, if not downright counterproductive.

On a somewhat more charitable account it may be objected, however, that delving into the perfect knowledge assumption *was* — in a tradition harking back to Menger — very much in line with Austrian preoccupations during the interwar years. It is, of course, true that such concerns licensed inquiry into a whole range of issues too parochial for Shackle's bold vision. It was Shackle himself, however, who granted that much in his definitive appraisal of Hayek's contribution as an economist: "[T]o have made knowledge . . . the central strand in the economic theoretician's skein of themes, shows Hayek as one of the great innovators. He . . . refers to other pioneers: to Ludwig von Mises, Frank Knight, Maynard Keynes and Gunnar Myrdal. His own achievement is to have brought all such suggestions to a focus and a verbal encapsulation" (Shackle, 1988, 187).

But Hayek, it should at once be added, was by no means alone among Viennese economists in subjecting the perfect knowledge assumption to a critical review; besides Mises, Hayek is indebted and pays tribute to the economists attached to the Mayer Circle, most notably to Morgenstern and Rosenstein-Rodan. That Hayek's concern with the subtle relations between the economics of knowledge and the knowledge of economics forms the centerpiece of his distinctive approach to social theory, and that it was therefore not merely an opportunistic flirtation, has been widely acknowledged. What has, however, not been generally appreciated in the burgeoning commentaries on Hayek's forays into the realm of knowledge is the extent to which he had benefited from vital inputs from his Austrian contemporaries (more on this later).

There is a curious lacuna in Shackle's exposition pointed out by Brian Loasby. Hayek's explanation of widespread unemployment as being engendered by false entrepreneurial conjectures (rather than by entre-preneurial ignorance, as in Keynes), nurtured in turn by an excessive monetary expansion driving the money rate of interest below the natural rate, had the potential for "providing the basis for an economics of uncertainty and disorder. One would very much like to hear Shackle's explanation as to why that basis remained unused" (Loasby, 1989, 11). As Loasby elaborates, Hayek's concept of equilibrium in terms of mutually consistent plans calls for a process of discovery for its attainment. Although Hayek emphatically insists on the need for a notion of the market as an open-ended, continuous discovery procedure, whose outcomes, by defi-nition, can never be predicted in any detail, he does not seriously entertain the possibility that left to its own devices the economy would get stuck, break down, or cumulatively destabilize. Unhampered market processes could be trusted with eventually overcoming the problems posed by dispersed and incomplete knowledge. Thus, Loasby concludes, "certainty is preserved at the system level" (ibid., 12).

What Shackle finds so irritating about Hayek is that in the latter's most austere account, in *Prices and Production* (1931), market forces could always be relied upon, barring monetary disturbances, to tend toward an equilibrium position. In Hayek's model of perfect foresight, things could go wrong but only for monetary reasons. Although the role of expectations is taken into account in later work, notably in *Profits, Interest and Investment* (1939), they are kept at arm's length on Shackle's view. While Hayek is content to focus attention on the gathering of information, Shackle is concerned with the origination of new possibilities. Whereas for Shackle most markets are "inherently restless," Hayek does not consider speculative markets at all (Shackle, 1988, 186).

Two final comments on Shackle's investigation are in order. The first relates to what he deems to be the major innovation in the *General Theory*: Keynes's concept of *liquidity preference*. It certainly comes as a surprise that Shackle fails to mention, in *The Years of High Theory* and elsewhere, Menger's theme of the "saleability," or "marketability," of commodities — a theme which would accord so well with his own concerns and on which Sir John Hicks, who had become something of a Menger convert toward the end of his career, commented: "What Menger had to say on liquidity is deeper than what was said by anyone before Keynes; indeed I think it is deeper than what is in Keynes. ... For Menger had grasped ... that the holding of liquid reserves ... is only one aspect (though no doubt the most important aspect) of a much more general kind of behaviour. *It is a matter of provision against an uncertain future ...*" (Hicks, 1976, 139; emphasis added).[14]

The second comment relates to Shackle's criticism of *marginalism*, by which he means "simply maximalism or minimalism ... in the formal mathematical sense" (Shackle, 1988, 140). It has been the central contention of Erich Streissler's that Menger's distinctive contribution to economics defies incorporation into a marginalist decision model, and that during the reign of Böhm-Bawerk and Wieser in the University of Vienna "much of what was genuinely Menger's tradition got lost" (Streissler, 1973, 164). Recalling Jaffé's often cited, vivid description of Mengerian man as "a bumbling, erring, ill-informed creature, plagued with uncertainty, forever hovering between alluring hopes and haunting fears, and congenitally incapable of making finely calibrated decisions in pursuit of satisfactions" (Jaffé, 1976, 321), one would have no difficulty in recognizing the familiar traits of Shacklean man.

Some Notable Contributions of the Mayer Circle

If one were to succinctly characterize the research agenda of the interwar Austrians, one might summarize it in two phrases: they were "wrestling with time" and "agonizing over equilibrium" (Currie and Steedman, 1989, 1990). Just as the introduction of the "dynamic element" by all the established schools of thought was the overriding theme among new developments during the interwar years, Viennese economists of all persuasions also seized upon and grappled with it. For the reconstruction of modern Austrian economic thought, however, the work emanating from the Mayer Circle assumes an added dimension.

Yet, attaching the label "dynamics" to Austrian analysis is not without pitfalls. Consider the following statement by T. W. Hutchison: "Mayer's insistence on a 'causal-genetic analysis' is, when trimmed of its metaphysics, an insistence on the need for dynamic analysis" (Hutchison, 1953, 327). Such a judgment may give rise to misunderstandings. As Oskar Morgenstern observes in a comparative appraisal of the Anglo-American, the Lausanne, and the Austrian versions of the theory of subjective value, the distinction between "statics" and "dynamics" could most fruitfully be applied to the Lausanne theory. It carried merely "secondary significance" for the Austrian approach, which defied such categories, precisely because it drew its strength from being capable to analyze the transition between equilibrium states *without having to undergo a change in its general form* (see Morgenstern, 1931, 41).

Morgenstern's 1931 survey article was designed to serve as the introductory chapter ("position paper," as one would today presumably call it) to a volume on the state of value theory, edited under the auspices of the *Verein für Sozialpolitik*. This preparatory volume formed the basis of wide-ranging discussions at the Verein's Dresden Meetings in 1932. In the present context, Morgenstern's piece is noteworthy for the following reasons. First, it represents an endorsement of the indispensability of a theory of value to the theory of relative prices, or more precisely, of the purely instrumental nature of a theory of value (see also Mayer, 1932, 225). Second, it is a major statement on the essential *unity* of the theory of subjective value as it had evolved from the 1870s onward, and as such, Morgenstern's account would seem to fit in well with Austrian self-portrayals sketched above. Third, the common conceptual structure notwithstanding, Morgenstern points to disparities in scope, emphasis, and style of presentation between the contending schools of thought. In line with the work produced by the economists of the Mayer group, he is particularly keen to identify the distinctiveness of the Viennese as against the Lausanne approach.

In his assessment, Morgenstern opts for the Austrian version as a benchmark, on the grounds that it was the most elaborate.[15] Moreover, in view of the progress that had been made especially in the 1920s, Morgenstern laments the fact that a great deal of the objections raised against Austrian theory in its 1880 incarnation were no longer justified. To convey something of the flavor of Morgenstern's considerations, I will broach a few selected issues.

One of the themes canvassed by Morgenstern relates to the problem of the interconnectedness of the parts composing the economic system and the method germane to its analysis. More specifically, in what sense, if at all, did the Austrians conceive of the economy as a sytem of mutually dependent price and quantity relationships? While there seems to be widespread agreement that Austrian economists of all generations, *in so far as they had something distinctive to say*, did not adhere to a conception of general equilibrium in the Walrasian sense and the associated efficiency criteria, views differ substantially with respect to the evaluation of this circumstance, and the suggested alternative framework of analysis.

As Morgenstern (1931, 34) indicates, on the issue of partial versus general economic analysis, the Austrians appear to be more on the side of the Anglo-Americans. Referring to Marshall's procedure of deriving individual demand curves from the principle of diminishing marginal utility, he is suprised at how utility considerations are translated into demand without further ado. Morgenstern further notes that for the determination of prices, market-demand curves are drawn up on the condition of given other prices, and in *this* regard the Austrian and Anglo-American traditions were akin to each other. Yet at the same time, Morgenstern contends, the issue of the general interrelatedness of the price system was much more prominent in the Austrian (and even more so in the Lausanne approach) than in the Anglo-American version of the theory. The starting point, Morgenstern goes on to maintain, would be the same, however, for all varieties of the theory: each and every individual has to establish her own equilibrium, but since interindividual actions are mutually dependent, equilibrium for the individual is only possible once the equilibrium for the economy as a whole has been secured by the system of relative prices.

To be sure, these are dark sayings crying out for elucidation and elaboration. First of all, it is rather odd to find Morgenstern bracketing Austrian and Anglo-American thought on the issue of partial equilibrium analysis, considering Hans Mayer's strictures on the use of that method (see, especially, Mayer, 1930).[16] Furthermore, the principle of the equalization of marginal utility per unit spent as a decision rule for the establishment of consumer equilibrium is a characteristic Lausanne device and has no use in the Austrian scheme. As Mayer, in particular, relentlessly insisted, the equimarginal principle does not contribute anything to an explanation of the formation of prices in real markets; it is an adjunct to the Walras-Pareto general equilibrium analysis (see, Mayer, 1932, 170–177). According to Jaffé (1976, 316), Walras's neglect of consumption analysis should be attributed to the fact that he focused his attention exclusively on the market place; Walras invoked marginal utility strictly in the context of his pure theory of the determination of prices under a hypothetical regime of free competition. The theory of needs and problems of individual valuation, which preoccupied Austrian theorists following Carl Menger especially during the interwar period, were thus relegated to the sidelines and treated as preliminary.

If Austrian theory is neither partial equilibrium analysis in the Marshallian nor general equilibrium analysis in the Walrasian sense, what is it? The standard response that it is a theory *sui generis* is merely a common rhetorical manoeuvre to circumvent the thorny issue and let it hang in midair. In view of their importance for the reconstruction of the history of Austrian economic thought, such questions have received surprisingly little detailed treatment. This is surely a prime area for future investigations.

It has justly been noted time and again that Austrian writers eschewed the setting up of a system of simultaneous equations for the mutual determination of all economic variables (Blaug, 1985, 296; Hutchison, 1953, 147−148). It has also been canon for commentators to aver that Austrian writers lacked the mathematical finesse to appreciate such a procedure. George Stigler, for example, ascribes to Böhm-Bawerk the "methodological misconception" of spurning the concept of mutual determination for "the older concept of cause and effect" (Stigler, 1941, 181).

An even more influential judgment stems from J. A. Schumpeter, who attributed the Austrians' failure to ascend the ladder furnished by the marginal utility principle to the level of the general equilibrium system to their "defective technique" and their inability to grasp the meaning of a set of simultaneous equations (Schumpeter, 1954, 918). As more recent research has brought to light, however, even Walras himself did not climb up from the doldrums of marginal utility to the plateau of general equilibrium; rather, the concept of *rareté* (mathematically analogous to the concept of marginal utility as understood by non-Austrians) became available to him only *after* he had succeeded in constructing the mathematical apparatus for dealing with a network of interrelated markets under competitive conditions (see Jaffé, 1976, 313). But Schumpeter's suggestion that "the Jevons-Menger utility theory" be considered "an embryonic theory of general equilibrium" is intriguing and certainly worth pondering (Schumpeter, 1954, 918).

Yet Schumpeter's thesis is inconclusive: it balks at the decisive hurdle. The difference between Walras, on the one hand, and Menger, on the other hand, runs much deeper. The point is not simply that Menger and his followers among the Austrians lacked the necessary mathematical training (which is, of course, true), but rather that they deliberately did not seek to emulate the construction of an economic cosmos of interdependent prices and quantities strung together by a system of simultaneous equations. Jaffé has thrown the contrast between the two men's method of research into high relief as turning on the distinction between *logical* and *generative* causality. While Walras was convinced that he had definitively proved that *rareté* was *the* cause of value,[17] with exact proportionality between *raretés* and prices being considered the epitome of causality, Menger insisted — in line with his "analytic-compositive method"[18] — that the complexity of market phenomena be traced back to their most elementary constituents (see Jaffé, 1976, 321–322).

Therefore, when Austrian writers of the interwar period, especially those attached to the Mayer Circle, disavowed any commitment to what is generally known as "Gossen's second law" and to the use of indifference curves, this was no empty gesture. It portended a propensity to cling to the cornerstone of the Austrian edifice, *individual valuation* (*Wertung* or *Wertschätzung*),[19] the attribution of subjective value as the epitome of the economic process. There is hardly anything imaginable that would be more alien to the spirit of the Austrian enterprise than to turn the individual actor into a pillar of salt. By instinct and inclination, Austrian theorists strove after the incorporation of what is sometimes euphemistically referred to as "the non-negligible agent," a notion current in treatments of imperfect competition in a general equilibrium context.

Accordingly, such diverse protagonists of the Austrian tradition as Hans Mayer and Ludwig M. Lachmann were fond of quoting Pareto's discussion of indifference curves in order to underscore what Austrian theory is *not*: "The individual can disappear, provided he leaves us this photograph of his tastes" (Pareto, 1972/1906, 120). Commenting on the same passage, Nicholas Georgescu-Roegen (as unsuspicious, as far as tribal affiliations are concerned, an economist as one could wish for) has likewise observed that "for a science of man to exclude altogether man from the picture is a patent incongruity. Nevertheless, standard economics takes special pride in operating with a man-less picture ... The logic is perfect: man is not an economic agent simply because there is no economic process. There is only a jigsaw puzzle of fitting given means to given ends, which requires a computer not an agent" (Georgescu-Roegen, 1971, 343).

More recent developments in neo-Walrasian general equilibrium analysis have certainly borne out earlier Austrian suspicions that the theory is at its pinnacle when the individual agent is of measure zero. That such a claim sits somewhat oddly with a discipline which in more relaxed settings constantly extols the virtues of "freedom of choice" may be put down, though, as just another instance of the lower ranks of the profession not being able to understand what the leading minds are saying.

In view of these well-worn misgivings over the Lausanne theory it would, however, be erroneous to conclude that the Austrian writers did not at all attend to the general nexus of market phenomena. It is merely to assert that they pursued a type of analysis that even by then prevailing standards of rigor was not "embryonic" of Walrasian general equilibrium theorizing: they followed an altogether different trail. What I shall presently sketch are not, however, the accomplishments of the Austrian line of inquiry, but rather the fond hopes nourished for it.

The problem of the universal mutual dependence of prices and quantities, while not remotely as strikingly displayed as in Walras's system, took on a varying significance in Austrian writings, all grappled with it in one way or another. In a sense, the issue posed itself perhaps most starkly in Carl Menger's case. In the absence of a central authority supervising, mediating and unifying individual trades,[20] Menger sensed the need for a general nexus transcending the set of isolated bargains, thus preventing the economy from disintegrating. In his quest for devices facilitating the "interrelatedness," or "connectedness" (Abele, 1978, 206), of the series of bilateral trades Menger assigned particular importance to institutions,[21] such as money, for providing a link between traders who do not yet know of each other. It is not for nothing, Abele justly holds (208), that Menger, having dwelt on the considerations governing individual decision making, elected to bring his *Principles* to a close with a chapter on the factors accounting for the differing degrees of "marketability" (liquidity) of commodities and a chapter on money.

In line with the Lausanne general equilibrium method the Austrian stance calls attention to the linkages between markets, as evidenced by its elaborate treatment of the hitherto neglected relations between factor and product markets. Just as in the Lausanne approach, the juxtaposition, in the Austrian scheme, of markets for goods of higher order and markets for goods of the lowest order entailed a decisive shift in the direction of economics by placing the theory of factor incomes on a novel footing. Yet, there remains a crucial difference: while the notion of *simultaneity* is alien to the Austrian mind-set, concurrent interdependence is at the very heart of the Walras-Pareto tradition.

In order to get a handle on what writers in the Austrian tradition found (and still find) so irritating about conceiving of economic phenomena as the exclusive study of mechanical forces in mutual balance under closed-system conditions, it may again prove most helpful to phrase the issue in Shackle's felicitous terms (see, Shackle, 1988, 8−11). The chief culprit, as ever, is "the time-exempt ideal," as consummately encapsulated in Pareto's theory of general static equilibrium. "General equilibrium" names the formal acknowledgment that there is a dilemma of concomitant choice: not everybody can choose last. The perfect universal prereconciliation of individual choices of actions is a solution to the dilemma posed by concomitant choice, albeit at a price; it can only be attained by squeezing historical time. As Shackle has time and again insisted, all-encompassing prereconciled choices are simultaneous choices; there is no yesterday and no tomorrow, no "earlier" and no "later," with respect to choice. That is to say, the whole system of choices refers to the same sole, self-contained moment;[22] it is in effect timeless. In such a system there is not a single actor anticipating any other on any given market by, for example, setting price.

A set of simultaneous equations is a set of conditions to be fulfilled. If the system conforms to a unique solution, the algebraist may rest content. But the economist will inevitably ask herself who in a noncollectivist polity may conceivably be in a position to ascertain, specify, and solve the equations incorporating the technological constraints and individual preferences prevalent in such a society. According to the Austrian viewpoint, the familiar recourse to a central *sub*-ordinating agent was out of the question; but, even more importantly, an anthropomorphic notion of "the market" as the embodiment of the aggregated bids and offers required for equilibration was ruled out as well. Harking back to Menger, and in a common-sensically realist vein (see Uskali Mäki, chapter 2, this volume), the starting point for Austrian analysis is not "the market" as such, but individual trades.[23] As is well known, when transactions are carried out in a situation of isolated exchange, the meaning of an overall balance of a highly segmented market becomes rather dubious. In the absence of an agency distributing the equilibrium price free of charge to would-be traders, bids and offers will be furnished with respect to special circumstances rather than market-wide conditions. In the absence of a uniform market-wide price, it makes no longer any sense to speak of "market supply," "market demand," and "market price."

The famed mutual dependence of economic magnitudes — even in the absence of direct interdependencies such as so-called "externalities" — in the Walrasian general equilibrium system is *imposed* on agents through the structural characteristics of the model economy, regardless of whether or not agents perceive such interdependencies. Usually, the agents' perception of interdependence is more or less limited. For example, a consumer in the Walrasian general equilibrium model is aware of his preferences, endowment, income, and current prices. No knowledge of market conditions is called for. And yet, as Hukukane Nikaido noted, "interdependent relationships among economic agents, including him, exist, *and are clear to the omniscient* and are embodied in the aggregate market demand and supply or excess demand functions. True, his taste is subjective and peculiar to him, but the aggregate market excess demand functions, which integrate the individual behaviors of all economic agents including his, *are given to the market in the objective sense*" (Nikaido, 1975, emphasis added).

The gist of the Austrian misgivings about simultaneous interdependence may be summarized in one tantalizing word: *time*.[24] To revert to Schumpeter's suggestion, the Austrian theory in the making is not "an embryonic theory of general equilibrium" but a budding economics *in* time, or perhaps even, in Shackle's phrase, a germinating economics of fallible expectation (pace Hutchison, 1953, 325). Confronted with a stark choice, with hindsight, between a conception of the order of the whole as engendered by an equilibrium price system and a view of the agent as a discernible entity not conforming to the dictates of "the market," and seeking to modify the objects and agents surrounding her, Austrian writers pursued the latter line of inquiry. As one commentator who was both a supremely gifted expositor of Austrian theory and a pioneer of economic theory in his own right (and who had first-hand experience of Viennese economics, to boot) judged: "Any genuine economic thinking is bound to tackle the equilibrium of interdependence. The Viennese School constructed its theory in a spirit which in many ways was contrary to that of the Lausanne School. It made a distinction, not without justification and using its own analytical instruments, between a halt in the flow of goods and the decisions of economic agents which by their interaction adjust supply and demand. As it took as its starting point the agent ... and the subjective theory of marginal utility ... the result could not be otherwise" (Perroux, 1980, 148−149). Indeed, Perroux's distinction between a general equilibrium of inert objects and a general balancing of activities of dissimilar and unequal agents animated by a drive for change, whose interactions in irreversible time give rise to *real tâtonnements*, may be highly relevant for the assessment of the distinctiveness of the Austrian contribution during the interwar years.

Unfortunately, it must be readily conceded that at the end of the day there is no crisp reckoning on these matters. In fairness, one must not forget, however, that the Austrian research agenda had still been in its infancy when it was aborted, to be resuscitated only some forty years later. Nonetheless, it seems possible, untainted by the smokescreen of words, to locate precisely where the Austrian and Lausanne schemes parted company. Mark Blaug's recent incisive characterization of the Austrian mode of theorizing as "total equilibrium" analysis would certainly have struck a chord with those concerned. By "total equilibrium" analysis Blaug means any analysis concerned with the interdependencies between markets, particularly factor and product markets (Blaug, 1990, 185). Viewed in this light, the Walrasian general equilibrium analysis would merely be one specific variant of total equilibrium analysis. It is perfectly possible, Blaug concludes, to engage in total equilibrium analysis without conceiving of the problem of the existence of multi-market equilibrium as the mathematical solution to a set of simultaneous equations.

In all but name this is precisely the gist of Morgenstern's 1931 intervention; and he was by no means alone in his judgment: Mayer (1930, 12) held out the prospect of an Austrian theory of the "genetical *Allzusammenhang* of all prices"; Mises (1966/1949, 392) used the term "general connexity of the prices of all goods and services" to denote market interdependencies; and, finally, Lachmann (1977, 55), in a retrospective assessment of the significance of the Austrian school, referred to the "general nexus of market phenomena" as certainly being acknowledged in Austrian theory, but as receding into the background as against the *adjustment of individual plans* to changing circumstances.

No doubt, both the Austrian and the Lausanne schemes focus on the connections between input and output markets. In contradistinction to the classical approach, both treat wage goods as a component of income, not of capital stock; that is, the real wages paid in the current period are generated by current production — "a hallmark of the new economics," as Robert Eagly, in a superb study of classical economic theory, observed (Eagly, 1974, 132). One may justifiably contend, however, that on the Austrian reasoning, given its explicitly stated objective to develop a theory of factor pricing on the basis of the "novel" theory of subjective value, the break with classical analysis is even more pronounced (see Walsh and Gram, 1980, 136–137).

But there remains a crucial difference overlooked by Eagly: factor and product markets are not conjoined simultaneously. The Janus-like nature of Austrian theory — starkly opposed to the classical theory of value and distribution on the one hand, but retaining vestiges of the classical sequential, step-wise method of analysis on the other — may be gleaned from its theory of imputation. The essential point about the theory of distribution through valuation by imputation is that the values and prices of goods of higher order are derived from the values and prices of the goods of lower order in whose production they serve. To state the issue somewhat more precisely, since the utilization of higher-order goods requires time, the value of higher-order goods depends on the *anticipated* want-satisfying power of the lower-order goods in whose production they are employed. "[T]he value of the goods of higher order is, in all cases, regulated by the prospective [*voraussichtlich*] value of the goods of lower order to whose production they have been or will be assigned by economizing men" (Menger, 1981/1871, 150).[25] As Adolf Nussbaumer commented, the

Austrian emphasis on uncertainty about future utilities was meant to foster an account of the principles of economic valuation (see Morgenstern, 1934); "it does not fit into Pareto's static system of general equilibrium on which a large part of the subsequent thought about utility theory has been founded" (Nussbaumer, 1973, 79).

It seems expedient at this point to consider briefly the role of the entrepreneur. In Walras's scheme, the entrepreneur is an intermediary connecting input and output markets by assuming the role of a buyer of productive services in input markets and of a seller of commodities in output markets (see Walker, 1986). As pointed out by Eagly (1974, 136), in the Walrasian setting the current hire of factors by entrepreneurs is linked to the current demand for commodities; whereas, in classical analysis the current hire of factors by capitalists is tied to accumulated stocks from past periods. In the Austrian setting, one might wish to add, the current hire of factors by entrepreneurs is likened to the *expected* demand for commodities. It should be noted, however, that the notion of the entrepreneur as someone providing linkages between markets, which has assumed, via the impact of Mises, central importance in contemporary Austrian economics, particularly in the work of Kirzner, is not at all spelt out in Menger.[26] It is indeed astounding and a matter of speculation that someone whose thinking on individual decision behavior was so consumed by notions of ignorance, error, and uncertainty should have failed to emphasize the entrepreneur's role in instigating and sustaining market processes — by buying goods (or means of producing goods) at a known price in order to sell at a price she cannot know when committing herself.[27]

Before concluding this selective report on the specific contributions of the Mayer Circle, I will refer to some further noteworthy individual performances. Any account of Austrian economic thought between the wars, however selective, would be seriously deficient without paying any attention to Morgenstern's work on expectations and perfect foresight — one of the major achievements coming out of the Mayer Circle.

Morgenstern was not only a member of the Mayer and Mises circles, but he also frequently attended the meetings of the Vienna Circle of logical empiricists and the Menger Colloquium. He moved decidedly away from the Paretian *ab initio* consistency of plans toward a consideration of strategic interaction. Already early on in his career he had been intrigued by the ways in which predictions influence the predicted events (Morgenstern, 1928) — a well-known problem in the social sciences, usually referred to as the "Thomas theorem": "If men define situations as real, they are real in their consequences" (Merton, 1968, 475). In his 1928 book, an epistemological study of forecasting, Morgenstern invoked the now familiar example of Professor Moriarty chasing Sherlock Holmes (98) in order to demonstrate the paralyzing implications of the perfect foresight assumption. It is an early example of a zero-sum, two-person game with no saddle point in pure strategies.[28] A player who would be required to disclose her pure strategy would be at a disadvantage, and the question is what would constitute, if at all feasible, an optimal move. The attempt to outguess each other by the train of thought: "I think that he thinks that I think that he thinks . . . ," would be doomed to resolve the dilemma.

Morgenstern continued to pursue the theme in a broader context in a long forgotten, but recently much appreciated *Zeitschrift* article (Morgenstern, 1935). He argued here that the notion of perfect foresight is fraught with logical inconsistencies rendering it inappropriate as a basis for equilibrium theory. For an individual agent to decide on a rational course of action in a system of interdependently acting individuals, perfect foresight is to include foresight of the intended actions of other agents, who are likewise assumed to be endowed with perfect foresight. As we have seen, either an infinite regress beckons, or equilibrium is instantaneously achieved, rendering *tâtonnement* redundant.

A further issue engaging Morgenstern (1935) is the exploration of the relationship between the assumed knowledge of economic theory among agents and the subsequent theory — a problem that has attracted a lot of attention among theorists under the rubric of "rational expectations." Thus it seems that Morgenstern was the first to pose the rational expectations problem and expose its logical limitations (as noted by, for example, Arrow, 1987, 210; Phelps, 1988, 457) a quarter-century before the concept was formally introduced by John Muth. The rational expectations literature has shown, however, that Morgenstern's problem would disappear *if* all agents in a "large" economy (only agents with measure zero) made their predictions using the same objectively correct model, and the rational expectations model would then form a Nash equilibrium in beliefs and actions (see Schotter, 1991, 20). But the common-model solution of rational expectations theory had already been dismissed by Morgenstern: "The necessity that any individual view with complete foresight all economic relationships — consequently, that he has to be master of theoretical economics — leads to a fact noteworthy for epistemology. Should complete foresight be an indispensable postulate for the erection of the theory of economic equilibrium, then, there results that wider paradox that the science has already posited the object that it is first to investigate; that, without this assumption, the object could not exist at all in the meaning specifically considered" (Morgenstern, 1976/1935, 175).

Another objection to the rational expectations solution concerns the large numbers assumption. The inconsistency between perfect foresight and equilibrium exposed by Morgenstern evaporates under perfectly competitive conditions; in such a regime, as is well known, no one can influence anybody. But Morgenstern's paradox surfaces as soon as we revert to the presupposition that an individual's future behavior influences the behavior of other agents — that is, under imperfectly competitive conditions, such as under duopoly or monopolistic competition, in which case equilibrium is no longer determinate (see Kim, 1988, 90).

The logical contradictions noted by Morgenstern could only be remedied by reconsidering the assumptions concerning the distribution of different degrees of foresight, or knowledge, among market participants (see Morgenstern, 1972, 1170–1171) — an idea pivotal for Hayek's line of reasoning. In his seminal article on "Economics and Knowledge," Hayek (1937) duly acknowledges his indebtedness to the work done by members of the Mayer Circle, especially by Morgenstern and Rosenstein-Rodan. For reasons unknown to me, the reprinted version of that article in *Individualism and Economic Order* (Hayek, 1949) does not include the following footnote, which is noteworthy, in regard of Hayek's position, in its own right:

> I should like to make it clear from the outset that I use the term "equilibrium analysis" throughout this paper in the narrower sense in which it is equivalent to what Professor Hans Mayer has christened the "functional" (as distinguished from the "causal-genetic") approach, and to what used to be loosely described as the "mathematical school". It is round this approach that most of the theoretical discussions of the past ten or fifteen years haven taken place. It is true that Professor Mayer has held out before us the prospect of another, "causal-genetic" approach, but it can hardly be denied that it is still largely a promise. It should, however, be mentioned here that some of the most stimulating suggestions on problems closely related to those treated here have come from this circle. (Hayek, 1937, n.1, 34–35)

Hayek then goes on to cite Mayer (1932) and Rosenstein-Rodan (1930; 1934). According to Mayer (1932), "functional" price theories are merely concerned with spelling out the conditions for the configuration of prices consistent with a state of equilibrium, incapable of explaining how prices are actually formed in real markets. By contrast, the task assumed by "causal-genetic" price theories is to explain how, in a given situation, a position of equilibrium may be reached — that is, to demonstrate how prices come into being, rather than to establish the configuration of prices securing and sustaining an equilibrium state. Mayer urged the economics profession to abandon the functional approach — as he held it to be exemplified in the equilibrium approaches of Cournot, Jevons, Walras,

Pareto, and Cassel — in favor of a theory of "causal process." His insistence on the irreversibility of economic processes and their unfolding in historical time have a strikingly contemporary ring. Mayer's important point (1932, 183–184) that a system of simultaneous equations must not be used to derive explanatory theories concerning adjustment processes prefigures Hayek's distinction in "Economics and Knowledge" between the Pure Logic of Choice and the "empirical" part of economics — consisting of, that is, in principle falsifiable propositions concerning the acquisition and dissemination of knowledge.

It must be readily acknowledged that Mayer (1932) is on much firmer ground in his criticism than in his more constructive efforts. Nonetheless, one may well hold that Mayer's work epitomizes the intellectual struggles Austrian economists of the interwar period had to put up with. The research program adumbrated by Mayer sixty years ago is still in its infancy, it may be surmised, but it is up to contemporary economists with an Austrian disposition to rectify the situation.

Concluding Remarks

Sir John Hicks (1976, 1979) has valuably distinguished between two Austrian doctrines which go a long way in accounting for the diversity of Austrianism during the interwar years. Although they need not be mutually exclusive, the distinction provides a useful frame of reference for the historiography of Austrian economic thought, both old and new.

The first doctrine can be traced back to Menger and has been revived by the economists of the Mayer Circle. It is represented by the principle of the supremacy of demand, or supremacy of "marginal utility," in the explanation of value. The second doctrine puts emphasis on production as a time-consuming process in which time is no more than a mathematical parameter. Or, the distinction can also be cast as the distinction between an economics *in* time (as represented by Menger) and an economics *of* time (as represented by Böhm-Bawerk). It is probably fair to say that in so far as there was an Austrian self-awareness during the interwar years, it was Mengerian rather than Böhm-Bawerkian in spirit.

Since the greater part of the historiography of the Austrian school during the interwar period is almost exclusively dictated by the latter perspective, especially when it has been written from an L.S.E. vantage point, the balance needs to be redressed. Besides, for present-day Austrian economics a deeper probing into the endeavors of the Mayer Circle could after all provide the "missing link."

Acknowledgments

A distant ancestor of this chapter was presented to the Carl Menger Conference at Duke University in April 1989. The present version has benefited from a discussion in the Austrian Economics Colloquium at New York University in January 1990, particularly from points raised by Boyan Jovanovic and Andrew Schotter. I am indebted to the Austrian Institute in New York and the NYU Economics Department for financial support and to Bruce Caldwell, Israel Kirzner, and Mario Rizzo for having made all this possible.

Notes

1. See, for example, Abele (1978); Alter (1982); Mirowski (1984); Negishi (1985, ch.13; 1989, ch.8); Walsh and Gram (1980, ch.5). Cp. also the contributions to a special issue of the *Atlantic Economic Journal* (September 1978).

2. This may *partly* explain the outright hostile reactions the revamped body of thought had to put up with initially.

3. The Austrian impact on L.S.E. is explored in O'Brien (1990); see also McCormick (in press) and Wiseman (1985).

4. That Mises did not change his mind over the years may be inferred from a 1932 statement, where he makes the point that the various neoclassical streams of thought did not so much differ in the substance of their teachings as in their terminology and style of presentation (see Mises, 1981/1933, 214).

5. Axel Leijonhufvud suggests the following explanation: "Economics in the interwar period did not have the technical equipment to bring deep-lying issues between 'schools' to sharp confrontation. The notion that the distinctive contributions of diverse schools would in time reach their confluence in one grand system would seem — and, one suspects, probably did seem — a most sensible attitude to adopt to most teachers" (Leijonhufvud, 1976, n. 42, 87).

6. Bruce Caldwell has recently drawn attention to the crucial role of the socialist calculation debate for "Hayek's transformation" (Caldwell, 1988).

7. In fact, much more is known about its clientele (see Craver, 1986, 15) than about its activities. Among other factors that could be adduced for the lacuna are: (a) the lack of a record of the topics discussed; (b) there was no specific journal associated with the circle; (c) it was an open group not committed to some "manifesto" along the lines of the Vienna Circle; and (d) there was no monograph or conference series attached to it. On the research preoccupations of the Mises Circle, see Boehm (1984).

8. The resident economists were, *inter alios*, Steffy Browne (Stephanie Braun), Gottfried Haberler, Friedrich Hayek, Fritz Machlup, Oskar Morgenstern, Paul Rosenstein-Rodan, and Richard Strigl.

9. It was originally conceived as a set of volumes honoring Wieser, but unfortunately, he didn't live long enough to see it published.

10. It is noteworthy in this connection that J. R. Hicks, as he was then, on the very first page of his seminal 1934 *Economica* paper "A Reconsideration of the Theory of Value"

(written jointly with R. G. D. Allen), paid tribute to the efforts of the Mayer Circle. As Loasby (1989, 12) points out, it is astounding that Shackle (1967) is hardly concerned with linking up the emerging trends in *value theory* with notions of uncertainty and imperfect knowledge.

11. Lest there be any misunderstandings, let it be emphasized that the following remarks should certainly not be misconstrued as a criticism of Professor Shackle's historical scholarship. Since his is not meant to be a conventional history of economic thought, but rather an account of new developments in the field that excited him in his formative period, this would amount to carrying coals to Newcastle. Yet, my claim is that there may well be a case for using *The Years of High Theory* as a rhetorical device to highlight precisely those issues that Shackle deemed, for whatever reason, *not* worth exploring. In any case, what is at stake here are nuances and different emphases that have no bearing on the substance of Shackle's findings.

12. Under Hayek's supervision, Shackle had been working on a thesis on Austrian capital theory when he was exposed to the new Wicksellianism by Brinley Thomas, who on his return from Sweden lectured on Myrdal and Lindahl at the L.S.E. in the Spring term of 1935. Having later that year been familiarized with, by Richard Kahn and Joan Robinson, an outline of the forthcoming *General Theory*, Shackle decided to switch topics (but not his supervisor) and to apply Myrdal's language of ex ante and ex post to Keynes's theory of general output and employment. The result was subsequently published as *Expectations, Investment and Income* (1938).

13. To my mind, there can be no doubt that Shackle's repeated criticisms of Hayek's equilibrium concept are the most incisive to have been offered yet. But given Shackle's continous insistence on the inherent antagonism between (expectational) time and reason (neoclassical perfect rationality based on demonstrative proof, as epitomized in modern versions of the Walras-Pareto general equilibrium model), it is somewhat paradoxical to find him lamenting Hayek's failure to cut the Gordian knot.

14. Menger's pivotal role in this respect had been noted by, for example, Richardson (1960, 157n.)

15. Morgenstern (1931, n.30a, 31) likens the comprehensiveness of the Austrian variant of marginal utility theory to its "typically *German national character*" (sic!).

16. Mayer extended the traditional Austrian tenet that demand is logically and genetically prior to supply by denying that the latter could be analyzed independently of the former, which amounted to a wholesale rejection of partial equilibrium analysis.

17. As Christopher Bliss valuably points out, in a general equilibrium context it does not make any sense to claim that "marginal utility is the cause of relative price," because marginal concepts, from the logical point of view (and in Walras's case, as we have seen, also from an historical point of view), are not prior but "highly derived" (see Bliss, 1975, 34–35).

18. Menger used this term in a letter to Walras. See Letter 602 in Jaffé (1965, vol. II, 2–6).

19. "[Value] is a judgment economizing men make about the importance of the goods at their disposal for the maintenance of their lives and well-being" (Menger, 1981 [1871], 121). For an illuminating account of the teachings of the "old" Austrians drawing on the central category of "valuation," see Ruppe-Streissler (1963).

20. Morgenstern (1972, 1173) points to Menger's focus on bilateral exchange and the associated "indeterminacy" of relative price ("price conflict") as prefiguring Edgeworth's analysis. But the analogy should not be overdone: for Menger, indeterminacy was related to incomplete knowledge rather than to the number of traders. In any case, as Chipman (1965, 443–444) notes, Menger's analysis was considerably marred by his conclusion that the

equilibrium price would obtain "half-way" between the limiting price ratios where trade would occur.

21. Menger's view of the role of institutions in securing social coherence is ably condensed in Zuidema (1988, 32).

22. It is, of course, compatible with a system of simultaneous equations that the events to which it refers occur at different dates.

23. As Mises insisted: "In view of popular errors it is expedient to emphasize that catallactics deals with the real prices as they are paid in definite transactions and not with imaginary prices. The concept of final prices is merely a mental tool for the grasp of a particular problem, the emergence of entrepreneurial profit and loss" (Mises, 1966 [1949], 332).

24. "In reality, there is no general interdependence, there are only various irreversible dependencies" (Rosenstein-Rodan, 1930, 142). Part of the argument of this article, which was actually published in the very first issue of the *Zeitschrift* in May 1929, has been used in Rosenstein-Rodan (1934).

25. In the posthumously published second edition of the *Grundsätze*, Menger (1923, 148) is, if anything, even more emphatic on this point. Menger's insistence that the value of goods of higher order depends not on the present value, but on the *expected* value of goods of lower order in whose production they are employed, buttresses Austrian criticisms of productivity theories of interest—a point often overlooked, as emphasized by Kirzner (1979, 87).

26. See Hennings (1986, 228); Kirzner (1979, ch.4).

27. See, however, Mises (1966 [1949], 334): "The operation of the market is actuated and kept in motion by the exertion of the promoting entrepreneurs, eager to profit from differences in the market prices of the factors of production and the expected prices of the products."

28. In games not strictly determined—that is, in games not having saddle points in *pure* strategies—a saddle point always exists if the players adhere to mixed strategies ("minimax theorem").

References

Abele, Hanns. 1978. "Toward a neo-Austrian Theory of Exchange." In *Equilibrium and Disequilibrium in Economic Theory*, G. Schwödiauer, (ed.) Dordrecht, The Netherlands: D. Reidel, 203−212.

Alter, Max. 1982. "Carl Menger and *Homo Oeconomicus*: Some Thoughts on Austrian Theory and Methodology," *Journal of Economic Issues* 16: 149−160.

Arrow, Kenneth J. 1987. "Rationality of Self and Others in an Economic System." In *Rational Choice: The Contrast between Economics and Psychology*, R. M. Hogarth and M. W. Reder, (eds.) Chicago: University of Chicago Press, 201−215.

Black, R. D. Collison, Coats, A. W., and Goodwin, Craufurd D. W., (eds.) 1973. *The Marginal Revolution in Economics: Interpretation and Evaluation.* Durham, NC: Duke University Press.

Blaug, Mark. 1985. *Economic Theory in Retrospect*, 4th ed. Cambridge: Cambridge University Press.

Blaug, Mark. 1990. "Comment on O'Brien's 'Lionel Robbins and the Austrian Connection'." In Caldwell (1990), 185–188.

Bliss, C. J. 1975. *Capital Theory and the Distribution of Income*. Amsterdam: North-Holland.

Boehm, Stephan. 1984. "The Private Seminar of Ludwig von Mises." Paper presented to the History of Economics Society Meetings at the University of Pittsburgh.

Bonar, James. (J.B.). 1926. "Austrian School of Economists." In *Palgrave's Dictionary of Political Economy*, Vol. 1, H. Higgs, (ed.) London: Macmillan, 73.

Caldwell, Bruce J. 1988. "Hayek's Transformation," *History of Political Economy* 20: 513–541.

Caldwell, Bruce J., (ed.) 1990. *Carl Menger and His Legacy in Economics*. Annual supplement to Volume 22, *History of Political Economy*. Durham, NC: Duke University Press.

Chipman, John S. 1965. "The Nature and Meaning of Equilibrium in Economic Theory." In *Functionalism in the Social Sciences*, D. Martindale, (ed.) American Academy of Political and Social Science, 35–64. (Page numbers refer to reprint in *Price Theory: Selected Readings*, H. Townsend, (ed.) 2d ed. Harmondsworth, UK: Penguin [1980], 435–467.)

Craver, Earlene. 1986. "The Emigration of Austrian Economists," *History of Political Economy* 18: 1–32.

Currie, Martin, and Steedman, Ian. 1989. "Agonising over Equilibrium: Hayek and Lindahl." *Quaderni di Storia dell'Economia Politica* 7: 75–99.

Currie, Martin, and Steedman, Ian. 1990. *Wrestling with Time: Problems in Economic Theory*. Manchester: Manchester University Press.

Eagly, Robert V. 1974. *The Structure of Classical Economic Theory*. New York: Oxford University Press.

Georgescu-Roegen, Nicholas. 1971. *The Entropy Law and the Economic Process*. Cambridge, MA: Harvard University Press.

Haberler, Gottfried. 1961. "Mises' Private Seminar." Reprinted in Ludwig von Mises, *Planning for Freedom*, 4th ed. South Holland, IL.: Libertarian Press (1980), 276–278.

Hayek, F. A. von. 1937. "Economics and Knowledge," *Economica*, n.s. 4: 33–54.

Hayek, Friedrich A. 1949. *Individualism and Economic Order*. London: Routledge & Kegan Paul.

Hayek, Friedrich A. v. 1965. "Wiener Schule," *Handwörterbuch der Sozialwissenschaften*, Vol. 12. Stuttgart: G. Fischer, 68–71.

Hennings, Klaus H. 1986. "The Exchange Paradigm and the Theory of Production and Distribution." In *Foundations of Economics: Structures of Inquiry and Economic Theory*, M. Baranzini and R. Scazzieri, (eds.) Oxford: Blackwell, 221–243.

Hicks, John R. 1976. "Some Questions of Time in Economics." In *Evolution, Welfare, and Time in Economics: Essays in Honor of Nicholas Georgescu-*

Roegen, A. M. Tang, F. M. Westfield, and J. S. Worley, (eds.) Lexington, MA.: D.C. Heath, 135-151.

Hicks, John R. 1979. "Is Interest the Price of a Factor of Production?" In *Time, Uncertainty, and Disequilibrium: Exploration of Austrian Themes*, M. J. Rizzo, (ed.) Lexington, MA.: D.C. Heath, 51-69.

Hicks, J. R., and Weber, W., (eds.) 1973. *Carl Menger and the Austrian School of Economics*. Oxford: Clarendon Press.

Hutchison, T. W. 1953. *A Review of Economic Doctrines, 1870-1929*. Oxford: Clarendon Press.

Jaffé, William, (ed.) 1965. *Correspondence of Léon Walras and Related Papers*, Vol. I-III. Amsterdam: North-Holland.

Jaffé, William. 1976. "Menger, Jevons, and Walras De-homogenized," *Economic Inquiry* 14: 511-524. (Page numbers refer to reprint in *William Jaffé's Essays on Walras*, D. A. Walker, (ed.) Cambridge: Cambridge University Press [1983], 311-325.)

Kim, Kyun. 1988. *Equilibrium Business Cycle Theory in Historical Perspective*. Cambridge: Cambridge University Press.

Kirzner, Israel. 1979. *Perception, Opportunity, and Profit: Studies in the Theory of Entrepreneurship*. Chicago: University of Chicago Press.

Kirzner, Israel M. 1987. "Austrian School of Economics." In *The New Palgrave: A Dictionary of Economics*, Vol. 1, J. Eatwell, M. Milgate, and P. Newman, (eds.) London: Macmillan, 145-151.

Kirzner, Israel M. 1988. "The Economic Calculation Debate: Lessons for Austrians," *Review of Austrian Economics* 2: 1-18.

Kirzner, Israel M. 1990. "Commentary on S. Boehm's 'The Austrian Tradition: Schumpeter and Mises'." In *Neoclassical Economic Theory, 1870 to 1930*, K. Hennings and W. J. Samuels, (eds.) Boston, MA.: Kluwer, 242-249.

Knight, Frank H. 1931. "Economics (History of Economic Thought): Marginal Utility Economics." In *Encyclopaedia of the Social Sciences*, Vol. 5, E. R. A. Seligman, (ed.) New York: Macmillan, 357-363.

Lachmann, Ludwig M. 1977. *Capital, Expectations, and the Market Process: Essays on the Theory of the Market Economy*, W. E. Grinder, (ed.) Kansas City: Sheed Andrews and McMeel.

Lachmann, Ludwig M. 1982. "The Salvage of Ideas." *Zeitschrift für die gesamte Staatswissenschaft* (*Journal of Institutional and Theoretical Economics*) 138: 629-645.

Lachmann, Ludwig M. 1983. "John Maynard Keynes: A View from an Austrian Window," *South African Journal of Economics* 51: 368-379.

Lachmann, Ludwig M. 1986. "Austrian Economics under Fire: The Hayek-Sraffa Duel in Retrospect." In *Austrian Economics: Historical and Philosophical Background*, W. Grassl and B. Smith, (eds.) London: Croom Helm, 225-242.

Leijonhufvud, Axel. 1976. "Schools, 'Revolutions,' and Research Programmes in Economic Theory." In *Method and Appraisal in Economics*, S. J. Latsis, (ed.) Cambridge: Cambridge University Press, 65-108.

Loasby, Brian J. 1989. *The Mind and Method of the Economist: A Critical*

Appraisal of Major Economists in the Twentieth Century. Aldershot, UK: Edward Elgar.

Machlup, Fritz. 1981. "Ludwig von Mises: The Academic Scholar Who Would Not Compromise," *Wirtschaftspolitische Blätter* 28(4): 6–14.

Mayer, Hans. 1930. "Die Wert- und Preisbildung der Produktionsmittel." In *Economia Politica Contemporanea: Saggi di Economia e Finanza in Onoro del Prof. Camillo Supino,* Vol. 2. Padova, 1–51.

Mayer, Hans. 1932. "Der Erkenntniswert der Funktionellen Preistheorien." In *Die Wirtschaftstheorie der Gegenwart,* Vol. 2, H. Mayer, F. A. Fetter, and R. Reisch, (eds.) Vienna: J. Springer, 147–239b.

McCormick, Brian J. (in press). *Hayek and the Keynesian Avalanche.*

Menger, Carl. 1923. *Grundsätze der Volkswirtschaftslehre,* 2d ed. K. Menger, (ed.) Vienna: Hölder-Pichler-Tempsky.

Menger, Carl. [1871] 1981. *Principles of Economics.* Trans. J. Dingwall and B. F. Hoselitz. New York: New York University Press.

Merton, Robert K. 1968. *Social Theory and Social Structure* (enlarged ed.) New York: Free Press.

Mirowski, Philip. 1984. "Physics and the 'Marginalist Revolution'," *Cambridge Journal of Economics* 8: 361–379.

Mises, Ludwig von. [1949] 1966. *Human Action: A Treatise on Economics,* 3d rev. ed. Chicago: H. Regnery.

Mises, Ludwig von. 1969. *The Historical Setting of the Austrian School of Economics.* New Rochelle, NY: Arlington House.

Mises, Ludwig von. [1933] 1981. *Epistemological Problems of Economics.* Trans. G. Reisman. New York: New York University Press.

Morgenstern, Oskar. 1928. *Wirtschaftsprognose. Eine Untersuchung ihrer Voraussetzungen und Möglichkeiten.* Vienna: J. Springer.

Morgenstern, Oskar. 1931. "Die drei Grundtypen der Theorie des Subjektiven Wertes." In *Probleme der Wertlehre,* L. Mises and A. Spiethoff, (eds.) Munich: Duncker & Humblot, 3–42.

Morgenstern, Oskar. 1934. "Das Zeitmoment in der Wertlehre," *Zeitschrift für Nationalökonomie* 5: 433–458. (Translated as "The Time Moment of Value Theory" in Schotter [1976], 151–167.)

Morgenstern, Oskar. 1935. "Vollkommene Voraussicht und Wirtschaftliches Gleichgewicht," *Zeitschrift für Nationalökonomie* 6: 337–357. (Translated by Frank Knight as "Perfect Foresight and Economic Equilibrium" in Schotter [1976], 169–183.)

Morgenstern, Oskar. [1934] 1937. *The Limits of Economics.* Trans. V. Smith. London: W. Hodge.

Morgenstern, Oskar. 1972. "Thirteen Critical Points in Contemporary Economic Theory: An Interpretation," *Journal of Economic Literature* 10: 1163–1189.

Negishi, Takashi. 1985. *Economic Theories in a non-Walrasian Tradition.* Cambridge: Cambridge University Press.

Negishi, Takashi. 1989. *History of Economic Theory.* Amsterdam: North-Holland.

Nikaido, Hukukane. 1975. *Monopolistic Competition and Effective Demand.*

Princeton, NJ: Princeton University Press.

Nussbaumer, Adolf. 1973. "On the Compatibility of Subjective and Objective Theories of Economic Value." In Hicks and Weber (1973), 75−91.

O'Brien, D.P. 1990. "Lionel Robbins and the Austrian Connection." In Caldwell (1990), 155−184.

Pareto, Vilfredo. [1906] 1972. *Manual of Political Economy*. Trans. A.S. Schwier, A.S. Schwier and A.N. Page, (eds.) London: Macmillan.

Perroux, François. 1980. "Peregrinations of an Economist and the Choice of His Route," *Banca Nazionale del Lavoro Quarterly Review* No. 133 (June 1980): 147−162.

Phelps, Edmund. 1988. "Comment on N. G. Mankiw's 'Recent Developments in Macroeconomics: A Very Quick Refresher Course'," *Journal of Money, Credit, and Banking* 20: 456−458.

Prendergast, Christopher. 1986. "Alfred Schutz and the Austrian School of Economics," *American Journal of Sociology* 92: 1−26.

Punzo, Lionello F. 1989. "Von Neumann and Karl Menger's Mathematical Colloquium." In *John von Neumann and Modern Economics*, M. Dore, S. Chakravarty, and R. Goodwin, (eds.) Oxford: Clarendon Press, 29−65.

Punzo, Lionello F. 1991. "The School of Mathematical Formalism and the Viennese Circle of Mathematical Economists." *Journal of the History of Economic Thought* 13: 1−18.

Richardson, G. B. 1960. *Information and Investment: A Study in the Working of the Competitive Economy*. London: Oxford University Press. (Reprinted by Clarendon Press in 1990.)

Rosenstein-Rodan, P. N. 1930. "Das Zeitmoment in der Mathematischen Theorie des Wirtschaftlichen Gleichgewichtes," *Zeitschrift für Nationalökonomie* 1: 129−142.

Rosenstein-Rodan, P. N. 1934. "The Rôle of Time in Economic Theory," *Economica* 1: 77−97.

Ruppe-Streissler, Monika. 1963. "Zum Begriff der Wertung in der Älteren Österreichischen Grenznutzenlehre," *Zeitschrift für Nationalökonomie* 22: 377−419.

Schotter, Andrew, (ed.) 1976. *Selected Economic Writings of Oskar Morgenstern*. New York: New York University Press.

Schotter, Andrew. 1991. "Oskar Morgenstern's Contribution to the Development of the Theory of Games," C.V. Starr Center for Applied Economics, New York University, Research Report #91−08. Forthcoming in *History of Political Economy* (annual supplement).

Schumpeter, Joseph A. 1954. *History of Economic Analysis*. Ed. from manuscript by E. Boody Schumpeter. New York: Oxford University Press.

Shackle, G. L. S. 1967. *The Years of High Theory: Invention and Tradition in Economic Thought, 1926−1939*. Cambridge: Cambridge University Press.

Shackle, G. L. S. 1988. *Business, Time and Thought: Selected Papers*, S. F. Frowen, (ed.) London: Macmillan.

Stigler, George J. 1941. *Production and Distribution Theories: The Formative*

Period. New York: Macmillan.

Streissler, Erich. 1973. "To What Extent Was the Austrian School Marginalist?" In Black, Coats, and Goodwin (1973), 160–175.

Sweezy, Alan R. 1933–34. "The Interpretation of Subjective Value Theory in the Writings of the Austrian Economists," *Review of Economic Studies* 1: 176–185.

Sweezy, Alan R. 1934. *The Austrian School and the Interpretation of Subjective Value*. Ph.D. thesis. Harvard University.

Walker, Donald A. 1986. "Walras's Theory of the Entrepreneur," *De Economist* 134: 1–24.

Walsh, Vivian, and Gram, Harvey. 1980. *Classical and Neoclassical Theories of General Equilibrium: Historical Origins and Mathematical Structure*. New York: Oxford University Press.

Weintraub, E. Roy. 1983. "On the Existence of the Competitive Equilibrium: 1930–1954," *Journal of Economic Literature* 21: 1–39.

Wieser, Friedrich von. (F. W.) 1926. "The Austrian School of Economists." In *Palgrave's Dictionary of Political Economy*, Vol. 1, H. Higgs, (ed.) London: Macmillan, pp. 814–818.

Wiseman, Jack. 1985. "Lionel Robbins, the Austrian School, and the LSE Tradition." In *Research in the History of Economic Thought and Methodology*, Vol. 3, W. J. Samuels, (ed.) 147–159.

Zuidema, J. R. 1988. "Carl Menger, Author of a Research Programme," *Journal of Economic Studies* 15 (3/4): 13–35.

COMMENTARY

Mark Blaug

I must confess to being slightly disappointed by Stephan Boehm's chapter on interwar Austrian economics. The title led me to expect an account of the virtual demise of Austrian economics by World War II, particularly in its three distinctive contributions to received economic doctrine, namely, capital theory, business cycle theory, and the economic theory of socialism. Since this is a story that has never really been told in detail, I had hoped that Boehm would finally give us a definitive account of how Böhm-Bawerk was vanquished by Frank Knight, how Hayek and Robbins were laid low by Sraffa and Kaldor, and how Mises was buried by Lange. What Boehm gives us instead is something else. What he does offer is very interesting but it seems more inspired by recent developments in the post-war neo-Austrian revival than by Austrian economics as it was perceived in the interwar period and particularly in the eventful decade of the 1930s.

Starting in 1933, Frank Knight launched a vitriolic attack on Austrian capital theory as misconceived in its very foundations: for all practical purposes, Knight argued, the time structure of production made no differ-ence and therefore a nation's capital stock might just as well be viewed as a homogeneous fund of productive capacity. By 1936, Knight's half-dozen lengthy diatribes, supported by a dozen or so other contributions, amounted to something like a campaign. The entire controversy was reviewed at length by Kaldor in 1937(1960); his ambiguous defence of the "average period of production" as "meaningful" but "irrelevant" to a dynamic economy only served to encourage what was now a widespread skepticism

31

about the Austrian theory of capital. By the time Friedrich Hayek published his long awaited *Pure Theory of Capital* (1941), mainstream economics had moved on to other topics and, besides, Hayek rejected the concept of an average period of either production or investment and instead adopted the notion of a multidimensional heterogeneous capital structure, leaving the reader to puzzle over what was left of the Austrian as against the Anglo-American approach to capital. In short, by then there seemed little left of the house that Böhm-Bawerk had built sixty years earlier.

Hicks (1967) has described the widespread appeal of the Austrian theory of business cycles in the early 1930s, at least on the eastern side of the Atlantic. Books like Hayek's *Prices and Production* (1931) and *Monetary Theory and the Trade Cycle* (1933), as well as Robbins' *The Great Depression* (1934), had familiarized an entire generation with the doctrine that business cycles are caused by undue periodic "lengthening" of the period of production in consequence of reckless credit-expansion in booms; hence, depression necessarily involved a long painful process of reducing the "roundaboutness" of production. This Austrian theory of business cycles was so intimately related to the Austrian theory of capital that Knight's onslaught on the latter was just as much an attack on the former. Sraffa's (1932) critique of Hayek's *Prices and Production* is sometimes regarded as having dealt the fatal body-blow to the Austrian theory of capital but in point of fact the decisive critique was not forthcoming until the end of the decade in two characteristically trenchant articles by Kaldor (1939, 1942). By then, however, the Keynesian Revolution had succeeded in producing the sort of Kuhnian paradigm-switch in which the Austrian theory of business cycles literally disappeared from view. The fact that both Hayek and Robbins kept silent about Keynes, or indeed any of the contentious issues of business cycle policy after 1934 (see Blaug, 1990), only served to confirm the death of the Austrian theory of business cycles. Despite Haberler (1946, chaps. 3, 13); Moss and Vaughn (1986); Kim (1988, ch. 2) and O'Brien (1988, ch. 8), there exists no detailed account of the rise and fall of Austrian cycle theory. The more the pity then that Boehm says so little about it.

However, the reputation of Austrian economics in the interwar period rested far more on the economic theory of socialism than on capital or business cycle theory. To most economists in, say, 1935 the name of Ludwig von Mises would have conjured up, not so much the monetary over-investment theory of the business cycle, as the proposition that rational economic calculation under socialism is impossible. The story of the Socialist Calculation Debate has been told by Vaughn (1980), Murrell (1983), and at greatest length by Lavoie (1985). Lange's *On the Economic*

Theory of Socialism (1936) was judged in its day to have provided a satisfactory formal answer to Mises, but in retrospect, it is evident that Lange won the battle for the wrong reasons and that Mises had the better case, a case, however, which he never managed to express convincingly. Be that as it may, Lange's book not only buried the Austrian critique of socialism but also promoted Walrasian general equilibrium theory as the appropriate framework for thinking about such issues as capitalism versus socialism. Hicks' *Value and Capital* (1939) was only a few years off, but already general equilibrium theory was becoming the standard for theoretical sophistication in microeconomics, in terms of which Austrian price theory stood condemned as antideluvian.

Hayek's appreciation of the learning and discovery aspects of the dynamic *process* of competition, as distinct from the static properties of the *end-state* of competitive equilibrium, in his *Collectivist Economic Planning* (1935; especially 201ff) and his seminal essay on "Economics and Knowledge" (1937), strikes us today as remarkably original and perceptive. At that time, however, they passed by without notice and even Hayek may not have realized how close he was to charting a whole different territory from that of Walrasian mainstream economics that was beginning to emerge in the late 1930s. Boehm's closing pages on the work of the Mayer Circle and the Mengerian, rather than Böhm-Bawerkian, roots of interwar Austrian economics clearly reflect a belief that the elements of Austrian economics that I have been emphasizing have commanded more attention from historians of economic thought than they deserve. That may well be true from the standpoint of recent developments in neo-Austrian economics (Kirznerian entrepreneurship, etc.), but if we truly seek to recapture the atmosphere of interwar economics in order to understand the almost irreversible decline of Austrian economics by World War II, we need to focus, not on the now trendy subjects of expectations and disequilibrium adjustments, but on such traditional topics as capital and interest, business cycles, and market socialism.

My complaint of Boehm's chapter, therefore, is that he failed to write the sort of paper I would have liked him to have written.

References

Blaug, Mark. 1990. "Comment on O'Brien's 'Lionel Robbins and the Austrian Connection'." In *Carl Menger and His Legacy in Economics*, B. J. Caldwell, (ed.) Durham, NC: Duke University Press, 185–88.

Haberler, Gottfried. 1946. *Prosperity and Depression*. New York: United Nations.

Hayek, Friedrich A., (ed.) 1935. *Collectivist Economic Planning*. London: Routledge and Kegan Paul.

Hicks, John. 1967. "The Hayek Story." In *Critical Essays in Monetary Theory*. Oxford: The Clarendon Press, 203–15.

Kaldor, Nicholas. 1939. "Capital Intensity and the Trade Cycle," *Economica*. Reprinted in *Essays on Economic Stability and Growth*. London: Gerald Duckworth, 120–47.

Kaldor, Nicholas. 1942. "Professor Hayek and the Concertina Effect," *Economica*. Reprinted in *ibid*: 148–76.

Kaldor, Nicholas. 1960. *Essays on Value and Distribution*. London: Gerald Duckworth, 153–205.

Kim, Kyun. 1988. *Equilibrium Business Cycle Theory in Historical Perspective*. Cambridge: Cambridge University Press.

Lavoie, Don. 1985. *Rivalry and Central Planning. The Socalist Calculation Debate Reconsidered*. Cambridge: Cambridge University Press.

Murrell, Peter. 1983. "Did the Theory of Market Socialism Answer the Challenge of Ludwig von Mises? A Reinterpretation of the Socialist Controversy," *History of Political Economy* 15(1), Spring: 92–105.

Moss, Laurence S. and Vaughn, Karen I. 1986. "Hayek's Ricardo Effect: A Second Look," *History of Political Economy* 18(4), Winter: 545–65.

O'Brien, Denis P. 1988. *Lionel Robbins*. London: Macmillian.

Sraffa, Piero. 1932. "Dr Hayek on Money and Capital," *Economic Journal* 42(1): 42–53.

Vaughn, Karen I. 1980. "Economic Calculation Under Socialism: the Austrian Contribution," *Economic Inquiry* 18(4), October: 535–54.

2 THE MARKET AS AN ISOLATED CAUSAL PROCESS: A METAPHYSICAL GROUND FOR REALISM

Uskali Mäki

Introduction

The battlefield of rival economic theories and approaches is colored by obscure assessments of whether this or that theory is "realistic" or "unrealistic" and whether it is legitimately so. It seems that, for the most part, economists espousing so-called Austrian theories think of those theories as being realistic, or at least more realistic than typical theories within neoclassical mainstream economics. I find two features disturbing in such assessments. First, the very predicates, "is realistic" and "is unrealistic," are extremely ambiguous, and although economists typically are content with living with this ambiguity, it has harmful consequences for the quality of the controversies in which they are involved. I have elsewhere attempted to dispel some of these ambiguities.[1] Secondly, the grounds for economists' assessments of the realisticness of a given theory are far from being completely clear and well grounded. More often than not, unreflected commonsense experience plays a crucial role in such assessments without having been accorded that role by sound method-ological argument. The present chapter suggests that analyses of the metaphysical structure of theories might also play a relevant role in this game.

This chapter does not deal with the issue of *realisticness* directly in the special sense of trying to answer the questions of whether Austrian theory is true and whether its postulated entities exist — that is, whether it is realistic in two important senses of the term. Instead, I am concerned

35

with its potential realisticness, that is, whether these two questions are the kind that are worthwhile asking, with some measure of optimism about the answers. In other words, this chapter proposes a strategy of beginning with an analysis of the preparatory question of whether *realism* is an appropriate philosophy for Austrian theory. My problem is whether Austrian theory is the kind of theory that may be true and the logically prior question of whether the entities it postulates may exist.

More particularly, I ask whether there are grounds for realism about Austrian theory that would be rooted in the general metaphysical structure and contents of the theory itself. It is suggested that there is indeed such a ground, and that it is related to the envisioning of the market as a discovery and communication process, and the emphatic rejection of the depiction of the market entirely in terms of the conditions of equilibrium states. I argue that in holding this theory, Austrian economists commit themselves to a special causalist and processual metaphysics, and that the theory has the structure of what may be called a *causal process theory*. It is then suggested that causal process theories are particularly appropriate for a realist interpretation. The underlying premise behind the reasoning is that we are more entitled to consider believing in the existence of the entities and properties postulated in a coherent and comprehensive causal process account than in the postulations of a static equilibrium account focusing on end states.

In earlier work I have argued, first, that Austrian invisible-hand explanations have a *causal* structure (Mäki, 1990a, 1991a). In particular, I have suggested that even though the outcomes of invisible-hand processes (such as the institution of money or a given structure of relative prices in an economy) are not the intended results of that action, they, nevertheless, are its causal consequences and, therefore, have to be causally explained (by theoretically redescribing them as such causal consequences). Secondly, I have also suggested that the total architecture of Austrian theory and its several elements are compatible with a *realist* theory of science with essentialist leanings (Mäki, 1989, 1990a, 1990b, 1991d). For example, I have argued that Austrian economics subscribes to commonsense realism about the economic actor and scientific realism about the invisible hand. In particular, I have suggested that Menger's theory of money invites an interpretation in terms of a realism about universals, real essence, causal powers, and necessities.

The present chapter combines these two suggestions about causality and realism. It analyzes in more detail the causal structure of the Austrian theory of the market process and suggests how this structure gives support to a realist philosophy of Austrian economics.

The Austrian theory of the market process does not tell the whole truth about the world. The causal process it proposes to depict is, at most, an isolated slice of what in fact takes place in the social world. For instance, it excludes factors such as the moral feelings of the market participants and state intervention in its various forms. In a sense, Austrian theory deforms our image of social reality by ignoring a vast number of ingredients in the total situation and by focusing exclusively on some others. In one important sense, then, Austrian theory is unrealistic. This feature of the theory will be met as a challenge to a realist interpretation of it. I will argue that the main suggestion of the paper survives this challenge, provided the theory of the market process is understood as a purportedly realistic representation of the essence of the market. This is my second major suggestion.

In sum, it is argued that even given its strongly isolative character the causal and processual structure of the Austrian theory of the market invites a realist reading. We have to be very careful with the import of this claim. It is not argued that the Austrian theory is thereby established as the true account of the market economy, but rather that the relatively detailed causal contents of the theory lend support to a realist reading of the theory. Finding ways of assessing the truth of the theory is another difficult problem. The following pages keep silent about this question that has preoccupied most commentators on the methodology of Austrian economics. The last section suggests briefly why such commentaries are misguided.

It is important to note that the general argument advanced in the present chapter can, in principle at least, be used for defending a realist reading of what also appear as causal process theories in other streams of economics, such as the post-Keynesian theory, the so-called real business cycle theories, and some strands of institutionalism. Austrian theory, with its consistent emphasis on the theoretical centrality of process, gives us an exceptionally good opportunity for pursuing this line of argument. Of course, this is not to say that there is something like a well-developed understanding of the concept of process available in Austrian economics (or elsewhere in economics, for that matter). Some clarification work has to be done on the notion of process itself.

"Ground for Realism"

It is advisable to begin with a brief clarification of the notion of *ground for realism* in or about an economic theory or a school of economic thought. The first important component in need of clarification in this notion is *realism*. By realism, in or about a theory or an approach generating such a theory, I here mean what may be called a *realist reading* of that theory. By a "realist reading" of a theory I mean an interpretation of the theory as putatively referring to entities that exist and as a systematic representation of the features of those entities, such that the theory has a chance of being either true, close to the truth, or carrying the promise of getting us closer to the truth of what it represents. Thus, a realist reading of a theory does not in itself entail the belief that the theory is true. It only entails the belief that the theory has a chance of being true, that is, that it is the kind of theory to which the vocabulary of veracity may sensibly apply. This means that the theory can be taken seriously as a candidate for capturing the truth of what exists and takes place in the world. In sum, a realist reading of T implies taking the objects of T as candidates for real existents and the major statements of T as candidates for true statements.

The distinction between realism and realisticness may help dispel any remaining confusion. It is one thing to hold realism about T and another to believe in the realisticness of T (at least on the standard specifications of "realisticness," such as truth). It is one thing to believe that T is the kind of theory to which the vocabulary of "true" and "false" may be legitimately applied, and it is another thing to believe that T is true. Of course, the latter belief implies the former, but not vice versa. The grounds for the two kinds of belief may also differ. The grounds for realism may consist of metaphysical considerations, while the grounds for belief in the truth of a theory should usually comprise other kinds of evidence as well.

Let us then clarify what I mean by the notion of a *ground* for realism. It is easier first to say what is *not* meant by this idea. I do not mean to ground a realist reading of a theory in appealing to the explicit meta-theoretical declarations of its proponents. It is not difficult to find interpretations of Austrian theory among the Austrian economists that would count as realist, or to find even more radical and ambitious allegations to the effect that the Austrian theory is *the true account* of the market economy. Such self-interpretations do not count here. By taking this stance I do not intend to deny that the self-understanding of economists may have something to do with the real nature of the objects of such self-understanding. I am here simply interested in a different kind of evidence for a realist reading of Austrian theory.

The relevant evidence has to do with *the general metaphysical structure of the theory* in question and *the kind of claims it appears to make or is used to make about the world.* It is here that the fact that Austrian theory appears to provide causal claims about the market process becomes relevant to the question of whether there are grounds for a realist reading of the theory. Note that I am talking about the *kind* or *type* of claims a given theory makes rather than about its specific claims.

This feature of the argument pursued here has an important consequence, namely: *the argument is neutral with respect to the detailed theoretical variations and controversies within and without Austrian economics.* I do not have to take sides in the debates about the adequacy of this or that particular detail in the theory of entrepreneurship or about whether the market process is ultimately teleologically convergent. Therefore, the fact that I use Israel Kirzner's version as an example should not be taken to imply anything like an idea of its superiority over alternatives. My argument stands or falls irrespective of the ultimate fate of Kirzner's version. The argument can be attempted in the case of all economic theories of the same metaphysical kind. It is the causal and processual character of a theory that suffices for my purposes; the evaluation of its many other, more specific, features may be bracketed at this stage, while keeping in mind that *they become crucial when assessing its truth.*

This strategy implies that *the grounds for realism are theory-type specific or approach-type specific.* This runs counter to those formulations and allegations concerning scientific realism according to which realism stands or falls as an overall thesis about all of science. I do not think that science, or the set of scientific theories, is homogenous enough to warrant such a globalizing attitude. As a descriptive thesis at least, I do not buy scientific realism as a universal thesis. A more local approach in checking its soundness seems more attractive. It is another question whether we have good grounds for espousing realism as a universal normative idea about science. In this essay I am interested in economics as it is.

Causal Process Theories

There are two necessary conditions for a theory to count as a causal process theory. First, it has to provide an account of a *process* as a sequence of events. Second, it has to depict the driving forces that set and keep the process in motion, that is, the *causes* of the motion from one event to another in the sequence. Not all descriptions of processes are causal descriptions and not all descriptions of causation are descriptions of process (even if it were the case that all processes are causal processes and that all causation involves process). Both the necessary conditions have to be satisfied in order for a theory to be categorized as a causal process account.

In order to understand the metaphysics of causal process theories, we need a perspective from which the concepts of process and cause mingle. This brings in some clarification concerning both of the key categories. Here we can draw upon Wesley Salmon's recent work on causation. He makes a distinction between two concepts of causation, namely that between "production" and "propagation" (Salmon, 1980; 1984, 139f.).

The following are examples of *causal production*. "When we say that the blow of a hammer drives a nail, we mean that the impact produces penetration of the nail into the wood. When we say that a horse pulls a cart, we mean that the force exerted by the horse produces the motion of the cart. When we say that lightning ignites a forest, we mean that the electrical discharge produces a fire." (Salmon, 1984, 139.) Causal production is a matter of bringing about effects. In our reconstructive interpretation of Austrian theory, it seems fruitful to view causal production as something generated by *causal agents*, that is, entities equipped with *causal powers*. Causal powers, ascribable to things of various kinds, are powers to bring about effects in the world.

Causal propagation is in question when, for example, "[e]xperiences that we had earlier in our lives affect our current behavior. By means of memory, the influence of these past events is transmitted to the present ... A sonic boom makes us aware of the passage of a jet airplane overhead; a disturbance in the air is propagated from the upper atmosphere to our location on the ground. Signals transmitted from a broadcasting station are received by the radio in our home. News or music reaches us because electromagnetic waves are propagated from the transmitter to the receiver." (Ibid.) Causal propagation is a matter of transmitting influences from one spatio-temporal location to another.

Causal processes, then, involve both causal production and causal propagation, both agency and transmission. There are several important characteristics that causal processes possess. Two of them are particularly relevant to our interpretation of Austrian theory. First, causal processes are *capable of transmitting signals or information* (ibid., 141). Not surprisingly, this will have a significant role in our interpretation of the notion of the market process. Second, causal processes are *self-determined* in that they are not parasitic upon causal influences exterior to the process itself (ibid., 144−145). Again, this will be crucial for our attempt to interpret a theory which has radically pro-market implications.

Salmon has much to say about the role of propagation in causal processes, but he is not very clear about the role of agency or production in such processes. It seems obvious, however, that we need both concepts of causation in theorizing about causal processes. We need to have an idea of a driving force pushing and keeping the self-sustained process in motion, and we need to have an idea of how the influences of the driving force are transmitted along the causal chain constituting the process. The first is causal production, the second is causal propagation. News or music does not reach us merely "because electromagnetic waves are propagated from the transmitter to the receiver" but also because those waves were generated and sent in the first place and because our radio is capable of receiving them and transforming them into intelligible sounds.

As I will show, the Austrian theory of the market process involves both notions of causation. Entrepreneurship involves causal power which serves as a productive agent; hence, causation as production is involved. Market prices function as carriers of the signals that transmit causal influences from one part of the economy to another; hence, causation as propagation is involved.

Austrian Theory of the Market as a Causal Process Theory

We then have to examine whether Austrian theory is a causal process theory in the above sense, since the suggestion that it invites a realist reading hinges upon its being such a theory. I argue that Austrian theory of the market process is a causal process theory in the required sense. It comprises both the idea of causal agency and the idea of causal propagation. Actors equipped with entrepreneurial alertness are the causal agents of the process, while price signals serve to transmit information across the economy. This means that it is the combination of the Misesian and Hayekian heritages that provides the composite notion of causal process. Note again that, given the character of my problem, I may keep silent about many of the disputed details of the economic theories under discussion; it is their general metaphysical characteristics that matter.

Let us begin with a brief examination of the notion of causal agency. A thing is a causal agent if it possesses a power to bring about effects in the world; therefore we have to clarify the concept of causal power (see, e.g., Harré & Madden, 1975). Having the power to act in a certain way is to be capable of acting that way; it is to be in a state of readiness to act that way; it is to act that way if the appropriate conditions obtain; and it is to act that way by virtue of an intrinsic nature. Causal powers in this sense are akin to tendencies, drives, capacities, propensities and the like. Things equipped with such powers are capable of causal production. Human powers, when embedded in preferences and plans, beliefs and expectations, make them causally efficacious. They are essential for defining ourselves as human agents.

On an earlier occasion, I have suggested that Kirzner's version of the Austrian theory of entrepreneurship postulates a causal power, namely entrepreneurial alertness (Mäki, 1991a, 158–161). I here repeat the grounds for this suggestion, drawing upon Kirzner's writings. He nowhere explicitly says that entrepreneurship involves a causal power, but I interpret his statements so as to make them support the suggestion, on each of the four conditions of the ascription of causal power:

1. *Having the power to act in a certain way is to be capable of acting that way.* This is what Kirzner is implying when he writes, for example, the following: "Entrepreneurial alertness consists, after all, in the *ability* to notice without search opportunities that have been hitherto overlooked." (Kirzner, 1979, 148; emphasis added.)

2. *Having the power to act in a certain way is to be in a state of readiness to act that way.* This condition seems to be satisfied by statements such as this: "Purposive human action involves a posture of alertness toward the discovery of as yet unperceived opportunities and their exploitation." (Kirzner, 1979, 109.)

3. *Having the power to act in a certain way is to act that way if the appropriate conditions obtain, that is, if the propensity is triggered or stimulated.* Again, textual support is available. Kirzner writes that entrepreneurial alertness is something that can be "*inspired*" by "the lure of market profits" (Kirzner, 1985, 61) and by "freedom of entrepreneurial entry" (ibid., 91); it can be "*tapped*" (ibid., 25) or "*switched on*" by the incentive of "the pure gain..." (ibid., 58–59; emphases added).

4. *Having the power to act in a certain way is to act that way by virtue of an intrinsic nature.* Kirzner does not have much to say about an intrinsic basis for the causal propensity built in entrepreneurship, but he does seem to imply that there is such a psychic basis when he talks about "the qualities that make for entrepreneurial alertness" and refers to "restive temperament, thirst for adventure, ambition, and imagination" (Kirzner, 1985, 26, 89), as well as "vision, boldness, determination, and creativity" (ibid., 64).

It would seem, then, that the notion of entrepreneurial alertness satisfies the conditions of purportedly denoting a causal power. If this is correct, then entrepreneurial alertness may be treated as a causal power, and human beings presumably having this property as causal agents. These agents are depicted as the producers of causal effects in the market process. Next, we have to examine how the idea of causal propagation is exemplified in Austrian theory.

The obvious candidate for the substance being propagated is information. Here the theory of entrepreneurship has to be combined with the Hayekian insight of the market process as a communication and learning process (Hayek, 1948). The actual market prices are exchange ratios in disequilibrium situations that are characterized by discoordination of the plans and actions of individuals and by the existence of price divergences. These price divergences are reflections of error and ignorance and asymmetric information among market participants; these gaps in prices deliver information about gaps in knowledge, functioning as signals of discoordination. The entrepreneur is alert to discover and utilize these profit opportunities, and by so doing she disseminates knowledge in society. "The market entrepreneur bridges the gaps in mutual knowledge, gaps that would otherwise permit prices to diverge with complete freedom." (Kirzner, 1985, 60).

Disequilibrium market prices are vehicles of conveying information across time and space. "On the one hand, these exchange ratios with all their imperfections reflect the discoveries made up until this moment by profit-seeking entrepreneurs. On the other hand, these ratios express entrepreneurial errors currently being made." (Kirzner, 1985, 133.) By engaging in profit-seeking activities, entrepreneurs, without intending to do so, both receive and send messages, that is, information of the relative scarcities, actual or anticipated, of goods and services now and in the future, and the past and present errors involved. By utilizing this information entrepreneurs thereby help correct the errors. This gives direction to the market process: the market process is a learning process. Agents learn that their expectations have been too optimistic or too pessimistic. The market process is a communication process whereby prices and price differentials transmit information which is utilized by alert entrepreneurs. Their profit-seeking actions unintentionally drive the process and give it direction.

While the accounts of causal process theories in physics usually depict energy as the substance being propagated, I am suggesting that in the Austrian picture of the economy the substance propagated is information. It is the transmission or communication via price signals of information from one part of the market to another that constitutes the aspect of causal propagation in the Austrian theory of the market process. It therefore seems that Austrian theory also satisfies the second condition of causal process theory.

It is also clear that the Austrian theory of the market process is supposed to preserve the idea of the self-determination of the process. "Our identification of decision making with alert, entrepreneurial human action has provided us with *an explanation for the market process that does not, in principle, depend for its general pattern, upon any extraeconomic factual considerations whatsoever.* The market process emerges as the necessary implication of the circumstances that people act, and that in their actions they err, discover their errors, and tend to revise their actions in a direction likely to be less erroneous than before." (Kirzner, 1979, 30; emphasis in the original.) "Spontaneous order," a popular term among Austrian economists, aptly captures the idea of self-determination. The market allegedly generates a spontaneous, reproductive order without the help of any external causal agent. The market process is represented as a self-supporting process.

In sum, the Austrian theory of the market process seems to be a genuine causal process theory in the required sense.

Theoretical Redescription of the Market Process

Let us refine the above interpretation of Austrian theory by employing the idea of *theoretical redescription*. Theoretical redescription is a matter of redescribing, in theoretical terms, what is already empirically or "phenomenologically" described, as really being something else — this something else constituting the "essence" of the object of (re)description. Take another look at Salmon's example: "When we say that lightning ignites a forest, we mean that the electrical discharge produces a fire." (Salmon, 1984, 139). Here, it is suggested that a causal agent be identified by theoretically redescribing as an electrical discharge a phenomenon that is empirically described as lightning. I suggest that both elements in the Austrian theory of the market as a causal process, namely, the notions of causal agency and causal propagation, involve such theoretical redescriptions. *The reason for the need for theoretical redescription is that the market does not appear to the common sense as a causal process of the kind conceptualized in Austrian theory.*[2]

The commonsense notion of the market is, I think, best formulated in terms of selling and buying. Selling and buying are intentional actions. They are directed to an end in the mind of the seller or buyer. In other words, selling and buying are accompanied by specific "spheres of intended-ness", that is, sets of ends, which it is the intention of market transactors to bring about by performing acts of exchange. The spheres of intendedness of the transactors belong to the realm of the common sense. This is the realm of phenomenological or empirical descriptions of what it is that takes place in the market. However, these descriptions do not capture all the essential facts about selling and buying. There is also a sphere of unintended facts involved in market exchange, that is, the sphere of the invisible hand. This is the proper realm of scientific theory. (See Mäki 1991a, 161–165). In other words, an empirical description of the market in terms of selling and buying does not make it evident that the market is a causal process of the Austrian kind. This can only be revealed by redescribing selling and buying as really being something else, namely, as exercises of entrepreneurial alertness and as discovery and communication of information.

Thus, the action of market agents is theoretically redescribed as a manifestation of entrepreneurial alertness and as a form of the communication of information. Only in this way can the causal contents of the notion of the market be revealed. Let me formulate the two redescriptions in the form of two *ontological identification statements*, one for causal agency, the other for causal propagation. It is the task of such identification statements to describe what, from the point of view of system coordination, *really or ultimately* takes place in the market, when acts of selling and buying *appear* to take place. An analogous identification statement asserts that "Lightning *is* a manifestation of an electrical discharge." Such statements maintain that the objects of the empirical description (lightning or selling and buying) really are the objects of the theoretical redescription following the expressions "is" or "are". "Are" (or in the singular, "is") means "are really", "are at bottom", "are ultimately", etc.

(CA)   Selling and buying in the market *are* manifestations of the causal agency of entrepreneurship.

(CP)   Selling and buying in the market *are* forms of the causal propagation of information.

Identification statement (CA) is meant to refer to those forms of selling and buying that involve arbitrage or speculation, that is, those that drive the causal process of the market. It may be taken to concern either actual selling and buying which manifest both entrepreneurial and "Robbinsian," and possibly other elements, or else pure entrepreneurial selling and buying, in which case they manifest nothing but entrepreneurial elements. In both cases, Kirzner's account subscribes to (CA).

Identification statement (CP) is meant to concern those cases of impersonal selling and buying where the exchange ratios approximately reflect the relative scarcities of goods. Again, it is these cases that are relevant for the idea of the market as a causal process. The statement reformulates the Hayekian idea of the market as a telecommunication process. On this interpretation, when Hayek suggested that the market is a discovery and communication process, by that token he subscribed to the theoretical redescription employing (CP).

In Contrast: Equilibrium Theory as a Model Theory

The above argument can be clarified by contrasting Austrian theory with Walrasian general equilibrium theory in its standard formulation. There are two assumptions characteristic of the latter which render it incompatible with the Austrian vision of process. One is the assumption that actors are equipped with complete information. Since it is the state of general equilibrium that is characterized by full information, there is no room and no need for the notion of the market process as a learning or discovery process. Another assumption that effectively excludes the idea of process is that of one (equilibrium) price on which all exchanges take place. In the Austrian theory it is vital that the market envisage a multiplicity of prices for one good. It is these price differentials that provide entrepreneurs with opportunities for arbitrage gain and thus stimulate them to generate the market process.

Before entering on a discussion of the connection between causal process theories and realism, let us introduce a simple contrast between two kinds of theories. This is the philosopher Brian Ellis's distinction between *model theory* and causal process theory. Ellis says that "causal process theories attempt to describe the basic causal processes of nature [... whereas] model theories define norms of behavior against which actual behavior may be compared and explained" (Ellis, 1985, 55; see also Ellis, 1957).

I have argued that Austrian theory is an example of causal process theory. There is a well-known interpretation of general equilibrium theory which makes it an obvious case of model theory in the above sense. I have in mind Frank Hahn's view that the Arrow-Debreu construction of general equilibrium "makes no formal or explicit causal claims at all" and that "no description of any particular process is involved" (Hahn, 1973, 7). Hahn then argues for a reading of the theory as what I would like to call a *critical ideal type*: since the theory is, he thinks, an adequate formalization of the notion of the invisible hand, it can be used to undermine claims about the blessings of the free market by showing that those claims thereby presuppose the premises of the theory, which we know are very far from the truth. "This negative role of Arrow-Debreu equilibrium I consider almost to be sufficient justification for it, since practical men and ill-trained theorists everywhere in the world do not understand what they are claiming to be the case when they claim a beneficent and coherent role for the invisible hand" (ibid., 14−15). In other words, it is not the task of the Arrow-Debreu construction to provide a true account of the workings of the world, but instead to inform us about what the world would need to be like for the "invisible hand," or rather what Hahn conceives of as the invisible hand, to hold. The problems with Hahn's suggestion notwithstanding, it fits well with the idea that the Arrow-Debreu construction is a model theory in Ellis's sense.

It should be noted that it does not follow from the above suggestion that Hahn's nonrealist reading of general equilibrium theory as a model theory is the only possible reading of all of its versions. For instance, in his numerous writings, Donald Walker (e.g., 1988) has argued, contrary to many other interpretations of Walras, that this founding father himself held a non-Hahnian view of his version of general equilibrium theory. Walker argues that Walras regarded his theory as a true representation of the processes of pricing and adjustment and the ultimate convergence to equilibrium in real markets, these processes involving essentially the role of entrepreneur. This is to suggest that Walras was a realist about his theory. If this is correct and if Walras was justified in holding this view, then it follows that the standard Austrian dichotomy between process theories and end-state theories of the market cannot be used for criticizing Walras's theory.

Causal Process Theories and Realism

There is a simple sense in which some market process theories are more "realistic" than equilibrium state theories: they add a further slice of economic reality to our theoretical picture of the economy, viz. the process connecting equilibrium states. Process theories are not at all, or not merely, about equilibria as end states but also, or merely, about the processes that tend to bring these states about and the driving forces that put the process in motion. Some process theories are therefore richer or more encompassing than equilibrium theories and in this special sense more "realistic." However, it is doubtful whether this circumstance, as such, is a virtue at all from a *realist* point of view. There has to be something special about the element of causal process to make it count when considering the prospects of realism in Austrian economics. I argue

that there is something especially apt in the notion of causal process.
Let us take a look at what Brian Ellis has to say on this matter.

> Now, the argument for scientific realism, insofar as it concerns the reality of
> theoretical entities, derives whatever force it has from taking causal process
> theories to be typical of scientific theories generally. For to accept that A is the
> cause of B is to accept that both A and B are real existents .... But no such
> argument applies to the theoretical entities of model theories, for the hypothetical
> entities of model theories are not the postulated *causes* of anything. Conse-
> quently, there is no parallel argument that to accept a model theory involves
> the belief that the entities to which it apparently refers really exist. ...
> Consequently, it does not matter whether these theories are literally true or
> false. What matters is whether they are adequate to the task for which they
> were devised. (Ellis, 1985, 55–56)

Thus, Ellis maintains that in the case of causal process theories, "the
postulated causes of the phenomena must be supposed to exist if the
theory is to be accepted as doing what it purports to do" (ibid., 57). I
have three specifications to add to this.

First, Ellis lacks an analysis of the notion of causal process, but we
already have one in rough outline. In its light, we may specify the idea of
the commitment to the existence of causes so as to make it apply to
causes in the twin roles of production and propagation.

Second, causes are to be taken as the proper objects of relevant
theoretical redescriptions that tell us what ultimately takes place in our
research object. Just as lightning is to be redescribed as electrical discharge,
buying and selling are to be redescribed by means of ontological identification statements (CA) and (CP) in order to capture the causal structure
of the respective processes.

Third, Ellis does not explicitly provide us with a general criterion of
existence, one that would discriminate between the objects of model
theories and causal process theories. The obvious candidate, of course, is
this: for something to exist, it has to be able to cause effects. The notion
of causation, of course, can be variously specified, but ours — causation as
comprising both production and propagation — can be used to provide a
particularly strong criterion of existence or hypothetical existence. Note
that the accomplishment of the task of the present essay does not require
a criterion of existence, but one of hypothetical existence. Since Ellis
talks about the acceptance of or belief in a theory, he needs the former.
Since we are interested in the grounds for a realist reading of a theory, we
may be content with the latter. Such a criterion seems to underlie the
intuitively plausible argument that, unlike model theories, causal process
theories invite a realist reading.

Causal process theories have been constructed for the purpose of providing accounts of the more or less detailed workings of the world with the promise or hope of delivering the truth about the causal agents and causal propagation. This is why such theories invite a realist reading. Other virtues such as coherence, predictive power, and heuristic suggestiveness may be possessed by theories which make no claims to truth. That certain statements logically cohere, that they help predict occurrences in the world, that they suggest strategies of modelling, or that they help uncover divergencies between the actual and the ideal — none of this compels or even encourages scientists literally to believe in or even to attempt to test the truth of the picture given by the theory composed of such statements.

On the other hand, the objects of causal process theories are candidates for real existents that hold definite roles in the causal order of the world. Acceptance of such a theory implies a belief in (at least the plausible possibility of) the existence of the things and properties postulated by the theory. Causal process theories hold the promise of capturing what exists in a particularly strong way in that they are not content with citing causes and effects within an event ontology, but instead give a detailed account of relevant causal powers and connections, consisting of both production and propagation. In other words, such theories inform us about *what* there is in the causes that make them able to generate certain effects and *how* they manage to generate those effects. Such theories are obvious candidates for true accounts of what really takes place in the world.[3]

Austrian Process Theory and Realism

I have argued that the Austrian theory of the market process is a causal process theory in the required sense. It involves a conception of the causal agent or the driving force of the process as well as a notion of the causal propagation of information along with the process. I am arguing that as a result Austrian theory invites a realist reading.

To make this argument more concrete, I now proceed to develop further the suggestion I have made earlier that Austrian economics subscribes to a combination of commonsense realism (in its conception of the economic agent) and scientific realism (in its conception of the invisible hand). (See Mäki 1990a, 336–338; 1990b, 301–304, 307–308.) The specification of this idea utilizes the suggested analysis of the causal and processual metaphysics of Austrian theory.

The set of questions relevant to realism comprises not only the question of existence and truth, pure and simple, but also that of the *causal relevance* or causal role of the presumed existents in the order of things.

We may be convinced that there are human beings and that they are equipped with faculties such as purposefulness, ignorance, alertness, and learning capacities. At the same time, we have little reason to doubt that humans are prone to reflexive and routine behavior and are often incapable of discovering opportunities or learning from errors. These judgements are based on commonsense experience; no scientific theory is required to inform us about such familiar facts about human beings. However, commonsense understanding alone does not provide us with much aid in deciding which of the human propensities are *causally relevant* for the emergence of the social entities with which our explanatory theories are concerned. In other words, our commonsense understanding is not sufficient for conceptualizing human beings as the causal agents of invisible-hand processes. It is here in our quest for understanding the role of facts about humans in the social order of things that we have to appeal to an explanatory scientific theory. In deciding on the causal relevance of this or that set of human propensities, we need a theory that links those propensities to a set of social outcomes as our *explananda*. A causal process theory serves precisely this purpose. It shows how a set of human propensities operating within a social framework brings about a process, possibly with potentialities for social outcomes of this or that kind.

The specification I have in mind should now be obvious. Austrian economics involves commonsense realism in its conception of economic actors in that it shares the folk psychological conceptualization of human action in intentional terms regarded as genuinely referential. That human beings exist and that they act purposefully and alertly to opportunities, commit errors and learn from them, buy and sell goods in the market, make profits and losses, and so on; all this is nothing new from the point of view of our commonsense view about humans. Of course, on the same commonsense basis, humans may truthfully be claimed to possess many other properties and to engage in many other activities as well. The simple attribution of existence and certain propensities and actions to human beings goes together with commonsense realism.

However, making such claims of existence and truth, pure and simple, within commonsense realism does not yet enable us to make any reliable judgements concerning the causal relevance of any of those existents from the point of view of the explanatory tasks of economics. To be able to attribute the further quality of causal relevance to some of the human propensities and actions, that is, in ascribing to them a crucial causal role in the social order of things, we need a scientific theory understood in a realist fashion. Austrian economists claim to possess this ability, and in doing so they subscribe to scientific realism. The existence of an invisible-hand process as a causal process is not an obvious fact from a commonsense point of view. The attribution of causal relevance and scientific realism thus go together.

Let the above distinction be misunderstood, let it be added that attributions of causal relevance belong also to the purview of folk psychology: the beliefs and desires of actors may be regarded as the causes of their actions, irrespective of what these beliefs, desires, and actions ultimately are, in neurophysiological or other noncommonsense terms. Economics, however, seems to have little interest in this circumstance as such, so I have ignored it here. Instead, I use "causal relevance" as a shorthand for "causal relevance in regard to the market process." It is the causal relevance of those mental qualities that help push and keep the market process in motion that are of interest here.

It is precisely the point of the theoretical redescription of buying and selling by means of identification statements (CA) and (CP) to specify those aspects of market transaction that are believed to have causal relevance. A materialist may identify market transaction with (or redescribe it as) certain kinds of neurophysiological process. This would not, however, reveal those aspects of transactions that would be regarded by Austrian economists as causally relevant to the market process. Similarly, redescribing lightning as Aristotle did would not be regarded by modern scientists as revealing the causation of a forest fire. It is the redescription of lightning as electrical discharge that is needed. Similarly, entrepreneurship and the discovery and communication of information are the relevant aspects of selling and buying in the causal process of the market.

The case of (observed) lightning identified with a manifestation of an (unobserved) electrical discharge is a matter of scientific realism. The question is whether electrical discharge as a theoretical entity exists and whether a theory about it comes close to the truth. The situation in regard to entrepreneurship and the discovery and communication of information as the theoretical entities of Austrian theory is different. The question of existence in this case is a matter of commonsense realism involved in folk psychology. It is the question of their causal relevance for the market process shaped by the invisible hand that is a matter of scientific realism. *This* is what I mean by suggesting that Austrian economics subscribes to a combination of commonsense realism and scientific realism.

Austrian Theory as an Isolative Theory

Causal process theories are hypothetical descriptions of causal processes in the world. By representing the causal history of an *explanandum*, or the causal process that results in the *explanandum*, a causal process theory provides us with a causal explanation. Not all scientific theories are causal process theories. Recall Brian Ellis's suggestion that there are other kinds of theory, such as those that he calls "model theories" (or, using the vocabulary familiar to the social scientist, we might call them also "ideal type theories"). They provide ideal norms of the state or behavior of some system. It is against these ideals which actual states or behavior may be compared so that the possible divergence between the two can be explained if required. (Ellis, 1985.)

It seems clear that on Hahn's interpretation, Walrasian general equilibrium theory is a model theory in the above sense. What is interesting about the Austrian process theory is that, as I will show next, it appears to have features characteristic of both model theories and causal process theories in the sense Ellis uses these terms. This has two interesting implications. First, it calls for a qualification in the distinction between causal process theory and model theory as a dichotomous distinction. Secondly, and more interestingly from our present point of view, the obvious fact that Austrian theory bears features of model theory poses a challenge to our realist reading. I am suggesting that the Austrian theory appears as a model theory in that the market process is described by the theory as an isolated process, as an "ideal norm".

Austrian theory isolates the market process from various "disturbing" influences, most notably from various kinds of state intervention. It is a theory of a causal process that is self-determined and able to bring about coordination in the economy, only provided no other significant causes intervene. In Kirzner's words, "an entrepreneurial discovery process . . . , in the absence of external changes in underlying conditions, fuels a tendency toward equilibrium" (Kirzner, 1985, 12). This is an implication of the allegation of the self-sustaining or spontaneously beneficial character of the market process. As a matter of actual fact, however, the market is hardly ever allowed to do its work spontaneously, undisturbed by intervening influences such as monetary expansion by the central bank, minimum-wage legislation, or rent control. Yet, the theory isolates the process from those influences. This is one feature characteristic of model theories shared by Austrian theory.[4]

Two kinds of empirical investigation practised by Austrian economists reflect the character of the theory as an isolative model theory. First, much research in Austrian economics addresses itself to explaining states and tendencies of discoordination in the economy as divergences from what the market process would allegedly have generated in isolation. This is accomplished by referring to those external influences that have actually intervened in the market process — a feature shared by model theories, according to Ellis.

There is another category of empirical research that reflects the character of the Austrian theory as an isolative theory. It is not mentioned by Ellis, but it is practised by Austrian economists. I have in mind the attempts to find actual cases in economic history where the major isolative assumptions of the theory have been true or close to the truth, that is, where the relevant isolations have actually materialized themselves or where the intervening influences have been negligible. One then attempts to show that in these cases the outcomes of the market process are spontaneously coordinated.

Now, it may be suggested that due to the fact that Austrian process theory is similar to neoclassical equilibrium theory, in that it has a strongly isolating and idealizing character, it has no more right to a realist reading than neoclassical equilibrium theory. This objection questions whether there is any genuine difference between Walrasian general equilibrium theory and Austrian theory in metaphysical and semantic terms. Both are, after all, representations of a counterfactual case, are they not? While Walrasian equilibrium theory describes an ideal state, Austrian theory describes an ideal process. The causal process represented by Austrian theory is often counterfactual in that, for example, the process takes place in the absence of state intervention, even though in actual economies the state more often than not intervenes in one way or another. As a consequence, there usually is a dicrepancy between the ideal process represented by the theory and the actual process. What is it that justifies our claiming that Austrian theory invites an interpretation as a hypothetical description of a real economic process?

In order to understand the difference between Walrasian theory in Hahn's interpretation and Austrian theory we have to see the distinction between real causal powers and tendencies on the one hand and their actual manifestations on the other. Austrian theory is about the market process as a causal process in the following sense. It depicts the fundamental driving forces or the causal powers and the tendencies they give rise to, and it follows the propagation of their influences through the market process, isolated from all disturbing factors. The actual process is not effectively or materially isolated, but is also moulded by many other factors, except for those that are included in the theory. Given such a reading of Austrian theory, it may be taken as a candidate for a true representation of real powers and tendencies and the process they would generate in the absence of intervening factors. The truth of Austrian theory would not be shattered merely by its being about the tendential features of the economy.

What about Walrasian theory in Hahn's interpretation? Why would it not be appropriate to interpret it in realist terms as well? Its counterfactual character should not in itself prevent such a reading, if it does not do so in the case of Austrian theory. It would appear that the crucial problem with equilibrium theory is that it is difficult to construe it as a theory about tendencies, for example, about the tendency towards the state of general equilibrium. The theory appears to be about a possible, nonactual state. The theory itself says nothing about whether there is a tendency inherent in the real forces of the economy towards the equilibrium or some other state. *Tendencies* may fail to actualize themselves without making theories of those tendencies false. But the permanent nonactuality of possible *states* as the sole objects of a theory does not give strong support to the idea that the theory might turn out to be true, or that truth is a relevant category in its context.

I will now suggest an essentialist specification of the idea pursued above. Let us take a look at a passage by Israel Kirzner in which he states that

> the dominant [equilibrium] theory, by emphasizing certain features of the market to the exclusion of others, has constructed a mental picture of the market that has virtually left out a number of elements that are of critical importance to a full understanding of its operation (Kirzner 1973, 4).

What is suggested here? Neoclassical equilibrium theory has excluded a number of elements of the market; the theory is isolative and in this sense unrealistic. But this would not serve as an effective criticism of the theory; any theory, Austrian theory included, is unrealistic in this sense. The crucial point is that neoclassical theory has excluded elements that are of "critical importance" to an understanding of the market. Kirzner expresses his point by saying that what is at stake is a "full understanding" of the market. There may be a possibility of misunderstanding here. I suggest the attribute "full" be understood as meaning not comprehensive or wide, but deep. It is ontological depth, not merely width, that is claimed to be gained by revising the isolations of neoclassical theory. The inclusion of emotions and moral feelings (or the shoe sizes) of market agents in the isolated field of the theory would increase its width, but Austrian economists refuse to take this step. Why? Because, I suggest, they think this would not increase the ontological depth of our theoretical account of the market. In other words, emotions, moral feelings, and shoe sizes are not regarded as causally relevant for the market process.

On the other hand, it is the inclusion of entrepreneurship in the isolated field of the theory that is believed to do the trick. Entrepreneurship is supposed to be constitutive of the essence of the market. By excluding entrepreneurship, neoclassical theory is alleged to lose the chance of understanding the essence of the market. I suggest the following: *The Austrian theory of the market process is a theory of the essence of the market.* The strongly isolative character of the theory serves precisely this idea. Instead of detaching the theory from reality, the revised isolation allegedly brings it closer to the essential aspects of reality. *Far from being in conflict with a realist reading of the theory, its isolative character in fact strengthens my case.* This argument also implies that we have to distinguish between model theories in Ellis's nonrealist sense and isolative theories in the present realist sense. Those features of Austrian theory that we have discussed suggest that it is not a model theory but only appears as such.

There are other deforming assumptions in some formulations of the theory that do not appear to have similar essentialist grounding. To these belongs the decision

> to view the market, in a world of production, *as if all* entrepreneurial activity were in fact carried on by producers; in other words, it now becomes convenient to think of resource owners and consumers as passive price-takers, exercising no entrepreneurial judgement of their own and simply reacting passively to the opportunities to sell and buy which the producer-entrepreneurs hold out to them directly. (Kirzner 1973, 18.)

Let us formulate this assumption as follows:

(P)   All entrepreneurial activity is carried on by producers.

It would seem from the above quotation that the decision to accept (P) is not primarily dictated by the beliefs of the Austrian economist about the structure of the world. Indeed, Kirzner states more explicitly that "[o]f course this is only an analytical convenience, but it will simplify much of the discussion and will help lay bare the inner workings of the market in the complex world of production." (ibid.) If this were the case, that is, if (P) were nothing but a simplification device, it would follow that (P) would not distort the theoretical image of the essence of the market.

The situation is a little more complicated though. Kirzner also says that producers constitute "a built-in group of entrepreneurs" and that "production involves a necessarily entrepreneurial type of market activity" (ibid.). This seems to imply that beliefs about the structure of reality do play a role in the decision to accept (P) after all, that is, assuming (P) is not a matter of mere theoretical convenience. All this is related to the concern about the essence of the market. The statement, "production involves a necessarily entrepreneurial type of market activity" says that production and entrepreneurship are connected by the relation of necessity.

We have to be careful with what this means. *Production necessarily involves entrepreneurial action. Entrepreneurial action does not necessarily involve production.* On the other hand, *consumption does not necessarily involve entrepreneurial action*, although it most often does, more or less. Entrepreneurship, then, is part of the essence of production. Production, on the other hand, is not part of the essence of entrepreneurship. But because entrepreneurship is not part of the essence of consumption, (P) is more in accord with reality than the assumption

(E)   All entrepreneurial activity is carried on by consumers.

We may then say that there is an important sense in which (P) is more realistic than (E). In any case, the conclusion is the same as with the premise that (P) is nothing but a simplifying device. The idea in both cases is that assumption (P) will not in any way distort the suggested theoretical comprehension of the essence of the market. On the contrary, the deforming assumption is introduced in order to help us see more clearly the role of entrepreneurship in the real constitution of the market process.

Conclusion

I have argued that (a) the Austrian theory of the market has the character of a causal process theory; (b) this supports a realist reading of the theory; and (c) the realist reading is not undermined by the theory also having the character of an isolative theory. Recall that the argument is not dependent on the details of the version of Austrian theory we have discussed. Any economic theory of the same metaphysical character should qualify for similar treatment.

We may ask how these suggestions relate to the standard discussion on the methodology of Austrian economics. As in economic methodology in general, this discussion has been mainly concerned with the issue of epistemic appraisal. The received view of the methodological character of Austrian economic theory is that it is accompanied by dogmatic insulation from criticism, that it is made immune to falsification and intact by empirical evidence (see, e.g., Blaug, 1980; Hutchison, 1981). Since such an epistemology of dogmatic nonfallibilism may be regarded as inconsistent with the fundamental standards of science, Austrian economics may appear as unscientific from such a perspective. On the other hand, since no consensus amongst economic methodologists or philosophers of science obtains over what the fundamental standards of science are, we may feel justified in adopting a less dogmatic call for critical appraisal, following Bruce Caldwell's "critical pluralism" (Caldwell, 1984, 1986; see the reactions by Rotwein, 1986 and Hirsch, 1986).

The suggestions of the present chapter can be used to support Caldwell's line and to specify it in the case of Austrian economics. If claims (a) to (c) are correct, then it follows that (i) metaphysical evidence (not merely empirical evidence) can be used to discriminate between theories as to the appropriate "reading," supposed to disclose their general character, and that (ii) the selection of whatever further evidence (including empirical evidence) is judged relevant for assessing a theory should depend on its "reading" as well as its detailed assertions. An assessment of a theory should depend on what it is.

To restate a point made on an earlier occasion (Mäki, 1990a, 338–339): if it is part of the character of the Austrian theory of the market that it is a purportedly true and explanatory, but nonpredictive isolative representation of causal processes that actually occur in open, nonisolated circumstances, then it should be assessed as such an attempt, and not as if it involved the pursuit of something else. If the metaphysically grounded realist reading is correct, then the further evidence should be such that it can be used to judge whether the Austrian theory has the realist virtues of being relevantly true or close to the relevant truth from an explanatory point of view.

It is one thing to appraise theories as to *how well* they attain the ends they are used to pursue; it is another thing to appraise *how good* those ends are. Before either of these tasks can be accomplished, we have to tackle the third problem of understanding *what* those ends are and *how* they are pursued. The foregoing is an attempt to promote such an understanding. It is also suggested that this idea should be more generally acknowledged in economic methodology.

Acknowledgments

I am grateful for comments on an earlier draft from Stephan Boehm, Bruce Caldwell, Wade Hands, Daniel Hausman, Israel Kirzner, Jukka-Pekka Piimies, and Heikki Taimio. Part of the work for this article was done during my Fellowship at SCASSS (Swedish Collegium for Advanced Study in the Social Sciences), for which I wish to express my thanks.

Notes

1. I distinguish between realism (as a philosophical doctrine) and realisticness (as an attribute of representations) — and nonrealism and unrealisticness, respectively — and their numerous varieties. For an analysis of some of the kinds of and interrelations between realism and realisticness, see Mäki, 1989, 1991b, 1992.

2. For a lengthy discussion of the idea of theoretical redescription in the context of Austrian explanation, see Mäki, 1990a.

3. My views are interestingly related to those of Nancy Cartwright's in her *How the Laws of Physics Lie* (1983). She argues that if an entity holds a causal role in our account of the world, this may be taken as a reason for believing in its existence. This much I am inclined to share with Cartwright. However, when she maintains that it is a characteristic of explanatory theories that they are false, our ways depart. It seems that this difference is at least partly rooted in different conceptions of the relation of truth to theoretical isolation, to be discussed in the section on "Austrian Theory as an Isolative Theory" below (see also Mäki, 1991c, 1992).

4. For a general discussion of the method of isolation and the related idealizations in economic theorizing, see Mäki, 1991d.

References

Blaug, Mark. 1980. *The Methodology of Economics: Or How Economists Explain.* Cambridge: Cambridge University Press.

Caldwell, Bruce. 1984. "Praxeology and its Critics: an Appraisal," *History of Political Economy* 16, 363–379.

Caldwell, Bruce. 1986. "Towards a broader conception of criticism," *History of Political Economy* 18, 675–681.

Cartwright, Nancy. 1983. *How the Laws of Physics Lie.* Oxford: Oxford University Press.

Ellis, Brian. 1957. "A Comparison of Process and Non-process Theories in the Physical Sciences," *British Journal for the Philosophy of Science* 8, 45–56.

Ellis, Brian. 1985. "What Science Aims to Do." In *Images of Science*, P. M. Churchland and C. A. Hooker, (eds.) Chicago: Chicago University Press.

Hahn, Frank. 1973. *On the Notion of Equilibrium in Economics.* Cambridge: Cambridge University Press.

Harré, R. and E. Madden. 1975. *Causal Powers.* Oxford: Basil Blackwell.

Hayek, F. A. 1948. Individualism and Economic Order. Chicago: University of Chicago Press.

Hirsch, Abraham. 1986. "Caldwell on Praxeology and its Critics: A Reappraisal," *History of Political Economy* 18, 661–668.

Hutchison, Terence. 1981. *The Politics and Philosophy of Economics.* Oxford: Basil Blackwell.

Kirzner, Israel. 1973. *Competition and Entrepreneurship.* Chicago: University of Chicago Press.

Kirzner, Israel. 1979. *Perception, Opportunity, and Profit*. Chicago: University of Chicago Press.

Kirzner, Israel. 1985. *Discovery and the Capitalist Process*. Chicago: University of Chicago Press.

Mäki, Uskali. 1989. "On the Problem of Realism in Economics," *Ricerche Economiche*, 43, 176–198. (To be reprinted in *The Philosophy and Methodology of Economics*, edited by Bruce Caldwell. Edward Elgar.)

Mäki, Uskali. 1990a. "Scientific Realism and Austrian Explanation," *Review of Political Economy* 2, 310–344.

Mäki, Uskali. 1990b. "Mengerian Economics in Realist Perspective." In *Carl Menger and His Legacy in Economics*, B. J. Caldwell, (e.d.) Annual Supplement to *History of Political Economy* 22, 289–310.

Mäki, Uskali. 1991a. "Practical Syllogism, Entrepreneurship, and the Invisible Hand." In *Economics and Hermeneutics*, D. Lavoie, (ed.) London: Routledge, 149–176.

Mäki, Uskali. 1991b. "Friedman and Realism," *Research in the History of Economic Thought and Methodology* 10: (forthcoming).

Mäki, Uskali. 1991c. "Comment on Hands." In *Appraising Modern Economics: Studies in the Methodology of Scientific Research Programmes*. Mark Blaug and Neil de Marchi, (eds.) Aldershot, UK: Edward Elgar, 85–90.

Mäki, Uskali. 1991d. "Universals and the *Methodenstreit*: Carl Menger's Conception of Economics as an Exact Science." Mimeo.

Mäki, Uskali. 1992. "On the Method of Isolation in Economics." In *Poznan Studies in the Philosophy of the Sciences and the Humanities* 25, Special issue on *Intelligibility in Science*, Craig Dilworth, (ed.), 319–354.

Rotwein, Eugene. 1986. "Flirting with Apriorism: Caldwell on Mises," *History of Political Economy* 18, 669–673.

Salmon, Wesley C. 1980. "Causality: Production and Propagation," *PSA 1980*, 2, 49–69.

Salmon, Wesley C. 1984. *Scientific Explanation and the Causal Structure of the World*. Princeton: Princeton University Press.

Walker, Donald. 1988. "Iteration in Walras's theory of tatonnement," *De Economist* 136, 299–316.

p35i # COMMENTARY

Bruce J. Caldwell

Uskali Mäki asks whether there are grounds for considering the Austrian theory of the market to be a realist one: Is the Austrian story about the market process the kind of theory about which it may be possible to say that its referents exist, and that it is true? He answers that there are grounds for such a claim. By picturing the market as a discovery and communication process, and by rejecting as inadequate the more common depiction of the market in terms of equilibrium states, the Austrians make certain metaphysical claims about the world. Mäki argues more specifically that the Austrians provide a "causal process" theory, and that such theories invite a realist interpretation, especially when they are contrasted with static equilibrium "model" theories. He also anticipates an important objection that all theories that purport to be realist must address. The theoretical redescription of a phenomenon is typically isolative, it focuses on only one part of reality. But a theory can still be a candidate for a realist interpretation if the part of reality that it focuses on is an essential aspect of the phenomenon in question. Mäki argues that Austrian theory remains a candidate for a realist interpretation because it claims to have isolated the essential features of the market process. Mäki appropriately avoids any discussion of whether this claim is in fact true. He addresses the logically prior question of whether Austrian theory is of a type that the claim could possibly be true.

In my critical remarks, I will focus on the causal production–causal propagation dichotomy, then on Mäki's important discussion of theoretical description and isolative theories.

60

Mäki draws on Wesley Salmon's distinction between causal production and causal propagation and applies them to, respectively, the Misesian notion of the entrepreneur and the Hayekian vision of the workings of the price system. Salmon's differentiation between the production and propagation of causes is clear enough, and I think that Mäki is correct to view the entrepreneur as a causal agent and the price system as a transmitter of information through space and time. It is with some of the details of the analysis that I had trouble.

1. Salmon's own examples of causal production versus causal propagation are drawn with the natural sciences in mind, and their transference to a theory of human action may be problematical. His example concerning memory is instructive. Salmon argues as follows:

> Causal propagation (or transmission) is equally familiar. Experiences that we had earlier in our lives affect current behavior. By means of memory, the influence of these past events is transmitted to the present. ... A sonic boom makes us aware of the passage of a jet airplane overhead; a disturbance in the air is propagated from the upper atmosphere to our location on the ground (Salmon, 1984, 139).

Salmon is saying that, just as the atmosphere permits a sonic boom to be transmitted through space, memory allows past experiences to be transmitted through time. He wishes to emphasize the symmetry between causal propagation in space and in time, and within the context of his discussion, his point is well taken. But if one is solely concerned with explaining human action, his example threatens to obfuscate the previously clear distinction between causal production and propagation. It seems to me that all purposeful human action, and more fundamentally human perception itself, is affected by past experiences that can be said to reach the present via memory. If this is true, then the present actions of entrepreneurs, because they are affected by past experiences, are examples of *both* causal production and causal propagation. If we take Salmon's own example seriously, it would seem that he has only further confused the already prickly problem of what is to count as a "cause" in a theory of human action.

2. Moving now to his application of Salmon's theory, I agree with Mäki that the entrepreneur takes the role of a causal agent within Austrian theory. And I think that Mäki is right that this holds true over a very broad range of possible characterizations of entrepreneurial behavior.

For example, imagine for a moment that, starting from the Kirznerian version, we reconstruct a new theory of the entrepreneur. The agent in this theory shares with his Kirznerian counterpart the function of coordinating markets, of spotting (and by his profit-seeking activities unintentionally correcting) past errors, by being ever alert to arbitrage possibilities. But our new agent does more than this. In particular, some of his actions are *sources* of error and discoordination. Thus we might append to the usual Kirznerian abilities of alertness and a thirst for adventure a Schumpeterian propensity to disrupt the economic environment by introducing innovations. We might insist that even alert and profit-hungry entrepreneurs are not immune from committing discoordinating errors of their own, so that there is no guarantee that in the aggregate entrepreneurs will play a coordinating role. We might point out that, in an environment in which many alert entrepreneurs are on the lookout for profit opportunities, such opportunities will be few. As such, an alternative way to make profits is to mislead one's trading partners about present and future relative scarcities. (Indeed, if some subset of entrepreneurial agents found it easier to mislead others than to seek out price divergencies, it would be a misuse of their native abilities were they to choose to seek out "real" arbitrage possibilities rather than to create them through deception.) We might finally add that, in models that include a government sector, alertness to rent-seeking opportunities would be included. This fuller theory of the entrepreneur, then, would not only allow one to represent the bold, imaginative individuals contained in the Kirznerian vision, but the Charles Keatings of the world, as well.

The imagined "theory of the entrepreneur" sketched above in no way resembles any Austrian theory of the entrepreneur with which I am familiar. But even so, the entrepreneur in my sketch still has causal powers, and indeed, he has richer powers than does his Kirznerian counterpart. This example is offered in support of Mäki's point: characterizing the Austrian entrepreneur as a causal agent does not depend on which version of the theory is under consideration.

There may be one exception to Mäki's point. In most (if not all) versions of the Austrian theory of the entrepreneur, "alertness" is a capacity that all humans possess, but that only a few at any given moment and place choose to exercise. However, one might wish to define alertness as a trait that is unique to specific agents. If such were the case, if only a subset of all agents qualified as entrepreneurs, then the existence of some such agents would have to be postulated in order for one to have a causal process theory.

3. I agree with Mäki that within Austrian theory the price system is a transmitter and that the substance transmitted is information. Mäki stresses the role of the market in transmitting information concerning *price divergencies*. Price divergencies represent differing assessments of relative

scarcities by market participants and occur due to ignorance, error, asymmetric information, and the like. His emphasis is appropriate, since one of the central claims of Austrian theory is that the actions of profit-seeking entrepreneurs help to eliminate such divergencies. Crucially, price divergencies cannot arise in models in which all agents have access to the same, objectively correct information, as is the case in many of the standard models of the market economy.

Mäki's exposition obscures two other important functions of the price system, however. One of these is well known to neoclassicals and Austrians alike: prices convey information about relative scarcities. This allows agents (both consumers and firms) to make better decisions concerning resource allocation, and as such it is one of the most significant functions of a price system. Mäki mentions relative scarcities but focuses on the error correction function of markets.

A third function of the price system that has been identified by Austrians is not mentioned by Mäki. The function is well captured by Hayek's phrase, "the market as a discovery process." Within a market system there are incentives for entrepreneurs to seek out new products, processes, and markets, to invent and innovate, to recombine inputs in new ways, to engage in the manifold activities that ultimately cause the economic environment to change.

This third function may cause additional problems for Salmon's sharp distinction between causal production and causal propagation. Imagine that (due to either natural or man-made causes) a once plentiful input becomes relatively scarce. This information is transmitted through the price system; that is, its price rises. The new higher price stimulates entrepreneurs to seek out new supplies of the input, to consider what alternative inputs might be viable substitutes, to rethink production processes or input combinations, and so on. This is a standard story within Austrian theory; price signals are a key stimulant of entrepreneurial action. But in Salmon's terms, the story suggests that causal propagation (of changing prices, reflecting changing relative scarcities) can "cause" causal production (entrepreneurial action).

My objections in this section are reducible to the complaint that Salmon's theory, at least in the necessarily abbreviated form it takes in Mäki's chapter, may be too thin a framework on which to hang the rather rich Austrian theory of the market process. This may not be a lethal objection, but it does suggest that Salmon's theory requires further articulation.

Mäki's handling of the concept of theoretical redescription is subtle and thought-provoking. It is a commonplace that theories abstract from reality, that they are isolative. The usual next step is to assert that this makes theories "unrealistic." Mäki's treatment differs. He argues convincingly that a theory that isolates the essence of a phenomenon is a viable candidate for a realist interpretation. In making his case, Mäki makes the following statement: *"[t]he reason for the need for theoretical redescription is that the market does not appear to the common sense as a causal process of the kind conceptualized in Austrian theory"* (44; emphasis in the original).

This statement gets at a key problem that economists face. Economists learn, fairly early on in their training, certain important things about the real economy that seem true. There are gains from trade. Price-fixing causes resources to be misallocated. Demand curves slope downwards. Most important, policies that fail to take these truths into account will have predictable and perverse effects.

One of the most frustrating things about being an economist is that the truth of such statements is not evident to noneconomists. Economists are good at explaining why so many groups appear hostile to these truths. Using models with self-interested agents, it is easy to show why union leaders, or firms seeking government protection from competition, or academics in competing disciplines looking for research funding, or government officials trying to get reelected, would challenge such statements. These models do not explain, however, how such a patently self-interested disregard of the truth could persist undetected (except by economists) for so long, or how it could come to be so widespread. The unpopularity, or inconvenience, of a message is not sufficient to explain its failure to be believed by so many for so long.

Mäki gets at another reason: what individuals actually experience when they engage in market behavior is quite different from the process that is identified by economists. This seems plausible. What economist has not groused (at least momentarily) at the high (indeed, unfairly high!) price of a favorite out-of-stock commodity, or about his (unjustly) low salary compared to that of the consulting-oriented business management professor down the hall. It takes a clear and convincing story to induce people to get out of their roles as consumers and wage-earners to see the larger workings of the market economy.

Ironically, one barrier to understanding have been the models of economists. For reasons that have been (in my view) nowhere well explained, economists in the twentieth century became infatuated with models possessing ever-increasing levels of mathematical sophistication. These models may have many benefits associated with their use, but they have not helped to foster a better comprehension among noneconomists of how the price system works. Indeed, Austrians believe that they undermine the understanding not just of lay people, but of economists, as well: this was one of the conclusions that they drew from the socialist calculation debate. The attractiveness of causal process stories is that they help economists and noneconomists alike to overcome this barrier.

The Austrians claim to be making true statements about essential elements of really existing causal social processes. One can question whether their claims are true. Or, even if they are accepted as true, one can question whether they capture the most important aspects of social reality. The latter question plagued Menger, and it is prudent to recall that currently the chief realist competitor of Austrian theory is a variant of Marxism. When Marxist realists look at a commodity or capital they see an exploitative social relationship; different realists find different essences in a market economy. Mäki wisely leaves to the side the all-important question in all of this: How are such incompatible but competing visions to be appraised?

Some may wish to deny, then, the truth of the Austrian theory. But if it is a realist theory, as Mäki argues, then one cannot deny its claim to be trying to say something that is true. And as such, one cannot simply dismiss Austrian theory, as can be done with so many other models of economists, as just another irrelevant (others, but not Mäki, would use the word "unrealistic" here) theoretical construct. This is an implication of Mäki's analysis, and it has significance for the battles that economists fight against their cultured despisers.

3 KIRZNER'S THEORY OF ENTREPRENEURSHIP — A CRITIQUE

Martin Ricketts

Introduction

Over the last thirty years, no economic theorist has devoted more attention to the role of the entrepreneur in economic life than has Israel Kirzner. From his early work on the historical evolution of the "economic point of view" (1960), through his detailed analyses of the importance of the entrepreneur in the competitive process (1973, 1979), to his recent concern with the implications of entrepreneurship for distributive justice, Kirzner has consistently and forcefully argued that a correct understanding of the way capitalist economies operate requires explicit consideration of the role of the entrepreneur. His work has been radical and inevitably subversive of the "mainstream" tradition in economics. Kirzner demonstrates that the methods of equilibrium theory (whether static or dynamic) implicitly overlook the entrepreneurial role and must, therefore, present a highly distorted picture of the economic system.

Kirzner's contribution goes far beyond the mere emphasis on entrepreneurship as a key component of economic theory however. Kirzner's conception of the role of the entrepreneur is a highly distinctive one, and gives to his work a character and underlying theme that sets it apart from that of all other writers in the area. Running through the entire corpus of Kirzner's work there is a unifying "leitmotif" that the exploitation of the gains from trade will not take place automatically. To achieve the advantages of coordination through exchange requires first that these potential gains are noticed. The entrepreneurial role is to be "alert" to as yet unexploited gains from trade.

It is from this fundamentally important insight that the strengths and weaknesses in the Kirznerian system all derive. Kirzner carefully unravels the logical implications of the seemingly innocuous proposition that entrepreneurs are alert to new opportunities, and in so doing creates a notably different theory of pure entrepreneurial profit from earlier writers on the subject.

In von Thünen's work in the first part of the 19th century and in Knight's (1921) work on profit can be found the idea that the entrepreneur receives a residual income. This is seen primarily as compensation for the bearing of uncertainty, however, and not as a result of "alertness." Knight (1921, 269–70) writes that "the confident and venturesome assume the risk or insure the doubtful and timid by guaranteeing to the latter a specified income in return for an assignment of the actual result." When it comes to the characteristics of entrepreneurs, it seems only fitting that Knight's should be bold, but there is no explicit recognition that they need be notably alert.

Schumpeter's (1943, 132) view of the entrepreneur, in contrast, emphasizes the forcing through of innovations. The function of the entrepreneur is "to reform or revolutionise the pattern of production by exploiting an invention or, more generally, an untried technological possibility . . . ." Schumpeter sees the personal qualities of energy, leadership, and determination as playing an important role. He compares the entrepreneurial character to that of "the medieval warlords, great or small" (133). Schumpeter's exposition has inevitably led to the impression that his conception of the entrepreneur has more in common with what the American "muckrakers" would have called the "robber barons" than with bold uncertainty-bearing knights. Neither approach, however, has quite the same flavour as that of Kirzner's, whose entrepreneur would perhaps be more likely to take the form of a humble pedlar at the fair than a contestant in the lists.

The Kirznerian Entrepreneur

For the purposes of this critique it will be necessary to concentrate on a few of the salient features of Kirzner's unique approach. The following propositions represent an attempt to summarise in a few lines the most distinctive elements in his system.

1. Pure entrepreneurial profit is a return to alertness. It is quite distinct from a reward for "waiting" and from any other conception of the "return to capital." It is not the same as a reward for bearing uncertainty. Neither is it related to the compensation for undertaking the superintendence

of production processes, nor is it the same as a "windfall" (a return to pure luck).

2. Unexploited gains from trade are revealed in arbitrage possibilities. By acting as a "middleman" the entrepreneur can put together new patterns of transactions between buyers and sellers. Differences between buying and selling prices enable the entrepreneur to achieve a pure profit. Trade in resources is therefore necessary to the realisation of a profit opportunity, but, Kirzner argues, it is not true that entrepreneurial profit is a return to personal wealth. Even a person totally lacking in personal wealth might, in principle, persuade a capitalist to advance the necessary funds and thus enable the entrepreneur to generate a pure profit. The return to "alertness" and the return to capital are quite different concepts. Thus "entrepreneurial profits ... are not captured by owners, in their capacity as owners, at all. They are captured, instead, by men who exercise pure entrepreneurship, for which ownership is *never* a condition" (1979, 94).

3. The gradual discovery and realisation of the gains from trade moves the economy away from disequilibrium and discoordination towards a situation of equilibrium and coordination. Neoclassical general equilibrium theory makes use of the concept of an imaginary "auctioneer" *outside* the system who, by a process of trial and error, establishes a set of prices that clear every market. Kirzner substitutes the entrepreneur *within* the system as the agent with the motivation and alertness to uncover the opportunities available. This process he perceives as a movement towards equilibrium. Thus "we have seen that the movement from disequilibrium to equilibrium is nothing but the entrepreneurial-competitive process ...." (1973, 218). Again, in the context of economic development Kirzner comments that "this contrast between Schumpeter's vision of the entrepreneur as a spontaneous force pushing the economy *away* from equilibrium and my view of the entrepreneur as the prime agent in the process from disequilibrium *to* equilibrium, is particularly important ...." (1979, 112).

4. Any ethical appraisal of capitalism requires that the nature of entrepreneurial profit is understood. Kirzner emphasises that income generated by pure entrepreneurship is *discovered* income. It is not, as in the traditional textbook accounts of production, the result of the application of known means to the achievement of given ends, but the result of noticing new opportunities. If entrepreneurial profit represents a "find" rather than something that is "produced," it is possible to argue that ethical appraisal should take account of its special character. In particular, Kirzner argues that, to the extent that the "finders-keepers" ethic is accepted, it should apply to entrepreneurial profit.

In the following sections several issues raised by these propositions are discussed. Section three takes issue with Kirzner's treatment of the capitalist and argues that, from the perspective of his own system, the pure capitalist is never an entrepreneur. In section four it is argued that the distinction between equilibrating and disequilibrating entrepreneurs is difficult to sustain within a subjectivist framework and that Kirzner's approach to the entrepreneur could survive without reference to the concept of equilibrium. In section five similar arguments lead to the conclusion that the rent seeker and the Kirznerian entrepreneur cannot be distinguished in the absence of clear agreement about the existing distribution of property rights. Section six takes up Kirzner's views on the justice of entrepreneurial profit, while in section seven further practical reflections on the relevance of Kirzner's approach to the processes of economic development are presented. A few suggestions are also mooted concerning the relationship between Kirzner's entrepreneurial processes and the behavioural and evolutionary approach to economics.

Entrepreneurship, Uncertainty, and the Capitalist

As has already been noted, Kirzner is quite clear that the entrepreneur and the capitalist are analytically distinct categories. He writes that "the key point is that *pure* entrepreneurship is exercised only in the *absence* of an initially owned asset" (1973, 16). Yet, Kirzner is equally clear that the capitalist cannot avoid exercising an entrepreneurial function. "The Misesian insight that every capitalist must at the same time be an entrepreneur permitted us to see how entrepreneurial competition among capitalists plays a vital role in the selection of which would-be entrepreneurs shall be entrusted with society's scarce and valuable capital resources" (1979, 105).

   Now, this statement is open to differing interpretations. The words "every capitalist must ... be an entrepreneur" might suggest that the proposition is either axiomatic or some logical inference from earlier propositions. It might, for example, derive from the Misesian view that "in any real and living economy every actor is always an entrepreneur" (1949, 253). Everyone is an entrepreneur and the capitalist is no exception. Alternatively, it might reflect an implicit process of reasoning such as — the entrepreneur is alert to unexploited gains from trade; all capitalists must, by the nature of their business, be alert to unexploited gains from trade; ergo all capitalists are entrepreneurs. Finally, it might reflect an empirical judgement such as "in practice, although the return to capital and entrepreneurial profit are theoretically quite distinct analytical categories, every capitalist's income contains elements of both."

It would seem reasonable, given the prominence accorded to the idea that capitalists must be entrepreneurs, to infer that this goes beyond an assertion of the Misesian view that all human action is inherently entrepreneurial. Further, it is not entirely clear why Kirzner should concur in such a view. It is, after all Kirzner himself who in pursuit of pure (Crusonian) profit carefully constructs alternative hypothetical situations in which the castaway luckily receives a windfall or carefully calculates the return to his effort and thereby receives income that "calls for nothing entrepreneurial in Crusoe's character" (1979, 160). For Kirzner, entrepreneurial profit requires the recognition of error, that is, that there exist alternative courses of action that will produce superior results to those derivable from existing ones. To the extent that it is accepted that some component of human action does not derive from a recognition of error, but can reasonably be seen as the result of a process of Robbinsian calculation or indeed of the perpetuation of mere routine, every actor is presumably *not* "always an entrepreneur." There is a big difference between the claim that any person *may* act as an entrepreneur and the view that every action is entrepreneurial.

The tension that can be sensed in Kirzner's work between the Misesian view that entrepreneurial action is all pervasive, and the view that it comprises only some portion of human action (though a crucially important and neglected one) is a theme that will recur throughout this critique. For the moment, we consider the possibility that the statement that all capitalists must be entrepreneurs is a reflection of the empirical judgement that, in practice, a "pure capitalist" will never be observed. As Kirzner would be the first to point out, such a statement leaves the analytical categories of entrepreneur and capitalist quite intact. The fact that the overall return to a capitalist's activities will comprise some component of pure entrepreneurial profit, as well as a return to uncertainty bearing and the simple provision of capital resources, does not prevent us from disentangling these components as a conceptual exercise. It would still be true that the pure Kirznerian capitalist, artificial construct though he or she may be, receives no entrepreneurial profit. In practice, after all, the pure Kirznerian entrepreneur is likely to be no less elusive. All entrepreneurs will be capitalists to some degree, even if their contribution of resources is limited to the cost of a telephone call to the capitalist, or indeed the opportunity cost of the time taken up in button-holing him in the street.

We are left now with the alternative that every capitalist decision must, by its very nature, involve an entrepreneurial element. There is some evidence that Kirzner wishes to be interpreted in this way. He writes that "the decision to lend capital is itself partly an entrepreneurial one, because it involves the possibility that the borrower may be unable to carry out his side of the contract" (1979, 97). This has always appeared to the present writer to sit uneasily with Kirzner's emphasis on *alertness* as the defining characteristic of the entrepreneur. It would seem more compatible with a Knightian conception of the entrepreneur as a person who shoulders uncertainty. Consider Crusoe's predicament as Friday appears on the scene. Friday rapidly notices the hunting potential of Crusoe's musket and realises that a certain type of edible bird that lives unknown to Crusoe on the other side of the island, and that has hitherto been out of reach of the available technology, will become easy game. He therefore suggests to Crusoe that a hunting party would be mutually beneficial. No doubt Crusoe may be uncertain about how much reliance to place on Friday's vision of the future. Is it a realistic possibility or the result of a deceptive calenture? But it is difficult to see where any particular alertness on Crusoe's part is involved. Like all capitalists he will have to assess Friday's character and credibility and will be uncertain about the outcome, but any entrepreneurial profit generated by the plan would more reasonably be labelled Fridavian than Crusonian.

Several writers have noted the fact that Kirzner's analytical framework insulates the entrepreneur from uncertainty bearing. Although Kirzner (1982) attempts to refine his concept of alertness to avoid the implication that the entrepreneur discovers immediate and certain gains, there is still no possibility within his system that the entrepreneur can incur losses. As High (1982, 166) notes in his comment on Kirzner's (1982) paper, Kirzner "has not particularly emphasised the role of losses in the market process." High goes on to ask the rhetorical question "if entrepreneurship is completely separate from ownership, is it meaningful to speak of entrepreneurial loss?" (166). There would appear to be no escaping the conclusion that entrepreneurs cannot lose *as entrepreneurs*. If I think that I have made a "find" that turns out to be worthless, I have lost nothing unless I have used my resources in attempting to develop it. In Kirzner's system, resource owners bear uncertainty, not the entrepreneur.

Entrepreneurship and Equilibrium

In this section we consider the role played by the concept of equilibrium in Kirzner's theory of the entrepreneurial process. It was noted above that Kirzner is consistent in regarding the entrepreneur as a coordinating force. "My own treatment of the entrepreneur emphasises the equilibrating aspects of his role." (1973, 73). Yet, it is by no means clear that, when taken together, all the components that go to make up Kirzner's approach to the market process are compatible with such an "equilibrating" conception of the entrepreneur.

The essential difficulty is in deciding whether the entrepreneur should be seen as operating within a given technological, scientific, and perhaps legal background—discovering all the opportunities for exchange latent in a certain "state of the arts"—or whether entrepreneurial alertness can be responsible for changing this background. In terms of neoclassical "textbook" concepts, Kirzner suggests that the entrepreneur moves the economy to a suitable point on the "production possibility frontier" where no further gains from trade exist. The frontier itself, which represents all the social possibilities attainable with given resources, is not objectively known by anyone and has to be discovered by entrepreneurial alertness, but there is a sense in which it exists, and in which its existence does not depend upon its discoverer. "I view the entrepreneur not as a source of innovative ideas ex nihilo, but as being *alert* to the opportunities that exist *already* and are waiting to be noticed ... as responding to opportunities rather than creating them" (1973, 74).

This conceptualisation of the entrepreneurial process has its drawbacks. In the first place it implies a tendency for the economic system to "run down" as opportunities are discovered unless some outside force intervenes to "create" more and more potential entrepreneurial discoveries. Second, this outside force, which we might call invention or scientific advance, has to be seen as nonentrepreneurial in character. Yet, much technical advance would appear to be quite entrepreneurial in Kirzner's sense of requiring alertness to new possibilities. When technical progress is called "induced," it is implied that existing market prices stimulate entrepreneurial efforts to do things in new ways. A famous historical example is the invention of Hargreaves' "spinning jenny," which has been related to high prices of yarn occasioned by developments in weaving. Such inventions, it could be argued, did not come "out of the blue" as a result of pure luck, neither did they arise from a purely Robbinsian process of maximisation, but they required alertness to the possibility of an unexploited opportunity. Price signals are perceived *ex post* as being important in appearing to "induce" the innovation, but this should not lead us to think of the process as being automatic. If ex ante prices and ex post profits appear to "explain" the pattern of technical change, this may simply reflect the point that big opportunities are more likely to be noticed than small ones.

I do not claim here that all scientific or technical advance is the result of entrepreneurial discovery. Perhaps great technical changes can derive from the findings of "basic research," which involves the pursuit of pure scientific knowledge rather than pure entrepreneurial profit. Once it is accepted that some component of innovation and even invention is entrepreneurial in Kirzner's sense, however, the idea of the equilibrating entrepreneur is no longer sustainable unless one is prepared, as Shackle puts it, to "rule a line under the sum of human knowledge, the total human inventive accomplishment" (1982, 255). As in section three, the issue here concerns the domain of entrepreneurship, whether it relates to all human action, including technical innovation, or whether it is possible to confine our conception to a more limited sphere. In section three it was argued that, in principle, human action could be envisaged that was non-entrepreneurial in Kirzner's, if not in Mises' sense. In contrast, I am in this section arguing that Kirzner's conception of entrepreneurship makes a clear distinction impossible between movements *towards* and movements *of* the production possibility curve, and that his implicit attempt to confine entrepreneurial movements to the former is unsuccessful.

It should be recognised that a wider reading of Kirzner suggests that he is himself unwilling to draw a very definite line between entrepreneurship and technical innovation, and that he has a rather broad conception of the role of the entrepreneur. For example, Kirzner writes that "it is the essence of our position throughout this book that exactly the same competitive-entrepreneurial market process is at work whether it manifests itself through prices adjusting toward general (or partial) equilibrium patterns or through the adjustment of commodity opportunities made available, techniques of production, or the organization of industry" (1973, 129). Further, in his later work he appears to move away from an explicitly "noncreative" conception of the entrepreneur. Quite the contrary — "the human agent can, by imaginative, bold leaps of faith and determination, in fact *create* the future for which his present acts are designed" (1982, 150: emphasis in original). In his work on distributive justice (1989, 40–44) Kirzner is even more explicit. He refers to "the basic unity shared by genuinely creative artistic and technological innovation on the one hand, and the more simple acts of discovery . . . on the other. To discover an opportunity, I have implied, is to create it (40)".

There would seem no way that the earlier simple view of the equilibrating entrepreneur can be made compatible with this later conception. On the other hand, Kirzner appears anxious to retain the notion of the entrepreneur as a co-ordinating force and distances himself from Shackle's nihilism. Shackle refers (1979, 31) to "the anarchy of history," whereas Kirzner wishes to draw attention to "the benign co-ordinative powers of the human imagination" (1982, 157). For Kirzner, it is unrewarding to see the world either as utterly chaotic or as a process of remorseless drive towards a final static equilibrium. It would, therefore, seem that the very notion of equilibrium is unhelpful and misleading when discussing the Kirznerian entrepreneur.

Kirzner's conception fits more into an evolutionary approach to economics than the standard neoclassical one, although it is to the latter that Kirzner most often directs his comparisons. Just as the natural world is in a perpetual state of change, change that is neither easily predictable nor entirely chaotic, so economic life may be envisaged, by analogy, to exhibit similar properties. The evolutionary models of Nelson and Winter, for example, generate time paths of economic variables on the basis of a "substitution of the 'search and selection' metaphor for the maximisation and equilibrium metaphor" (1982, 227). Firms, in their approach, adopt "routines" (the genetic material of the institution), which given the environment in which they are placed, result in varying levels of profit. Profits influence the expansion or contraction of the firm, again through the application of rules, while these routines may themselves be modified by the process of "search" — the counterpart of genetic mutation in evolutionary theory" (18). As it stands, this is far from being a Kirznerian conception. Search for Nelson and Winter has itself a "routine" aspect that would appear to make the "mutation" analogy extremely forced. If the comparison with "mutation" is to be used, however, it might well be thought that mutation through the intervention of Kirzner's entrepreneur is a more reasonable interpretation. This would emphasise that, in the case of the economic system, "blind watchmakers" do not make good metaphors.[1] The evolutionary process is not completely "blind," but is influenced by the ability of entrepreneurs to peer ahead and "to formulate an image of the future" (Kirzner 1982, 149) in a conscious attempt to create it.

Entrepreneurship, Rent-Seeking, and Efficiency

Kirzner devotes very little attention to rent seeking. Given his emphasis on alertness to gains from trade as the defining characteristic of the entrepreneur, the lack of interest in behaviour that involves no such gains might seem understandable. But other writers, neither ignorant of nor unsympathetic to subjectivist traditions in economics,[2] have noted that alertness to the possibilities of *personal* gain may not always imply *social* gain. It may instead simply result in the "discovery" of ways of diverting resources from one person to another. In the following paragraphs it is argued that Kirzner's lack of interest in rent seeking leads him to attach the term "entrepreneurship" to activities that may not justify it.

The analysis of monopoly is an area in which this dispute has been particularly intense. Kirzner points out (1973, ch. 5) that it would be a mistake to consider monopoly from an entirely static point of view. An entrepreneur may gain control of the entire supply of some resource. From the point of view of the present moment he is a monopolist and his return is monopoly rent. But from a longer run and more dynamic perspective this rent may derive from a thoroughly *entrepreneurial* decision to appropriate the resource – a decision not imitated by others and presumably unnoticed. This part of Kirzner's argument is entirely compatible with Littlechild's (1981) critique of the misleading nature of calculations of the social cost of monopoly. Taking issue with Cowling and Mueller's (1978) estimates, Littlechild pointed out that their methodology implied that all monopoly profit represented efficiency losses. Cowling and Mueller made absolutely no allowance for the Kirznerian possibility that the observed profit was an entrepreneurial return and actually represented social gains, gains that in the absence of the entrepreneur would have remained entirely unexploited.

It is one of the most enjoyable features of Kirzner's writing that he tries out his ideas even under the most unfavourable circumstances, rather as a physical component of a new product might be tested to destruction to assess its reliability. Kirzner (1979, 222–223) considers the appropriation by one of a group of travelers (by means of racing ahead of the others) "of the unheld sole water hole in the desert which *everyone* in a group of travelers knows about." Even this, argues Kirzner, might be seen as entrepreneurial discovery. To the present writer, however, it seems that if this can be seen as entrepreneurial discovery, there is *nothing* that cannot be seen as entrepreneurial discovery. The other travelers, argues Kirzner, might equally have raced ahead. Perhaps this indicates the want of alertness or the lack of appreciation of the "true market value of the unheld water". Perhaps they wrongly assumed that no-one could get to the water before them, or they overestimated the quantity of water available, or "gave the water no thought at all."

Perhaps the root of my disagreement with Kirzner at this point concerns his lack of any close attention to the nature of property rights. He describes the water as simply "unheld" although known to everyone. The physical existence of the water had presumably been discovered at an earlier time and the knowledge of its whereabouts distributed to all potential users. In these circumstances I would assert that it is inconceivable that the group of travelers would regard the water as "unheld" and therefore available for entrepreneurial appropriation. They would instead regard the water as a communal asset with a clear right of individual *use* implied. Kirzner is able to come to his startling conclusions only by postulating a set of circumstances that are mutually incompatible, namely general knowledge of both the existence and economic uses of an asset combined with lack of *any* conception of rights to its use. Of course, it may well be true that *private and exchangeable* rights to the asset are not held, but Kirzner is led into error by the implicit assumption that property rights either take this strong private form or otherwise are entirely absent.

Once the existence of weaker "communal" rights to resources is recognised, even if supported, as Alchian (1965, 129) puts it, "by the force of etiquette, social custom, (and) ostracism," rather than any more specific coercive powers of the State, the activities of the fleet-footed water grabber are revealed as rent seeking. By appropriating the water, he has infringed the property rights of the other travelers.

It must be admitted, however, that the case can still give rise to difficulties. Suppose that the water resource is being over-used by travelers exercising their communal rights. The quality and quantity of the water is deteriorating, the surrounding verdure is wilting, and the general amenity value of the watering place is declining. A person contacts each of those in the group that, by custom, is considered to have a right of use and persuades them to relinquish any claim. This person, unlike other members of the group, may have spotted the great economic value of a properly managed resource, and should he gain control through agreement, some of the social gains will appear as pure entrepreneurial profit. No rights have been infringed, and the social gains from greater coordination achieved.

Now suppose, however, that the resource is not over-used, and that it bestows its benefits on all passers-by freely and efficiently as a gift of nature. Along comes our putative entrepreneur and by some noncoercive means manages to gain control. He does not run ahead of the other travelers but merely gets them drunk by the camp fire and so induces them to part with their rights. Is this person a Kirznerian entrepreneur? He has certainly been more alert than the others. He may certainly have perceived the possible market value of the water if only access could be restricted. Further, my objection concerning the infringement of implied property rights no longer applies.

There is a genuine (and possibly irresolvable) dilemma here. Since no property rights have been coercively challenged, the returns in this case could be seen as entrepreneurial. Yet we might be tempted to argue that this entrepreneur can gain only by restricting the use of the water, reducing the use of this particular route across the desert, and diverting the consumers' surplus, hitherto enjoyed by the traveler to himself in the form of a payment for what had always been received without charge. The entrepreneur, it might be claimed, has been alert merely to the possibilities of successful deception, and the other members of the group will have recieved less in payment for their rights than they will in future be returning to the entrepreneur for water supplies.

Once it is clear that no uncompensated transfers of property rights have taken place, however, Kirzner is in a stronger position to counter these points. The problem with this reasoning is that it introduces an "objectivity" into the situation that is not warranted. How do we know that deception has anything to do with the case? Perhaps the exchanges negotiated between the entrepreneur and the other members of the group reflected the true judgements of all the participants. Further, the implicit assumption of the "objectivist," that there can be no net social advantage derivable from the pattern of exchanges described and that, therefore, there *must* be some legerdemain involved, may be untrue. Perhaps the entrepreneur has spotted the potential of the surrounding land for the purposes of tourism or agriculture, and recognises that the entrepreneurial profits will be greater, and imitation more difficult, if he can secure control of the supplies of necessary water.

To summarise, rent seeking can either be defined in terms of activities that infringe established property rights, or in terms of activities that result in social losses. Kirzner is a consistent subjectivist and his writing clearly implies the impossibility of identifying social waste objectively. But his somewhat casual treatment of concepts of property seems to the present writer to lead to a neglect of the possibility of rent seeking, (interpreted as action that infringes property rights) and to the impression that all alertness may be entrepreneurial, even the alertness of the shop-lifter. The Kirznerian entrepreneur can act only within a given structure of rights. This status quo may be difficult to define and may give rise to disagreement, but without a careful appraisal of the nature and distribution of property rights within a community it will be impossible to distinguish the Kirznerian entrepreneur from the rent seeker. Further consideration is given to this point at the end of section seven.

Entrepreneurship and Distributive Justice

In his treatment of distributive justice, Kirzner uses the special nature of entrepreneurial profit to question the applicability of conventional "end state" concepts of justice to the ethical evaluation of capitalist income. Most treatments of distributive justice, he argues, are based on the analogy of sharing out a given pie. Even those more sophisticated treatments that link the size of the pie with the distributive rule adopted, see the problem as one of choosing among various alternatives that are already known, and that imply predictable maximising behaviour on the part of economic agents. This approach cannot cope with the justice of a form of income that depends upon the *discovery* of new opportunities. A finders-keepers ethic would be more applicable to this situation. Indeed, Kirzner goes further to argue that it is possible to reconsider the philosophical problem of establishing original just title to natural resources by accepting the discovery element inherent in their appropriation.

Kirzner makes it clear, however, that his major interest is not to take issue with the ethics of existing discussions of distributive justice, but to establish that they are based on a mistaken view of capitalist income. He writes, "My disagreement with the existing literature will, then, turn out to be not a disagreement in ethics but a disagreement in economics" (1989, 3). The existing approaches are not based on a "valid positive understanding" of the way capitalism works because they overlook the importance of pure entrepreneurial profit and the return to alertness.

Produced versus Discovered Pies

A major problem that Kirzner appears not to resolve, however, is the quantitative significance of his observation. Kirzner's economics may be "positive" in that it is concerned with how capitalism actually works, but his subjectivist methodology does not permit the identification and measurement of empirical counterparts to theoretical concepts such as pure profit. How are we to tell at any point in time what part of a person's income is the result of entrepreneurial alertness, and what part is the result of Robbinsian maximising behaviour? The question would appear to be irresolvable. At some points Kirzner writes as if all income is in a meaningful sense "discovered." "Every penny which the resource owner in fact obtains in exchange for his resources is thus a 'find'" (1989, 116). At other points, the Kirzner of the early chapters of *Competition and Entrepreneurship* reasserts himself. "Resource incomes present aspects both of discoveries and of simple entitlement-generated resource proceeds" (1989, 126). "I would not ... deny that, besides these discovery elements in capitalism, inextricably intertwined with them, are elements of fairly stable repetitive patterns" (176).

Much of the tension in Kirzner's work between the view that all income is discovered and the alternative view that only a certain proportion represents newly discovered gains from trade derives, it might be argued, from the issues discussed in section three. The Misesian argument that every decision is inherently speculative might well lead to the designation of all income as entrepreneurial in nature. Yet, I have already argued that the specifically Kirznerian insight that entrepreneurial income is *discovered* does not, in spite of Kirzner's attempts, necessarily result in such a conclusion. When a resource owner agrees to sell, argues Kirzner, (1989, 116) "he is taking a daring entrepreneurial gamble"; perhaps he is missing better opportunities elsewhere; or his decision "may be, in an entrepreneurial sense, an embarkation on a *losing* venture." But what have the acceptance of daring gambles and the risk of *losses* to do with alertness? Is this not the job of the capitalist and resource owner? Kirzner appears at these points to risk confounding the distinctions, so painstakingly established, between alertness to new opportunities and the bearing of inevitable uncertainty. If, after all, Kirzner has concluded that these distinctions are unsustainable, his system loses many of its distinctive properties.

The Market and the Graspers-Keepers Ethic

Suppose for the moment that a return to conscious, purposeful, alertness can be distinguished from other types of income. It is still not clear that the alert discoverer of an opportunity will gain the profit. *Realization* of an entrepreneurial opportunity requires resources, so that it is by no means obvious that the first discoverer of an opportunity will reap the reward. Kirzner draws the analogy with the pursuit of an animal and argues that apportioning legal rights between original pursuer and final slayer is a matter of convention. He offers the opinion, however, that "the first one taking possession should, I would argue, really be recognised as the first genuine discoverer of the economic value of the unowned resource" (1989, 172). Where the quarry is not some physical resource, but "the gains from new patterns of exchange," it is difficult to see how these could accrue to anyone *but* the final person who *realizes* the opportunity. In market processes, the spoils go to those who grasp them rather than to those who first notice them. Yet, somehow the phrase "graspers-keepers" has a less persuasive appeal as an ethical principle than "finders-keepers," even though it more accurately reflects the realities of the market. Kirzner circumvents the problem by defining it away. The grasper *is* the finder. Without the grasp, where is the evidence that anything has been found? The distinction between finder and grasper may still have significance in the moral thinking of many people, however.

Consider the celebrated recent takeover battle between Guinness and Argyll for control of Distillers in the United Kingdom. The chairman of

Guinness, Ernest Saunders, was found to have misappropriated Guinness shareholders' funds in his efforts to fund a share support operation, thus keeping the price of Guinness shares "artificially" high. He won the battle for control of Distillers but was later imprisoned. A Guinness shareholder wrote to *the Times* (August 30, 1990) that, as a direct result of the takeover of Distillers, the company had gone from strength to strength and that he could not see any sense in which he could be said to have suffered a loss by theft. Further "Ernest Saunders was the one who saw the opportunity and went for it." James Gulliver, the defeated Argyll chairman replied the following day "A letter in *The Times* yesterday talks about Ernest Saunders identifying the opportunity. He did not. It was identified, analysed and a strategy developed by Argyll" (23). As far as Gulliver was concerned it was not the Guinness shareholders but those of Argyll who were robbed. His complaint mainly concerned the means used by his opponent to gain victory, but it is impossible to mistake the implicit extra claim that prior discovery gave Argyll some sort of additional title to the quarry.

Some Concluding Comments

Kirzner's insights concerning the role of entrepreneurship in economic development are of more than purely philosophical significance. The persuasiveness of his approach rests not on its coherence as a purely metaphysical system, but on its ability to make sense of our observations of the world. As we survey the ruins of the planned economies in Eastern Europe, their failure cannot be explained merely by reference to techno-logical considerations. They failed because their structure ignored Kirzner's "positive understanding" of the way the market economy they were supposed to replace and supplant actually worked.

An entrepreneurial perspective also helps in the understanding of other historical cases. From 1965 to 1980 Rhodesia was faced with economic sanctions imposed by the United Nations. Over the period, however, it diversified its agriculture, attained the highest rate of growth in Africa, and developed export markets in a whole range of new crops (Harris, 1990). If necessity is said to be the mother of invention, it seems equally true that adversity is often the precursor of entrepreneurship. On the other hand, as Witt (1989, 414) points out, Kirzner gives us no well-articulated theory of alertness to explain these and other phenomena. His attention is so focused on the *rationale* of the entrepreneur that the circumstances most favourable to the realization of entrepreneurial talent are not really explored. "A more profound theoretical basis could indicate which factors possibly affect the incentive to be alert, to search for new opportunities, or the time it takes for competition to erode the 'alertness' rent."

It is less easy to see how Kirzner's theory of entrepreneurship can be used normatively as an aid to policy formulation. Clearly, the exercise of entrepreneurship requires the ability to trade in property rights. But there are other important questions to address. For example, although a regime of purely private and exchangeable property rights is most conducive to entrepreneurial alertness, does it follow that alternative regimes are necessarily less desirable? Is greater scope for entrepreneurship always preferable to less?

Because Kirzner's conception of the entrepreneur is so intimately associated with the gains from trade, it is easy to assume that the greater the recognition of "error" the better. But the arbitrage conception of the entrepreneur requires that the *durability* of exchange relationships is always precarious and may be disturbed at any time by alert entrepreneurial intervention. This disturbance may harm none if everyone accepts that agreements are entered into only for the duration of each moment. If, however, long standing agreements to trade in a certain way are in existence, and if assurances concerning the durability of such agreements were required to make them initially acceptable, entrepreneurial intervention could prove very destructive. Kirzner's theory of the entrepreneur, in other words, does not take account of the *relational* or *obligational* aspects involved in long-term contract.[3]

Even though the entrepreneur may achieve pure profits from putting together new exchange relationships, he may not have recognised true "error" in Kirzner's sense. Recontracting may have harmed some of those who invested specific resources in the existing relationship. If the entrepreneur's profit is not sufficient to compensate those harmed, it is difficult to argue that any error would have been involved in resisting change. Even if the newly spotted opportunity is so productive that *all* could be compensated, and real Kirznerian error would be associated with continuing with present arrangements, grasping the new prospect may not be socially desirable unless compensation is actually paid to the losers. In the absence of such compensation, economic agents would be less prepared to tolerate a position of dependence on others. Establishing rights in such situations may be extremely difficult, however, and we again see the importance of correctly establishing the framework of property rights and social conventions within which the entrepreneur is assumed to operate. A society in which new opportunities are always immediately graspable may be one that is incapable of achieving the benefits of long term associations because no one will be prepared to commit specific resources to maintaining them. An agreement *not* to trade with a newcomer over a certain period of time may be necessary if the confidence to make specific investments and endure economic vulnerability is to be developed. The corollary of this observation is that economic progress depends not only on giving scope for entrepreneurial alertness and the recognition of error, but also, in appropriate circumstances, on giving protection from entrepreneurial intervention and encouraging a certain degree of acceptance of error.

Notes

1. The metaphor is used by Dawkins (1986).
2. See, for example, Buchanan et al. (1980).
3. The problems of trading frequently over long periods in the presence of "asset specificity" have figured prominently in the work of writers such as Oliver Williamson who argue that such factors determine the form of "governance" required for transactional relations. See, for example, Williamson (1985) and Goldberg (1976).

References

Alchian, A. A. 1965. "Some Economics of Property Rights," *Il Politico* 30(4): 816–29.

Buchanan, J. M., Tollison, R. D. and Tullock, G., (eds.) 1980. *Toward a Theory of the Rent Seeking Society*. College Station: Texas A&M University Press.

Cowling, K. and Mueller, D. C. 1978. "The Social Cost of Monopoly Power," *Economic Journal* 88(4): 727–748.

Dawkins, R. 1986. *The Blind Watchmaker*. New York: Longman.

Goldberg, V. 1976. "Toward an Expanded Economic Theory of Contract," *Journal of Economic Issues* 10, 1: 45–61.

Gulliver, J. 1990. "How Scotland Lost Out to Hammersmith Flyover," *The Times*, August 31, 23.

Harris, M. 1990. *Economic Sanctions and Rhodesia*. Unpublished M. Phil Thesis, University of Buckingham.

High, J. 1982. "Alertness and Judgment: Comment on Kirzner." In *Method, Process, and Austrian Economics*, Kirzner, I. M. (ed.) Lexington, MA: D.C. Heath, 161–168.

Kirzner, I. M. 1960. *The Economic Point of View: An Essay in the History of Economic Thought*. Kansas City: Sheed and Ward.

———. 1973. *Competition and Entrepreneurship*. Chicago and London: University of Chicago Press.

————. 1979. *Perception, Opportunity, and Profit: Studies in the Theory of Entrepreneurship*. Chicago and London: University of Chicago Press.

————. 1982. "Uncertainty, Discovery and Human Action: A Study of the Entrepreneurial Profile in the Misesian System." In *Method, Process, and Austrian Economics*, Kirzner, I. M. (ed.) Lexington, MA: D.C. Heath, 139–159.

————. 1989. *Discovery, Capitalism and Distributive Justice*. Oxford: Blackwell.

Knight, F. H. 1921. *Risk, Uncertainty and Profit*. Boston: Houghton Mifflin.

Littlechild, S. C. 1981. "Misleading Calculations of the Social Cost of Monopoly Power," *Economic Journal* 9(2): 348–363.

Mises, Ludwig. 1949. *Human Action*. London: William Hodge.

Nelson, R. R. and Winter, S. G. 1982. *An Evolutionary Theory of Economic Change*. Cambridge, MA: Harvard University Press.

Schumpeter, J. A. 1943. *Capitalism, Socialism and Democracy*. London: Unwin University Books.

Shackle, G. L. S. 1979 "Imagination, Formalism and Choice." In *Time, Uncertainty, and Disequilibrium: Exploration of Austrian Themes*, Rizzo, Mario J. (ed.) Lexington, MA: D.C. Heath, 19–31.

————. 1982. "Means and Meaning in Economic Theory." *Scottish Journal of Political Economy* 29(3): 223–234.

Williamson, O. E. 1985. *The Economic Institutions of Capitalism: Firms, Markets, Relational Contracting*. London: Collier Macmillan.

Witt, U. 1989. "Subjectivism in Economics—A Suggested Reorientation." In *Understanding Economic Behaviour*, Grunert, K. G. and Ölander, F., (eds.) Dordrecht: Kluwer Academic Publishers, 409–431.

p 89; COMMENTARY

Entrepreneurship, Uncertainty and Austrian Economics

Israel M. Kirzner

I am most grateful for Martin Ricketts' perceptive and generous critique of my work on the theory of entrepreneurship. I must also express similar appreciation for Martin Ricketts' recent review of my *Discovery, Capitalism, and Distributive Justice*;[1] the ideas expressed in this commentary have been valuably stimulated by both of these essays.

Ricketts has raised a number of highly interesting, often subtle points in his critique. It will not be possible to address all of them in this response, and I apologize for this. It seems wisest for me to try to restate certain aspects of my understanding of the entrepreneurial role from a somewhat fresh perspective. This restatement may prove to be helpful in addressing several of the key objections raised by Ricketts, by emphasizing certain debatable features of his (otherwise superb and accurate) presentation of my position.

Opportunities: Noticed and Unnoticed

Standard microeconomics proceeds by postulating an array of known, alternative opportunities for action confronting the individual decision-maker, — permitting him, indeed requiring him, to adopt the optimal one. The very existence of opportunities is treated as synonymous with their having being already perceived. The optimizing or maximizing requirement thus ensures that the best opportunity will in fact be exploited. The entrepreneurial perspective on human action emphasizes the arbitrariness

85

of this set of assumptions. In particular it calls attention (1) to the possibility that an opportunity may exist but not have been perceived to exist, and (2) to social and market forces that tend to make it, nonetheless, reasonable for economists to postulate a *tendency* for available opportunities to become perceived by those for whom they are in fact attractive.

It will be useful to examine some differences between the meaning of a perceived opportunity and an unperceived opportunity. If an individual perceives an opportunity *with certainty*, this means that he sees the pleasant outcome offered by the opportunity as *already within his grasp* (contingent only on his taking appropriate action). Although the actual enjoyment promised by the opportunity has of course not yet been experienced, he already "possesses" it, since he fully controls the ability to enjoy it at will. It is as if he has ice cream in his freezer, available for consumption whenever he chooses. It is, as it were, "in his pocket."

Consider someone who sees with certainty how he can acquire ice cream. He does not have ice cream in his freezer, but he has money in his wallet, a well-functioning car in his driveway, and a well-stocked supermarket a short distance away; if he has complete confidence in his wallet, his car, and his supermarket, then he already *now* feels, within his grasp, the power to consume the ice cream (or, at least, to do so in about a half hour). When he in fact consumes the ice cream, the enjoyment he experiences is simply the actualization of a fully anticipated, and assured, experience. No element of happy surprise whatever is attached to it. A plan has been successfully completed, that is all. The certainty with which that success had been anticipated ensures the absence of any sense of pleasant novelty in its successful outcome.

The unperceived opportunity is, of course, quite different. So long as it remains wholly unperceived, the opportunity simply does not exist — at any rate for the unsuspecting potential beneficiary. At the moment when this opportunity comes to be noticed, its existence impinges upon its potential beneficiary as a flash of light, as a discovery. This flash of light transforms the enjoyment (afforded by the opportunity) from being nothing more than the fully anticipated outcome of a plan always believed to promise success with certainty — into a fortunate, even exciting, surprise. The glimpsing of this unanticipated enjoyment lifts one out of the routine sequence of everyday experience. It is in the nature of a windfall — with one crucial difference.

This crucial difference arises out of the purely lucky character of the windfall, contrasted with the human discovery source of the suddenly-perceived opportunity. When we think of a windfall, we are thinking of a fortunate situation enjoyed by its beneficiary without it being in any way traceable to that beneficiary's actions or discoveries. But the newly discovered opportunity opens up an avenue for an enjoyment that its discoverer can justly attribute, at least in part, to his own "entrepreneurial" alertness. Had it not been for his alertness, this opportunity may have remained forever hidden and unexploited. He, not blind luck, is to be credited with the successful outcome.

Because we attribute to human beings a tendency — an "entrepreneurial" tendency — to notice that in their environment which is likely to be of use to them, we find the idea of a *permanently* unnoticed opportunity difficult to swallow. Sooner or later, we are sure, this opportunity will come to be discovered. The dark night of sheer ignorance that is responsible for the unnoticed character of an opportunity, will sooner or later give way to the light of dawn. At that moment it will "dawn" on the individual decision maker that he has available to him a hitherto unnoticed prize. And it is because of our confidence in this tendency for opportunities to be noticed, sooner or later, that we employ the metaphor of equilibration to the process of opportunity discovery. An unnoticed attractive opportunity is, in the context of the individual, a disequilibrium phenomenon. In this sense the discovery of an opportunity is seen as an equilibrating step. It is of course true that at any given moment, for each individual, there will exist many opportunities that he has as yet not perceived. We do not really find it easy to imagine an individual in full equilibrium (that is, with no fog of ignorance preventing him from realizing all available opportunities). Nonetheless, it seems useful to recognize the tendency for human beings to come to notice that which it is in their interest to notice, as an equilibrative tendency. A good deal of the changing patterns of human activity can, we believe, be explained in terms of this all-pervasive entrepreneurial tendency.

Thus far, we have contrasted the case of the opportunity already perceived with certainty with that shrouded in *complete* ignorance. The discovery of this latter kind of opportunity, we saw, was in the nature of a flash of light illuminating a scene otherwise hidden in complete darkness. We hasten to emphasize that these two cases (that of complete certainty, and that of complete ignorance) are merely polar cases in a continuous spectrum. The uncertainty of life is unlikely to leave many cases in which an opportunity is perceived as being one hundred percent assured of success. On the other hand relatively few of our actions are inspired by the flash of light that impinges on *complete* darkness. Most of our decisions, taken indeed under uncertainty, are nonetheless inspired, in part, by a fairly confident general assessment of the relevant possibilities. Most of our actions, taken indeed with reasonable assurance of success, are nonetheless beclouded by our awareness of how little is certain in this world. Let us more carefully consider these more realistic classes of opportunities perceived through a cloud of subjective uncertainty.

The Opportunity Seen With Uncertainty

The typical example is something like the following. At 2:45 A.M. a person, suddenly craving ice cream, considers whether he should drive to the twenty-four hour supermarket to buy some ice cream. At 3:00 A.M. he finally decides to do so. There has been no sudden flash of light illuminating any utter ignorance. Everybody knows that the supermarket is two miles away, and is open twenty-four hours a day. Everybody knows the approximate cost of a pint of ice cream. Everybody knows how to get to the supermarket by car. Nonetheless, there may have been good reason for the prospective ice cream patron to have decided at 3:00 A.M. *not* to buy ice cream (quite apart from the obvious possibility that he might, at 3:00 A.M. especially, have ranked sleep more highly than ice cream). After all, the supermarket might (for some reason yet unknown to him) in fact turn out to be closed (or, at any rate, to have run out of ice cream); or the price of ice cream may, just possibly, have increased so as to render it a substantially less attractive buy; or the chances of one's car breaking down (or of becoming involved in an accident caused by some inebriated party-goer returning home); or the ice cream found to cause cancer, are perhaps not entirely negligible. The uncertainties combine to make the opportunity to buy ice cream at 3:00 A.M. in the supermarket something less than an altogether sure desirable, thing. It is possible that our ice cream afficionado might have decided *not* to drive to the supermarket because of these uncertainties. But we have supposed that eventually he does decide to drive to the supermarket after all — and successfully brings home the ice cream. His earlier failure to drive to buy ice cream is revealed to have been a mistake. The uncertainties that fueled that failure are now revealed to have obscured the true state of affairs.

What has happened, clearly, is (1) that the opportunity to drive to the store and buy ice cream at 3:00 A.M. did in fact exist, and (2) that our insomniac ice cream enthusiast did finally correctly perceive this opportunity — despite the uncertainty surrounding it. At 2:45 A.M. he had, because of these uncertainties, not quite made up his mind to forage for ice cream; we may wish to say that he had, at 3:00 A.M., discovered an opportunity he had previously not quite fully perceived. The fog of uncertainty had rendered him blind, or at any rate, hazy-sighted, to the real possibility of buying ice cream in the early hours. While his "discovery" at 3:00 A.M. was thus somewhat short of being a case of illuminating a previously total darkness (since the principal elements making up the opportunity were fully known long before 3:00 A.M.), nonetheless, it is reasonable to recognize that something of a discovery did occur at that time. Up until then the uncertainties surrounding the drive to the super-market had appeared to be so menacing as to render this opportunity no opportunity at all (since there was a sufficient chance of failure to cancel out the opportunity value of any attempted drive to the store). At 3:35 A.M. our insomniac saw (as it turned out correctly) that an attempted drive to buy ice cream was, despite the uncertainties, a worthwhile venture, after all. His enjoyment, at 3:45 A.M., of his nocturnally acquired ice cream was not really an anticipated possibility at 2:45 A.M. (since at that time he had not yet become convinced that the drive to the store was a good idea; at 2:45 A.M. he did not believe — with sufficient confidence to undertake the expedition — that such a trip would provide ice cream for 3:45 A.M. consumption).

The "discovery" that inspired the 3:00 A.M. decision was thus in the nature of *overcoming* uncertainty, of *seeing through* the fog of uncertainty. It is not that our hero has accepted the burden of uncertainty but that he has conquered it. He does not shoulder uncertainty; he shoulders it aside. Where pure entrepreneurial discovery (of an opportunity hitherto hidden by utter ignorance) is in the nature of a flash of light illuminating what had previously been complete darkness, the decision finally to act in an uncertain situation constitutes the discernment of an opportunity which has, up until now, been revealed (through the fog of uncertainty) only in incomplete outline. If we see the essence of entrepreneurial discovery to consist in the glimpsing of that which was previously not seen, then we should recognize an entrepreneurial element, at least, in the decision made under uncertainty. This entrepreneurial element consists in finally being able to see the complete contours of a worthwhile opportunity where, until now, significant segments of these contours had not been glimpsed through the fog.

The achievement attained through successfully grasping an opportunity in the face of uncertainty can hardly be viewed as a complete, exciting, surprise (as was the case, we saw, with the success won through a suddenly perceived opportunity hitherto shrouded in complete darkness). Even at 2:45 A.M. (when our insomniac had not yet clearly seen the decisive worthwhileness of driving to the store for ice cream) he certainly realized that such a trip *could* quite possibly lead to ice cream. So the ice cream he acquires soon after 3:00 A.M. is hardly in the nature of a totally unexpected pleasure. This is quite true. But we must also emphasize, on the other hand, that we can hardly view the enjoyment of this ice cream (or the success achieved through any opportunity grasped under uncertainty) as merely part of a routinely expected future that is unfolding in preordained and fully anticipated pattern. There *is*, after all, an *element* of surprise, or at least of discovery, in the achieved success. When our sleepless ice cream seeker enjoys his purchase, he can congratulate himself on having seen an opportunity that had not been completely visible. Apparently, the successful outcome of an opportunity grasped under uncertainty, is *both* surprising *and* unsurprising; it bears the characteristics both of the unanticipated discovery *and* of the deliberately adopted goal.

Notice that this inherent ambivalence cannot be resolved into two clearly defined, separable portions. One cannot say that one portion of the ice cream was fully anticipated, and the remaining portion is a total surprise. *All* ice cream is, in some degree, anticipated: *all* the ice cream is, in some degree, discovered. The presence of the entrepreneurial element in the case of the uncertain opportunity (expressed in the successful grasping of the opportunity *despite* the uncertainty) has transformed the successful outcome — all of it — into a (partial) discovery. Each ounce of ice cream consumed partakes, to a degree, of the character of an entrepreneurial discovery.

Once we have recognized this discovery element in the successful outcome of the opportunity grasped under uncertainty, we should also recognize the operation of that same "equilibrative tendency" of which we took earlier notice (in the context of the discovery of the hitherto wholly unperceived opportunity). If there is a tendency for individuals to notice that which it is in their interest to notice, then it is plausible that this tendency be operative also in the case of the opportunity, hitherto only partially glimpsed through the fog of uncertainty. The entrepreneurial propensities possessed by individuals enable them to live reasonably successfully in an uncertain world by continually revealing to them the worthwhileness of emerging opportunities hitherto (or otherwise) shrouded in the fog of uncertainty (if not in the night of utter ignorance). The incentive that switches on the entrepreneurial alertness that enables individuals to overcome uncertainty is the prospect of gaining that which had not been clearly anticipated. Uncertainty indeed discourages many worthwhile undertakings (or, at any rate, undertakings which hindsight reveals to have been worthwhile). But life must go on even under uncertainty; individuals are in fact compelled to do the best they can in peering ahead through the fog, and it is their entrepreneurial sense that guides them, in the face of uncertainty, to undertake the actions that do in fact make it possible for life to go on with reasonable success.

Until now our discussion of opportunities, perceived and unperceived, brightly etched in an imagined certainty, or shrouded in the realistic fog of uncertainty, has been conducted entirely from the perspective of the individual. We have not considered the impact of these perceptions (or lack of perception) upon any social economic processes. (Although we talked of an individual contemplating buying ice cream in a store at 3:00 A.M., we might just as well have been talking of a Crusoe contemplating an expedition, in the dead of night, to the other side of his island, to forage for strawberries). But our interest in the entrepreneurial element (which, in the context of the individual, consists in noticing the existence of real opportunities despite the presence of discouraging uncertainties) in fact stems from our conviction as economists that it is upon this entrepreneurial element that the working of the market process depends. The opportunities that market entrepreneurs perceive and exploit are created by earlier coordination failures among market participants. The tendency for such opportunities to be noticed and exploited is (not only the process through which individual entrepreneurs come to notice what is profitable for them, but also) the process through which the market tends to coordinate the actions and decisions of countless market participants. Let us take note of certain peculiarities that surround the idea of an opportunity within the social context.

Opportunities in Society: The Role of Rights and Institutions

In the Crusoe context an opportunity exists in the configuration of physical resources and available and known technological possibilities. But in the social context an opportunity (available to a given individual) is marked out not only by the configuration of physical possibilities but also by the configuration of the anticipated actions of others (and by the individual's own convictions concerning the ethical significance of the interplay between his own actions and those of others.) The actions that others are likely to take is partly a function (and expression) of the institutions that these others support and/or take as given. (The same is true concerning the individual's own ethical evaluations.) In particular the rights of property are crucial in marking out what constitutes an available opportunity and what does not. Where an individual recognizes the private property rights of others, he will perceive opportunities only as these are marked out by the relevant rights (of himself and of others). Where an individual fails to see a well-enforced rights system (and where his own ethical constraints do not lead him to respect such a system) he may see and grasp opportunities for what others might consider and denounce as theft. Or, again, where an individual sees the possibility of profitably *modifying* an existing institutional structure we must recognize such institutional change as an entrepreneurial opportunity for him.

A similar ambiguity may also relate, it should be observed, to the welfare economist assessing the social efficiency of a given pattern of resource allocation. To the extent that the economist accepts some specified societal assignment of rights as an unquestioned, morally-relevant given, he may assess the efficiency of a market generated pattern of resource allocation only against the background and within the framework of that pattern of rights assignment. From this perspective it will be idle and irrelevant — in fact, almost meaningless — to speculate concerning the possible welfare advantages to society of abolishing or modifying the rights system itself. But it may be that the welfare economist does *not* take the existing system of rights as a given. He will then assess the welfare consequences not merely of economic changes that leave that rights system intact, but also of possible modifications in that rights system itself.

All this has relevance for the question of whether to describe the entrepreneurial process in the market context as socially equilibrative[2] (in the same way that we saw that the exercise of entrepreneurship could be considered equilibrative at the individual level.) Social equilibration and coordination are notions that depend, for their meaning, upon the given social framework within which they are being defined and considered. If one wishes to consider the possibility of changes in this given framework itself, one can talk of an equilibrative character of such changes (or absence of such a character) only in the context of some meta-framework. The possibility of such a meta-framework (and even the possibility that changes in the data be seen as disequilibrative with respect to such a meta-framework) does not in any way diminish the possible relevance of the circumstance that these changes may, within the *originally* given social framework, be equilibrative in character.

But the ideas expressed in the previous paragraph may be turned around. Once we appreciate how the entrepreneurial grasping of an opportunity by an individual can be understood as equilibrative (in the "individual" sense explained in an earlier section), and once we appreciate how the entrepreneurial process (carried on within a given market-institutional framework of private property) can be understood as socially equilibrative (within that given social-institutional framework), we should be able to recognize that the "evolutionary" perspective and the "equilibrative" perspective are mutually complementary rather than mutually substitutive. The analytical power conferred by our insights into the equilibrative character of market processes, need not be surrendered in order to appreciate the possibly evolutionary character of those (longer-run?) processes through which institutional frameworks may themselves change. Moreover, a sensitivity to the analytical fruitfulness of the equilibrative perspective can alert us to the possibility that evolutionary changes in frameworks may themselves be understood as *possibly* "equilibrative"—within the context of relevant even-more-primordial social meta-frameworks.

It is quite true that individual entrepreneurial acts may take "rent-seeking" forms that may include the exploitation of weaknesses in the institutional guarantees for private property rights. Certainly such entrepreneurial acts may be judged to be categorically different, in their social-welfare implications, from those acts of arbitrage whose socially coordinative properties this writer has emphasized. No one claims that all opportunities grasped entrepreneurially must be socially coordinative. But it remains the case, surely, that a tendency towards the grasping of arbitrage opportunities, as they emerge *within the institutional framework of a market system*, does represent a socially coordinative tendency, *viewed from the perspective of that institutional framework*. In much of my own work, dealing with the operation of the market, entrepreneurship has been explored against the background of that institutional framework which permits markets to function. It followed, therefore, that a primary example of entrepreneurial opportunity perception was that of the successful arbitrageur, and it was in the tendency for arbitrage profits so to be competitively eroded that we saw the typical operation of the market coordinative process. Moreover, our concentration on the market context meant that the coordinative (i.e., the "gains-from-trade") advantages of that entrepreneurial process coincided with the plausible applicability of a finders-keepers ethic for justification of the entrepreneurial profit so won. It came to appear that entrepreneurship is necessarily identified with an entrepreneurial gain which is both directly justifiable on ethical grounds and socially beneficial in the coordinative sense. This work may fairly be criticized, perhaps, for failing sufficiently to emphasize that these apparently benign ethical and social consequences of entrepreneurship arise strictly within the market-institutional context. But a careful understanding of these benign consequences of market entrepreneurship should not, surely, lead one to infer similarly benign consequences for the entrepreneurial grasping of opportunities within other institutional contexts. Where property rights are not well defined, not fully protected, or otherwise not complete enough to satisfy the conditions for a fully private enterprise economy, opportunities for gain may be noticed by alert entrepreneurs where the gain may indeed be able to be denounced as infringing on the rights of others. Certainly, it is a legitimate research objective for Ricketts to explore the exercise of entrepreneurial alertness within property rights frameworks that provide scope for rent-seeking behavior.

The Pure Capitalist and the Pure Entrepreneur

The foregoing discussions presented key aspects of this writer's view of entrepreneurship and the entrepreneurial process, in a way seeking to respond, directly or indirectly, to a number of the points raised critically and valuably by Ricketts. In particular, our discussion of the meaning of equilibration, both at the level of the individual and at the societal level, was designed to address at least some of the questions posed, on subjectivist grounds, by Ricketts' fourth section. And our discussion of the role of the institutional (and, in particular, the property rights) framework within which equilibration is being defined, was designed to throw some light on the extent to which entrepreneurship and the entrepreneurial market process can be held to be socially beneficial, in response to criticisms expressed in Ricketts' fifth and seventh sections. In the present section and in the next one, we pursue some implications of our preceding discussions in order explicitly to address matters raised by Ricketts in his third section. This will warrant special and explicit attention because in Ricketts' view these matters involve a theme that recurs throughout his critique, viz. the tension that he senses in my work "between the Misesian view that entrepreneurial action is all pervasive, and the view that it comprises only some portion of human action (though a crucially important and neglected one)." This theme gains additional importance by having been also prominently noted in his review article (mentioned at the outset of this essay) of a recent book of mine. Ricketts has, indeed, identified an apparent ambiguity (if not an outright inconsistency) in my treatment of the entrepreneurial role. I believe, however, that no inconsistency is involved and that this apparent ambiguity can be clarified. I shall attempt to provide this clarification in this section and the next.

The problem identified by Ricketts is the following one. Especially in my earlier work on the entrepreneurial role, use was made of a model of the market process in which there were two kinds of players, pure "Robbinsian" decisionmakers and pure (Misesian) entrepreneurs. Robbinsian decisionmakers made their "mechanical" maximizing decisions within given frameworks of certain prices. No ounce of entrepreneurship was called for in order to make these maximizing decisions; the analysis began with these given frameworks having already been revealed to these decisionmakers with certainty. These Robbinsian decisionmakers were seen to include all resource owners and all consumers. The second kind of players, the pure entrepreneurs, were, in this model, seen as alertly taking advantage of price discrepancies implicit in the diverse expectations of the Robbinsian resource owners and consumers. That is, the pure entrepreneurs bought inputs from resource owners at prices which, offered to resource owners as certain and unalterable options, added up to costs of production possibly lower than the prices (similarly certain and unalterable) at which these entrepreneurs offered to sell the product to consumers. Within this model the income earned by the resource owner was a pure productivity return, containing no element of entrepreneurial profit. While the model admitted only these analytically pure categories of decisionmakers, the model was presented as somehow capturing important features of real-world markets. In these real world markets there are, of course, no pure Robbinsian resource owners, and no *purely* entrepreneurial intermediators between resource owners and consumers. All resource owners and all consumers, in the real world, do exercise at least some entrepreneurial alertness to changed opportunities. All real world entrepreneurs do own, to some extent, some factor services of their own (and, moreover, recognize some aspects of their environment as relatively stable, offering little to the alertest of opportunity-watchers.) So that, from the point of view of these analytical models of the market, a real world resource owner's gross income would include (besides the more significant component of purely nonentrepreneurial marginal productivity return) some component of pure entrepreneurial profit. Most significantly, however, (for the problem identified by Ricketts) the major portion, or at the very least, an important portion of the real world resource owner's income is seen as consisting in a pure "Robbinsian" resource revenue component, containing no element of pure profit. The significant portion of the real-world resource owner's income could not, in this perspective, be explained, or ethically justified, along the lines that might be used, in particular, for the explanation and/or ethical justification of pure profit.

It is as against this picture of the real world—one seen as a collage formed out of analytically pure roles, both entrepreneurial and non-entrepreneurial—that Ricketts finds a second, rather different picture of the real world set out (or implied) in other parts of my work. In this second picture the entrepreneurial aspect inevitably present in the activity of any real-world decisionmaker—in particular the inescapable radical uncertainty confronting real-world decisionmakers—transforms the *entire* resource revenue earned by real-world resource owners into a form of entrepreneurial profit. Every penny of the wages earned by the laborer in the real world can, from this perspective, be seen as a species of entrepreneurial profit, calling, at least to some degree, for the very same economic and ethical evaluations accorded to the category of pure entrepreneurial profit itself. Although this latter perspective has been articulated only in my more recent work, Ricketts apparently finds (what he believes to be) disturbing premonitions of this view already in an earlier paper of mine[3] on entrepreneurship, in which I pointed out, following Mises,[4] that every real-world capitalist must, in the nature of his activities, be exercising entrepreneurship. Ricketts is puzzled and disturbed by this assertion of mine, which he apparently reads as being at variance with my own insistence (at least in my earlier writings on entrepreneurship) on the importance, for analytical purposes, of the notion of the pure capitalist role as distinct from that of the pure entrepreneur. In particular, he finds this assertion confusing in the light of his attribution to me of the (Schumpeterian[5]) position that "resource owners bear uncertainty, not the entrepreneurs."

Now, while the above mentioned ambiguity that Ricketts detects in my work certainly warrants attention (see the following section in this commentary), it should be pointed out that the passage cited (from my 1979 book) to the effect that each real world capitalist is also, to some degree, an entrepreneur, should in no way be seen as tainted by that ambiguity. Although Ricketts, rather surprisingly, canvasses an array of apparently alternative interpretations[6] of this latter cited passage, the simple interpretation of it (viz., that it draws attention to the conflation in the real world make-up of the typical "empirical" capitalist investor, of elements both of the pure capitalist and of the pure entrepreneur) is in fact made abundantly clear in the paper from which the passage was cited. There is nothing in that cited passage that might obscure the identification of a pure resource-revenue income with the pure resource owner's role (and of pure entrepreneurial profit with the pure entrepreneurial role).

Nonetheless, it will be useful to refer to aspects of Ricketts' discussion of this cited passage of mine (attributing a significant element of entrepreneurship to the real world capitalist) in order to help clear up the above cited ambiguity that Ricketts has perceptively noted as arising out of some of my recent work in this area. To this we now turn.

The Pure and the Impure: A Clarification

As mentioned, Ricketts has interpreted me as seeing the pure entrepreneur — he who is alert to new opportunities — as in no way bearing uncertainty. He finds this at odds, however, with a recent passage[7] in which I point out that a resource owner is, typically, taking a daring entrepreneurial gamble. (Because when a resource owner sells, he knows that he may be missing better selling opportunities elsewhere, that is, he may be embarking upon a losing venture.) What, Ricketts asks, "have the acceptance of daring gambles and the risk of *losses* to do with alertness?" I submit that not only is there a straightforward answer to this question, but that this answer can direct us toward the clarification of the apparent ambiguity in my position, identified in the preceding section.

It is true that exposing oneself to the risk of a loss is not at all the same thing as being alert to a new opportunity. However, it is also true that the very notion of being alert to opportunities is conceivable only in the context of an uncertain world, that is, in a Knightian world within which one is inevitably exposed to the uninsurable risk of loss. And here is the nub of the matter. Although the essence of the entrepreneurial function does not lie in the bearing of the burden of sleepless nights (occasioned by worry about losses), this function would evaporate entirely in a world unclouded by uncertainty. One can act entrepreneurially only in an uncertain world; conversely, as we shall see, to act in an uncertain world must mean to exercise, at least to some degree, one's capacity for entrepreneurship. As Mises put it (in explaining why, in the real world, everyone is an entrepreneur), "one must never forget that every action is embedded in the flux of time and therefore involves a speculation."[8]

Now, as discussed in one of the earlier sections of this commentary, action in the face of uncertainty does seem to involve exactly that same notion of discovery as occurs in the case of a hitherto unglimpsed opportunity suddenly being noticed by the alert entrepreneur. Uncertainty obscures key features of a developing situation; what is in fact a gainful opportunity may not be seen as such, the chances of costly failure may loom so prominently in the vision of the prospective agent that it may appear prudent *not* to attempt to grasp for possible gain. To act in the face of uncertainty is thus to believe — correctly or otherwise — that one *has* seen a genuine opportunity through the fog that almost obscured it. Such action in the face of uncertainty requires, that is, a degree of alertness to what is "around the corner" (i.e., hidden behind the fog of uncertainty) — in other words, it requires the exercise of the human entrepreneurial propensity.

It follows that in our real world of uncertainty, every action by a resource owner is, at least to some extent, in the nature of an entrepreneurial gamble; that is, it consists in the alert grasping of an opportunity dimly perceived through the fog of radical uncertainty. It is true that the entrepreneurial function of exercising alertness (to hitherto existing but unperceived opportunities) is not, in itself, a matter of being exposed to the risk of losses. But, on the other hand, it is also true that wherever such uninsurable risk of loss exists, action must presuppose the exercise of entrepreneurial alertness.

What we wish to emphasize, however, is not so much this insight itself, but rather the difficulties this insight must entail for the model (outlined in the preceding section) in which the world of uncertainty is pictured as a collage formed exclusively out of analytically pure roles, entrepreneurial and nonentrepreneurial, respectively. Can we still maintain that the real world investor is part pure entrepreneur and part pure capitalist? Can we still maintain that his income consists of one distinct pure profit component together with a second distinct pure interest component? The position developed in my more recent work, in which I have argued that every penny of a resource owner's income in an uncertain world can be seen to some extent as being the fruit of entrepreneurial alertness, (and, thus, defensible on the basis of the same ethical principles used to depend the legitimacy of pure entrepreneurial profit), clearly answers these latter questions in the negative. Are we then to reject completely that model of the market process (used particularly in my own earlier work on entrepreneurship) in which pure entrepreneurs who owned no resources whatever were conceived of as offering deals to pure "Robbinsian" resource owners and consumers (who display no entrepreneurship whatsoever)? I wish to submit that we do not need to, and should not, reject that model out of hand. There are analytical purposes for which that model is illuminating and instructive—despite those features of it that render it incompletely faithful to and expressive of the complex realities of the real world of uncertainty. But, I further submit, at the same time we must be careful not to permit use of that model, valuable though it may be for its own purposes, to mislead us into overlooking those features of the real world that that model suppresses—in contexts where it is precisely those features which may be of significance. In other words, there are some analytical purposes that are usefully served by viewing real world resource owners *as if* they are combination pure "Robbinsian" resource owners and pure entrepreneurs; there are other purposes for which, such a fiction would obscure significant features of reality. The ambiguity Ricketts has identified is a real one, but it involves no tension; it presents no inconsistencies and no problems. All this warrants some elaboration.

In order to understand the entrepreneur-driven market process, it is useful to focus on the pure entrepreneurial role. Such a focus is the more sharply attained if we adopt the device of treating resource owners and consumers as exercising no entrepreneurship whatsoever. Nothing is lost, in regard to our understanding of how markets work through continual entrepreneurial discovery (of gaps in existing market coordination), by imagining that, at each instant, the pure entrepreneurs are offering the nonentrepreneurs deals with complete certainty.

But there are other purposes—such as that of reaching an adequate ethical evaluation of real world resource owners' incomes—where it will simply not do to treat resource owners as if they operated in a world different from what it really is. For these purposes it is necessary to recognize that no one, in the real world, can wholly escape uncertainty. As Mises taught us, in the real world of uncertainty each acting human being *is* an entrepreneur. And, to the extent that resource owners do operate in the real world of open-ended, uninsurable uncertainty, their incomes—every penny of their incomes—must be recognized as partaking, to some degree, of the discovered quality we attribute to pure entrepreneurial profit. As noticed at length in an earlier section of this commentary, most real world situations display aspects of unanticipated discovery *and* aspects of plan-fulfilling attainment of anticipated outcomes. However, as explained in that section, the nature of the ambivalence (inherent in most real world situations) is such that it does *not* permit one to identify, in the revenue won through action in the face of typical uncertainty, a purely routine component and a distinct, purely entrepreneurial component. The Misesian insight that all human action is entrepreneurial has thus led us to recognize that all market incomes—every penny of them—display, to greater or lesser degree, the character of pure profit.[9]

The considerations we have advanced to clarify the ambiguity noticed by Ricketts may perhaps be usefully summarized as follows:

1. Real-world situations in which market participants act offer us aspects in which these acts are (as a result of uncertainty) in the nature of the spontaneous grasping of hitherto unanticipated discoveries, and also offer aspects in which these acts constitute the plan-fulfilling attainment of anticipated outcomes (because the uncertainty is seen as being bounded).

2. Economics seeks understanding of what occurs in real-world market processes by reference to models of market equilibrium, and also seeks to derive concepts of market processes of equilibration (as they may occur in the real world of disequilibrium).

3. Models of equilibrium can in no way reflect those aspects of real world situations that arise out of the uncertainty of disequilibrium and the entrepreneurial grappling with such uncertainty; such models can reflect only those aspects (of real-world situations) that express the boundedness of uncertainty (even in disequilibrium).

4. In order to understand those aspects of the real world that arise out

of the boundedness of uncertainty, we therefore focus on the way those aspects would in fact constitute the *whole* of the situations portrayed in our models of equilibrium. Resource owners' incomes are thus portrayed as pure marginal productivity incomes.

5. In order to understand market processes that arise in real-world disequilibrium, we focus precisely on those entrepreneurial (i.e., uncertainty-driven) elements that have *no* place in the equilibrium models. In order to highlight these entrepreneurial elements we generally conceive the *non*entrepreneurial elements in the real world as if these were in fact *purely* nonentrepreneurial. But in so doing we are, inconsistently, conflating an equilibrium picture with a disequilibrium picture. For purposes of conceptualizing the dynamic market process such a conflation does no harm. This conflation is designed to focus analytical attention on one real world element — the key element that drives the market process; it does so with greater impact by deliberately imagining away certain real world aspects of the resource owner and consumer roles. In this context resource owner incomes appear as purely Robbinsian, purely nonentrepreneurial outcomes.

6. When we wish to consider the ethics and economics of real world resource owner incomes in their own right (that is, not merely as part of an effort with the primary objective of understanding the market process itself), it becomes necessary to recognize those entrepreneurial aspects of real-world resource ownership from which it had been expedient (in seeking understanding of the market process) to abstract. It is then no longer possible to see resource owners' incomes — not even any fraction of them — as wholly planned outcomes; an element of entrepreneurial discovery is seen as attached to every penny of such incomes.

The Entrepreneurial Perspective and Austrian Economics

It may be useful to conclude these rather rambling observations, inspired by Ricketts' valuable critique, by pointing out how the emphasis on entrepreneurship in much of the modern Austrian literature reinforces and deepens those insights that have, from its earliest Mengerian roots, characterized the Austrian School. The subjectivism of Austrian economics meant that it saw economic phenomena, market prices, incomes and resource allocation patterns rather differently than other schools of economic thought. For Austrians these were seen, not as inevitable consequences of physical needs and resource constraints, not as the outcome of an interplay between physical resources and human rankings of preference, — but as the results of the ways in which deliberate human decisions, both in isolation and in society, impinge upon and shape a given physical world.

There were times, during the twentieth century history of Austrian economics, when this vision was confined to a "Robbinsian" understanding of human decisions, that is, with human beings seen as entering the economic arena with pre-assigned perceptions of the possibilities open to them. It was the signal merit of Mises's notion of human action that it deepened the Austrian vision to include, as a dominant factor influencing economic outcomes, that active element in human decision making that perceives and identifies what the possibilities and options for choice are seen to be. As a result of this work of Mises, and of a distinct series of insights concerning knowledge explicated by Hayek, modern Austrian economics has come to recognize that this entrepreneurial element (identified by Mises) plays the crucial role in achieving the market's tendencies towards coordination. It is not merely that awareness of the entrepreneurial element enhances our appreciation for the subjectivist perspective central to the Austrian tradition. It is our awareness of the entrepreneurial element that enriches our understanding of the coordinative properties of markets. As Ricketts has identified the central theme that has inspired my own work on entrepreneurship, "the exploitation of the gains from trade will not take place automatically. To achieve the advantages of co-ordination through exchange requires first that these potential gains are noticed." The deepened Austrian subjectivism that recognizes the manner in which economic phenomena express such noticing of potential gains, is at the same time the source of our deepened Austrian understanding of the social process of "co-ordination through exchange" which markets make possible.

Notes

1. *Journal des Economistes et des Etudes Humaines*, Vol. 1, No. 2, June 1990, 179–182.

2. Whereas we have, somewhat idiosyncratically, used the notion of an "equilibrative tendency" at the level of the individual to refer to the tendency of an individual sooner or later to come to realize what it is in fact best for him to do, we use here the notion of an "equilibrative tendency," in the social context, in a far more conventional manner. In the market context the equilibrative tendency consists in those many entrepreneurial steps of mutual discovery through which market participants are led more accurately to anticipate what others are able and motivated to do, thus bringing the pattern of exchanges gradually closer to that pattern that would exhaust all possible mutually gainful opportunities. (It will be noticed that this social process of equilibration is made up of series upon series of

individual opportunity discoveries, with each such discovery being the manifestation of the equilibrative tendency we found operating at the individual level.)

3. *Perception, Opportunity, and Profit.* Chicago: University of Chicago Press, 1979, ch. 6.

4. L. Mises, *Human Action.* New Haven: Yale University Press, 1949, 254

5. See, for example, Joseph A. Schumpeter, *The Theory of Economic Development.* Cambridge: Harvard University Press, 1934, 75, 137.

6. However, see Note 9.

7. Israel M. Kirzner, *Discovery, Capitalism, and Distributive Justice.* Oxford: Basil Blackwell, 1989, 116.

8. L. Mises, *Human Action*, op. cit., ibid.

9. It should be noted that the Misesian insight that, "in any real and living economy every actor is always an entrepreneur," is simply an implication of what it means to live in a real world of radical uncertainty. The empirical circumstance of ubiquitous uncertainty entails the impossibility of finding, in real life, individuals whose decisions wholly fit those of the pure "Robbinsian" maximizer (for whom the ends-means framework is given with certainty). It thus follows that the alternative interpretations Ricketts suggests for this writer's assertion that real-world capitalists are engaged in entrepreneurial competition, in fact, all turn out to be simply different ways of expressing the identical circumstance — the inescapable uncertainty surrounding the human condition.

4 SUBJECTIVISM, EXPLANATION AND THE AUSTRIAN TRADITION

Jeremy Shearmur

Introduction

My aim in this chapter is to stimulate and provoke. I have tried to raise some problems in the expectation that this may lead my discussant into offering some telling responses. In writing, I have presupposed a broad knowledge of the work of the subjectivist writers in the Austrian tradition. Not only are many good secondary accounts available, but there is no substitute for reading the works of the key figures themselves. I have also, and by conscious decision, written in an impressionistic manner, and I have not attempted to provide a full account of, or to engage with all of the — often important — secondary literature. To have done this would have been an interesting task, but it is not mine on the present occasion. Rather, my aim has been to tweak the tail of a venerable and mighty lion — in the hope that we may be both impressed and inspired by the resulting roar.

The chapter starts gently with a problem that has struck many readers of the Austrians. Why is it that they both place such emphasis upon the subjective and yet take such pains to dissociate their concerns from those of psychology? I attempt to explain this and also offer a little critical discussion. I then discuss another minor issue: how is it that Karl Popper, who shares so much with the Austrian subjectivists, is so opposed to subjectivism in the context of the theory of explanation?

After this gentle start, things heat up a little. In the next three sections, I suggest, first, that many Austrian subjectivists share with many neoclassical

103

economists some views that seem to me very dubious: a noncognitivist approach to value; the view that we cannot know the preferences of other people except insofar as they are exhibited in their action; and the idea that there can be no intersubjective comparisons of utility. Such views, as I explain, seem to me overstatements, and their proponents typically ignore the fact that we, as a matter of course, behave in ways other than they suggest is possible in the conduct of our day-to-day lives. This, in my view, is significant just because these issues are of importance for public policy—a sphere that, by setting real-world explanatory problems, gave rise to economics, but from which economists seem to me to have emancipated themselves, to the detriment of economic theory.

Second, I argue that insofar as subjectivists criticize more orthodox economics for a lack of realism (in the sense of its premises not being descriptively correct concerning human action, the market process, and so on), it is vital that they do not lose sight of the explanatory task of economics. In the context of our offering explanations, there is nothing, in principle, wrong with our offering models that simplify. An objection to such models has a point only insofar as it helps us to produce a better explanation of the phenomena in which we are interested.

Third, I discuss what seems to me an important divergence within subjectivism—a divergence, which I suggest we may look at as stemming from the different views of Mises and of Weber, between what I call a praxeological and a historical or institutional subjectivism. The former may be characterized by its use of a model of human action that is understood as universal in its scope, but which is purely formal in its character. The latter depicts the agent as acting on the basis of an historically or locally specific motive—whether some specific ideal or goal, some rule, or some institutional or cultural practise. Against the former of these, I rehearse the well-known charges of nihilism and explanatory sterility, and gently commend the latter. (I argue *en passant* that such figures as Hayek and Buchanan, who do not use this approach, have in fact given us good reasons to take it seriously.)

However, I then suggest that my argument for historical or institutional ideal types should be regarded only as permissive, in the sense that it suggests that there is nothing wrong with our making use of such things, rather than telling us that we have to do so. The reason for this is, again, because the prime concern of economics should, in my view, be the exploration and solving of extra-theoretical problems. (Clearly, problems generated by our theories themselves may be of immense interest; but it seems to me that we stand in need of an argument that the theories themselves genuinely help us to gain some handle upon the real world before we should give ourselves over to the single-minded pursuit of such concerns.) Further, what may be relevant for the task of solving such problems of explanation and understanding is not directly given to us by our commonsense knowledge, by historical knowledge, or, say, by whatever is given to us concerning the meaningful actions of other people by some theory of understanding or of hermeneutics. For, such knowledge does not, of itself, tell us *what* items of such knowledge should be selected for the purposes of the theoretical comprehension of economic phenomena as the unintended consequences of human action; at what level of aggregation we should be working; how different elements of commonsense knowledge should be bundled together, or how such knowledge should be represented in a simplified form in our models. The pursuit of these ideas, in turn, leads me into a brief discussion of the proper character of methodological discourse, and to break a lance for a (nonfoundationalist) approach to methodology, against some currently fashionable antimethodological views.

I conclude with a few suggestions about how we might judge when it may be important to take into account the considerations that subjectivists have emphasized.

Subjectivism and Psychology

One of the more striking themes in the Austrian tradition of subjectivism is its concern to distance itself from psychology. There are, in my view, three aspects to this.

The first is illustrated by Mises' emphasis that the Austrian approach to marginalism was not dependent upon particular theories of human psychology, such as Gossen's Law or the Weber-Fechner Law.[1] In respect of this, Mises was surely correct; and there was a point to his argument, since in earlier presentations of marginalism there appears to have been some ambiguity about this issue. At the same time, we need to bear in mind that the Austrian approach—in common with neoclassical economics—does not say anything distinctive about the formation of taste; and if we wish to understand that, psychological theories may clearly be of importance. (Hayek, for example, seemed quite happy that psychology may have a role in the explanation of conscious action; it was just that he considered this to be a different task from the task of social science as he understood it, which was concerned with the unintended consequences of human action.[2])

Second, there is what might be called the redundancy objection. The concern of the Austrian tradition is typically with the consequences of meaningful human action. From that point of view, it is enough that we know that individuals act, and — to a greater or lesser extent — to understand what they are doing when they act as being subjectively rational: that we grasp the subjective meaning of their actions. In this context, knowledge about the aetiology of the action is beside the point. Or at least, it is beside the point if such knowledge serves to explain the action in question without correcting the way in which we initially understood it. For the purposes of the subjectivist, it does not matter what happened prior to the action's taking place: that is strictly beside the point, for his explanatory purposes. As J.H. Runde has put it: "Most Austrians are likely to say that economics and psychology are separate disciplines and should remain so. This position stems from a reliance on their version of the rationality postulate."[3]

However, it *is* possible that the commonsensical account of human action, based on the rationality principle, may be corrected. Here, it seems to me that the Austrians' arguments have suffered, in that they have discussed challenges to the rationality principle as if the only terms in which we might alter it would involve its complete rejection. Karl Popper (whose views on the methodology of social science at some points are an interesting reworking of Weberian and Hayekian themes in the light of his own philosophical views) is here not untypical. In his "Rationality and the Status of the Rationality Principle,"[4] he suggested that we would be ill-advised to give up the idea that people act rationally on the basis of a knowledge of their situation as they see it, in the event that some model that is animated by this idea gets into empirical difficulties. He made this suggestion even though he agreed that this assumption — the rationality principle — is not, strictly speaking, true, but only a good approximation to the truth. His reason for arguing in this way was that he thought that this reduces the arbitrariness of our models.

It is indeed difficult to understand how accounts of human behavior as weakly rational are to be explained and corrected so that human action is understood in fact not to be rational action at all — other than in exceptional cases (as, say, when what was in fact some kind of a fit had been taken to be an instance of human action; for example, a spiritualist medium going into a trance). However, it would seem perfectly possible that we might develop an explanation, which draws upon cognitive psychology, of the way in which some individual's behavior deviated from our more ordinary understanding of subjective rationality (such that it is, in this instance, the rationality principle that we need to modify in a specific manner, rather than the model in connection with which we had been using it). We would, however, here be involved in a modification of the rationality principle, rather than its complete replacement.

In the context of explanations in economics — where we are typically concerned with the actions of many rather than of one individual — it is possible that work of the kind that Herbert Simon has done may correct our more usual picture of what agents are doing when they are acting rationally. We may, for example, be led by it to see that they are, and quite rationally, taking into account fewer options than we had assumed a rational person would.

Such work may lead us to question whether certain formal accounts of decision making are realistic representations of what individuals are doing when they are making decisions. However, this does not necessarily imply that these formal accounts should be discarded *as parts of our explanatory models*. For, as I argue in more detail later, our models may legitimately utilize assumptions that we know to be false. I would even (wildly) conjecture that this point may throw some light on an interesting issue in contemporary economics, which was inspired by work in psychology: the problem of preference reversal. I would suggest that the correct question to ask concerning the premises from which economists argue is their role in explanatory models, rather than as descriptively correct accounts of the phenomena with which they are dealing. Accordingly, it seems to me that while psychology-inspired criticism of the assumptions of theoretical economics may be of use, three conditions need to be satisfied before it is telling: first, that it discloses to us some premises as being incorrect; second, that this turns out to be of explanatory relevance — that it makes a difference; and third, that we can replace our older model by one that takes into account the criticism, in such a way that we are left with something of at least as much explanatory power as we had before.

Third among the objections of the Austrians to psychology is what might be called the cultural objection. This is the insistence by subjectivists that human action is culturally constituted and has a content that cannot be understood without reference to social institutions and conventions. This, in turn, is the basis of a critique of the idea that a naturalistic psychology could, in some sense, replace weakly rational explanation. This is not, however, in any way intended to rule out the idea that work in cognitive psychology could throw important light on how we understand the world and that it may not correct our more commonsensical ways of understanding ourselves. It does, however, explain why Popper was so insistent that methodological individualism — explanation in terms of weakly rational action — is not the same as psychologism, which is understood as reduction to a naturalistic psychology.

Popper Versus Subjectivism in the Theory of Explanation

One additional point may also usefully be made here. It concerns Popper's critique of subjectivism in the context of the theory of explanation. For Popper, an explanation is a cultural or "world 3" object.[5] The task of explaining something is to produce such an object. From appropriate premises, it should be possible to logically deduce a statement describing that which one wishes to explain. What is being produced in the social sciences will, on Popper's account, be compatible with methodological individualism and with the rationality principle. These, indeed, are public representations of the kind of things with which those subjectivists who are the subjects of the present chapter are concerned. However, for Popper it is also the case that the explanation has to satisfy other requirements, too.

First, it must be acceptable as a logical construction. It must indeed be the case that a statement of what one is trying to explain follows from the premises that are put up to explain it. Second, the explanation should, ideally, be testable and if not testable, open to criticism. Popper's own account of explanation in the social sciences changes over time — in the sense that in his earliest writings he stressed the role of universal laws; while later, he in effect argued that explanations using the "rationality principle" construction could fit the same formal conditions of adequacy.

Once these matters are understood, there should not be much serious disagreement between Popper and subjectivists in the "Austrian" tradition. For Popper was, essentially, concerned that explanation should be intersubjectively acceptable, and also that it should not be *ad hoc*. There are, to be sure, some differences — not least being the way in which Mises sometimes attempts to *demonstrate* the correctness of one explanation by eliminating others.[6] Of course, an eliminative approach is not something with which Popper would have any quarrel. However, he would stress that one has, by such means, only eliminated the alternatives that one has thought of — that we are typically not in a position to imagine every possible explanation of some phenomenon. (Compare the big problem facing Keynes's approach to probabilistic induction: one does not raise the probability of one horse winning a race by shooting other horses, if there are indefinitely many horses in the race.)

"Basic" Subjectivism, Noncognitivism and Privacy

Subjectivists, along with neo-classical economists, generally, have offered an account of individuals as acting on the basis of their preferences. Two points are worth making here concerning views that are shared between subjectivists and more mainstream neoclassical economists, but which are more contestable than either group seem to consider.

The first of these concerns the noncognitivism that is often taken on board as part of this account. It is by no means a necessary part of such a view, for our judgements about matters concerning which there is clearly truth or falsity (say, the population of Iowa on a particular date) may equally form part of the grounds upon which we act. Nonetheless, there is a marked predisposition on the part of many economists to treat individuals' preferences as matters of sheer brute fact, rather than, say, as opinions that people have only because they believe it to be *correct* for them to hold such views, and which they hold only insofar as they are able to defend them on the basis of what they believe to be the appropriate criteria. This is of some importance, since if economists are incorrect on this point, they will misunderstand the character of certain social institutions. For example, we will appraise differently some procedure concerning the formation of consensus, depending upon whether we appraise it in terms of the satisfaction of the individuals' prior preferences, or see it as a process through which preferences are themselves to be formed or validated.

The second concerns the view that we cannot tell what other people's preferences are until they act, and that we are not able to undertake intersubjective comparisons of well being. Now such views seem to me grotesquely false. If they *were* true, it would be difficult to imagine how most of everyday human life could take place—how we could interact with one another, speak a shared language, and so on. Why economists hold views of this sort is itself something that seems to me to require some explanation. My conjecture is that it is the twin product of the uncritical adoption of the kind of positivism that was fashionable earlier in this century, together with a disregarding of the respects in which the individuals with the consequences of whose actions they are dealing are members of the same biological species, and typically share much in common, culturally.[7] Now, it is of course true that our tastes may differ, such that we may not always be able to judge the preferences of our fellows; but that is an important piece of *knowledge* about the members of our species, rather than a matter of our inability to know anything about the preferences of our fellows until they are expressed. One does not need to be told how people feel if they are short of food or water, and we know roughly what to expect if we hear that the fleet has just come into port. A good shopkeeper will know a lot about what will, and will not, appeal to his customers. And markets would simply not work unless we were able to anticipate one another's preferences fairly well in this fashion. After all, we could hardly depend for our bread upon the self-interest of the baker if he was not able to anticipate reasonably well what we might want in advance of our asking for it. (You want bread? said the baker, startled!) He is clearly not in the same situation as he would be if facing for the first time beings of some other species, people from some other culture, or even people other than those with whom he had dealt, previously, upon a fairly regular basis. At the same time, his knowledge about the variability in our tastes is itself important information that he will need, if his business is to be a success.

What our knowledge in these areas does not give us, of course, is a Bentham-style method of rendering commensurable all forms of human well being onto a single scale, or of giving it a precise form of numerical representation. But why should anyone (apart from Bentham) have supposed that our concerns could be rendered into such a form? We seem in danger of reaching the absurd situation in which discussion of welfare in economics has little or nothing to say about the kinds of real-world problems from which it started, and in which economists, who, quite properly, have important things to say about markets and their relation to human well-being, find that they can say little or nothing about this issue when wearing their hats as economists.

Now, two economists who read an earlier version of this chapter objected in almost identical terms to my argument in this section. Both suggested that I had misrepresented economists' objections to interpersonal comparisons of utilities. It was not to the idea that such interpersonal comparisons can be made, they suggested, that economists object, but rather to the idea that such comparisons can have the status of *science*.

I am unmoved by this objection. It is, to be sure, in some sense gratifying for a "Popperian" philosopher of science to find two practitioners of economics so concerned about problems of demarcation. But Popper has himself come to place increasing emphasis upon the importance for science of openness to criticism, of which falsifiability is a particular, and dramatic, case. Given that the claim that interpersonal comparisons of utility are possible — as well as specific instances of such claims — are clearly open to criticism, it is difficult to understand why economists should be so concerned about making them. Indeed, economics is replete with claims about demand curves, preference structures, and so on — which are no more directly open to observation than are claims about the interpersonal comparison of utility. Accordingly, it is difficult to take seriously the idea that economists should be worried about these things on *epistemological* grounds. More plausible is the idea that their concern is with making value judgements.

If that is what is at the bottom of the economist's concern, he should be reminded that to use the Pareto criterion is, emphatically, *not* to avoid making value judgements. And if his reason for wishing to avoid making value judgements is that he is concerned that these will gain a false legitimacy from association with the predictive successes of "scientific" economics, I would suggest that he look again at the dismal history of the dismal science.

Let me put my point in more serious terms. It is not clear to me that once we accept the conjectural character of scientific knowledge and the fact that much theoretical economics is at best open to criticism but not to rigorous testing, there is any point in seeking to avoid making value judgements, and intersubjective comparisons of utility, provided that these are each made in ways that are open to intersubjective appraisal and criticism.

Sophisticated Subjectivism and Explanation

Subjectivists within the Austrian tradition, and others close to them, stress the way in which individuals act upon the basis of their own — and perhaps distinctive — appraisal of the situations that they are in. They act on the basis of what to them seems the best option. But their view of this may be very different from that of other people — not least because they may have all kinds of distinctive ideas about what might be done, which differ from those of other people, and they might give different weightings to these things.

Subjectivists also stress the way in which individuals act on the basis of their own understanding of the situation that they are in and that this may be false. Individuals may make incorrect appraisals of the circumstances in which they are acting; the theories that they are entertaining about the character of the social or the natural world may be incorrect, and so on.

Subjectivists also stress the way in which individuals may be acting on the basis of incomplete information. This may be a matter of their not having full information about a situation that is, in fact, fully determinate. Or it may be the case that the world itself is not fully determinate, in that what will happen in the future may be genuinely open.

In respect to these last three points, though, I wish to suggest that two different questions may be asked: first, are the subjectivists correct about the world; and second, is their point of relevance for theoretical economics. It might seem that this is an odd distinction to make, or that to make it lines one up with a Chicago "nothing matters except that the predictions come out ok" approach. But this is not the case.

One of my contentions in the present chapter is that subjectivists often seem to be involved in a confusion between reality and the characteristics of models that are useful for the purposes of explanation. My argument here is that, if we are interested in explaining real-world phenomena, such as the occurrence of trade cycles, the conditions that foster economic growth, or the effects of changes in taxation policy or of changes in the money supply, we need to make use of models that involve simplification. The reason for this is threefold.

First, what we have knowledge of concerning the social world — the actions of particular individuals — is typically at the wrong level of aggregation for us to use it for explanatory purposes. The phenomena with which we are concerned, such as trade cycles, are the products of the actions of many individuals in social situations. What we require is a representation of what the appropriate "typical" actions are in "typical" situations that bring about the effects in question. And our knowledge of the particular concrete actors and their situations of which we are aware (or of which we may gain knowledge through some process of investigation) does not of itself supply us with this information.

Second, our concern will be to throw light upon the causal processes involved, and this aim may legitimately involve us in making simplifications which we know, strictly speaking, to be incorrect. Just as, say, Newton was to depict the masses of the planets as if they were located at a single point in the center of the planets when explaining the motion of the solar system, so, it seems to me, it is perfectly legitimate for the economist to make simplifying assumptions that may help us get at the mechanisms responsible for the effect in which he is interested.

Third, a key point to be considered here is that we cannot tell independently of our explanatory theories which aggregation and which simplification is appropriate. What we should pick out, what we should ignore, and what we should disregard when offering a simplified model is not something that we can discover by, as it were, staring hard at the individual phenomena of which we have more direct knowledge. Rather, what we select, how we group it, what we include, and what we cut out: these decisions are all driven by our explanatory theories, and our selections are thus to be appraised on the basis of what is and what is not successful as an explanation.

This is *not* instrumentalism, for there is good reason to suppose that we may need to pay attention to the realism of our assumptions. What this argument does show is that subjectivists are incorrect if they think that just because social reality or human action has certain characteristics, these should also appear in our models. Indeed, one characteristic of the approach of many subjectivists is to suggest that, in the interests of descriptive realism, we should weaken assumptions that are being worked with in the models of more orthodox economists. But from weaker premises, less can be deduced, and it should not surprise us that this particular path has led towards nihilism.

It is perhaps worthwhile for subjectivist economists to bear in mind that Newtonian theory was immensely informative while being deterministic in its character, despite the fact that there are arguments to the effect that many of the phenomena with which it was dealing were indeterministic in their more detailed character. It may be the case that there is *no* informative general theory that is able to deal with the phenomena in which we are interested in full detail, yet a simpler model, which we know to rest on assumptions that are at best an approximation to the truth, may, nonetheless, be highly informative.

If I am right, subjectivist economics, insofar as it offers us arguments that more orthodox economic theory is unacceptable because its assumptions are not true, may exhibit a massive misunderstanding of the character of theoretical science. This is not to say, of course, that subjectivism may not make contributions of the greatest importance when its objections to more orthodox theory in fact lead us to be able to explain phenomena with which more orthodox theory cannot cope. But that, it seems to me, does not happen as often as subjectivists might have us believe.

Praxeological and Historical Subjectivism

Subjectivism within the Austrian tradition may be understood as falling into two parts. These stem from different reactions to the *Methodenstreit*: those of Ludwig von Mises and those of Max Weber. To condense: in the writings of each there is an account, in many ways similar, of individual human action as rational in a weak sense, or as subjectively meaningful.[8] They were, further, in agreement concerning the significance of this analysis for the social sciences. They differ, however, on one important point. For Weber, we are dealing — in economics — with what is, essentially, a historical ideal type. For Mises, there is one universal category of human action.[9]

Now the point at issue between them is of considerable historical interest. The issue takes us back at least to the work of Adam Smith. For in Smith's writings, or so it seems to me, the relation between the analysis that he offers in *The Wealth of Nations*, and his "four stages" approach to the understanding of history and human character, is not fully sorted out. In *The Wealth of Nations* Smith's approach is, for the most part, ahistorical in its character, with the conduct of hunter-gatherers being offered as illustrations of Smith's more general themes. But in his *Theory of Moral Sentiments* and *Lectures on Jurisprudence*, Smith offers us an account in which what one might call the basic character of human beings is the same in all circumstances, yet their characters as we experience them are shaped by the *kind* of society in which they are living. How a person is motivated, and many features of the society in which he lives, are to be understood as a product of the mode of subsistence within which he lives. It might, in such circumstances, be tempting to represent *The Wealth of Nations* as giving us an account of the behavior of man in the last of Smith's stages of history, "commercial society." But, as I have indicated, Smith does not take this route, and it looks as if much of the "four stages" typology is dropped in that volume. However, this leaves open the following unresolved issue: if man's behavior may indeed differ significantly from society to society, and if we are interested in understanding phenomena in the social sciences as the unintended consequences of human action, should we not be concerned with exploring the unintended consequences of different specific forms of human conduct, rather than with a model of human action which depicts it as essentially the same everywhere? All this is of more than purely historical interest, in that it signals a difference which has reverberations up to the present day. To put the matter bluntly, consider the two forms of subjectivism to which I referred above.

One of these may be seen as a Misesian or quasi-Misesian view. One can give an account of its development through Mises, Hayek, *some* parts of Lachmann, Wiseman, Buchanan, and Kirzner. Essentially, it starts from something akin to the regular neoclassical account of human action as rational maximization. Mises offers a richer account of the structure of human action than is to be found in neoclassical writings. But it is formal and universal in its character — in the sense of describing a structure that is supposed to be the same for all agents.[10] Those who take this view hold that theoretical social science is not properly concerned with the specific content of individuals' motivations.

However, there is more to this lack of concern for specific content than merely a lack of interest (or the view that this is to be filled in when we are dealing with specific pieces of history, rather than with social theory). For Mises — along with Robbins, Buchanan, and Kirzner — often express the view that we cannot have knowledge of the content of others' preferences: that they, and subjective costs, are known only to those who experience them. All that we can know is the particular choices and actions that they perform. This form of subjectivism, as it has developed, emphasized the subjective (and hence, it was suggested, private) character of preferences and costs. Further with Hayek, and then yet further with Lachmann, emphasis was placed upon the subjective character of our knowledge, although as I will suggest below, Lachmann is an important figure in the *other* branch of subjectivism, too. It was stressed that knowledge is socially divided, tacit and often incorrect, that individuals have expectations that also may not be correct, and so on. Great emphasis was further placed—notably in Wiseman and Buchanan—on the subjective character of cost.

All of this was interesting. It certainly drew our attention to phenomena that were, at best, simplified away in neoclassical theory, both within general equilibrium theory and within Chicago-style microeconomics. What is not so clear is what an emphasis upon such points is supposed to lead us to.

If our concern is greater descriptive realism, then, to be sure, assumptions revised in light of such points are more realistic than were the oversimplified representations of human action that occur within more standard neoclassical theory. However, the big issue for economics is: what can one *explain* using such ideas? One problem that arises here is logical. It is a problem from which we are often distracted by commentators discussing, for example, the move away from ideas of general equilibrium, as if it was a completely separate aspect of the work of the theorists with whom we are here concerned. For it is at least in part not so much an additional move as a consequence of the moves that they had made with respect to the premises from which they were reasoning. As compared with the assumptions of neoclassical theorists, their move in the direction of descriptive realism was a move that weakened the logical strength of the models that they were using; from weaker assumptions, less follows: one can explain less.

Now to be sure, one may characterize the situation differently. What is interesting, it may be claimed, is the process through which the economy adjusts itself—the market process. But what, in fact, does subjectivism tell us *about* this? What does it *explain* and in what terms? It seems to me that subjectivism of this first, praxeological, kind is at times left facing an abyss. A lot of emphasis is placed upon the subjective character of costs—only for the proponents of this theory then to say that their subjective character implies that we can know nothing of them.

For example, Israel Kirzner, in his "Another Look at the Subjectivism of Costs,"[11] after spending some time in distinguishing objective and subjective notions of costs, then says: "the subjective notion of the term 'cost' is necessarily always private."[12] But if this is the case, it is not clear what the economist can further say about it.

It could be objected that the whole point of the subjective theory is political—that under a subjectivist interpretation of cost it is only the individual decision maker who can know what cost is, and that therefore there is no case for overriding the market.[13] However, this argument seems to me vulnerable at both ends. On the one hand, and as I have already suggested, it seems to me a gross overstatement to say that we are not able to judge the subjective costs of an action. (If we were not, it would suggest that awards of damages by courts for, say, personal injury, are of necessity *completely* arbitrary, which is surely an overstatement.) On the other, if we take subjectivism *really* seriously and accept that individuals may well be completely wrong in their understanding of the world, and in their anticipation of the value to them of the outcomes of different courses of action, and so on, the political argument starts to look weaker, in that it is not so clear that they will do better for themselves than will the politicians.

Indeed, let us put public choice considerations about benevolent despots (which, in fact, seem to me completely telling) to one side for the purpose of the present argument. It could presumably be argued that it is just in those cases in which the knowledge of the government is likely to be better—that is, where they can draw upon a consensus of experts concerning matters that affect the well-being of many people—that it should act. While in matters that concern particular individuals and in which radical differences in their preferences may be important, such as much consumer choice, decision making should be in individuals' hands.

The "nihilism" that some discerned in Lachmann's work seems the logical end-point of an approach that puts stress on models that attribute error and ignorance to individuals: it is not clear what more one can say in completely general terms about the results of human interaction when human action is thus characterized. Indeed, the comment made by James Buchanan in his "Jack Wiseman: A Personal Appreciation" seems to me to hit the nail on the head:[14]

> In one sense, however, Jack Wiseman was too unorthodox; he could not, even for pragmatic purposes, work within a paradigm that he despised. We [Buchanan and Wiseman] shared a sympathy for Shackle's radical subjectivism, but Jack Wiseman found himself boxed in, like Shackle himself, by the implied nihilism of the extreme subjectivist stance. As a result he, along with Steve Littlechild, could never finish the textbook-treatise on subjectivist economics that they started.

That there was a problem here was well known to Wiseman himself. In his "Beyond Positive Economics—Dream and Reality,"[15] he is explicit that his complaint against orthodox economics is *not* "that the received doctrine is wrong because the assumptions from which it proceeds are 'unrealistic.'" It was, he continued, "the *nature* of the simplifying assumptions that is crucial. Can we really expect models that assume the future to be known, whether perfectly or in an objective-probabilistic fashion, to provide satisfactory explanations of human behavior in a world in which the future is not knowable and people are not surprised when the outcome of their plans differs from their predictions?" He then, however, poses the key question:[16] "Can we do better?", and responds: "It is not an easy question to answer." Wiseman does offer a number of interesting suggestions, but it is not easy to see how his programmatic ideas could lead us to explanatory theory, other than where he started to explore ideas of a more institutional character — which naturally brings us to the other part of the subjectivist tradition.

But what of the second strand in subjectivism? This is an *historical* or institutional theory of ideal types. It says, in effect, that it is proper for us *qua* theorists to pay attention to the *content* of people's motivation. Those who took such a view often also argued (and I think, very plausibly) that this content *is* in principle accessible to others. Such an approach would allow that there could be some universal formal structure to individual action — some notion of rule following or weak rationality, or whatever. It would suggest that the content of the rules that people follow might be different in different settings and that this could be of *explanatory* significance. Such a view was to be found in Lachmann himself (Indeed, it is interesting to note in this context *his* characterization of Mises' *Human Action*:[17] "In reading this book we must never forget that it is the work of Max Weber that is being carried on here."), and it was almost the running motif in the Lachmann *Festschrift* that Kirzner edited (Kirzner, 1986a).

In particular, stress was placed by contributors to that *Festschrift* upon the way in which individual agents make use of rules and ideal types to "understand and anticipate the conduct of others".[18] Further, it was mooted that institutions serve to provide some stability for agents, among the uncertainties of the world depicted by Lachmann and Shackle. These things, in their turn, have consequences for the way in which individual behavior may be understood by theorists. O'Driscoll and Rizzo, for example, in *The Economics of Time and Ignorance*, urge that there should be a shift from modeling actors as maximizing to modeling them as: "following rules of thumb or 'routines' at one end of the behavioral continuum, or as engaging in entrepreneurial discovery at the other end."[19] (They refer to Nelson and Winter and also to Hayek in connection with rule following; to Kirzner in connection with entrepreneurship.)

My suggestion, however, is that such rules of thumb and routines should be understood as tied up with local, and possibly historically specific institutions. This is not, of course, to suggest that within these settings individuals may not be understood as following out their own aims and purposes. It is, rather, that aims and purposes are to be understood in terms of individuals' participation in, and perhaps even by their being partly constituted by, particular social institutions.[20] Their conduct is thus, in part, to be understood in terms of those rules and institutions that may be more or less tight as they constrain conduct — and in part, of course, as the more unstructured pursuit of personal interest, not least through the opportunistic breaking of rules and departures from settled ways of doing things.

Now, Mises, in arguing that Weber's interpretation of economics as involving an historical ideal type was not acceptable, was in my view upholding a view which is widely shared among economists. For, economists seem exceedingly reluctant to embrace historical or institutional ideal types, even when they have themselves provided good reasons for believing that this is how individuals' behavior is to be understood. What do I mean by this last point?

Consider Hayek's economics. As far as I know — although I would be delighted to be corrected on this — nowhere does he actually *use* historical or institutional ideal types in his explanatory work *in economics*. In his "Economics and Knowledge" he explicitly asserts that the empirical content of economics comes with our theories about learning — and, in effect, institutions — and that if we wish to explain anything we will have to use "ideal types" (which in context one has to understand as historical ideal types, as opposed to Mises' praxeological representations of human action).[21] But this is not, as far as I know, something that Hayek himself ever follows up. Similarly, the noneconomic writings of Hayek are full of ideas about individuals following specific rules. But I do not think that he has recourse to such things when offering explanations of economic phenomena.

A similar point might be made about Buchanan and Vanberg's work in constitutional economics.[22] They are concerned with the rationale that individuals have to follow particular constitutional rules. But if they are correct, and offer this as an explanation of moral and legal order where we have it and as a suggestion as to how things might be improved upon, may we not use these ideas (of behavior that follows particular rules) in an explanatory context, too? It is beside the point that Buchanan and Vanberg would argue that the explanation for why these rules are adopted is a matter of agents' self-interest. For, even if they are right, this is not of importance here — for the very reasons that the Austrians advanced against some claims made for the relevance of psychology to economics (and which we reviewed earlier in this chapter). Rather, if peoples' conduct involves the following of, or is constrained by, specific rules or patterns of institutionally-related conduct, why should not an acknowledgment of this, rather than pure maximization, inform our models? (It is, of course, possible that these theorists could respond: there is no reason in principle why we should not do this; it is just that *in practice* such ideas do not make for good explanations of the material with which economists are concerned. This we will discuss further on in the chapter.)

The proponent of a historical or institutional interpretation of subjectivism might also address the following objections to the subjectivist praxeologist:

1. It is not odd that you think that you can tell us about the structure of *all* human action, while at the same time suggesting that we cannot have access to the content of any action other than our own? (Just how, he might ask, is it that you have all this structural information about what you are otherwise saying is a closed book?) Further, is not human subjective experience mediated by an intersubjectively shared language; and as Adam Smith suggested in *The Theory of Moral Sentiments* do we not discover qualities of our self through the reactions of others? Or to put this another way, while there may be something that is both important and subjective in the sense of being "inner" to each of us, is it not in many ways structured by what serves as the public currency of intersubjective discourse in the society in which we are living?

2. The consequences of earlier human actions stand as an objective setting within which we act, and have effects back upon us much as do physical objects, such as tables and chairs. While, if a subjectivist so wished, he could make a big deal of the idea that there is no such thing as "the" interest rate, it is clear that such things as interest rates and prices do have a thing-like character, and set survival conditions upon the success of many of our activities. Nozick is thus correct in arguing that a pure, subjectivist methodological individualism may be insufficient if we are trying to explain phenomena that are constituted by the interaction between individuals and such "objects," serving as "filter mechanisms".[23]

Let me now conclude my comments on these two forms of subjectivism. There seems to me a danger that purely praxeological subjectivism leads us to explanatory nihilism; while there seems no reason why, in principle, we may not use historical or institutional ideal types. To put this another way, there may indeed be a praxeological structure to human action which, (if due note is also taken of filter mechanisms) can be of great importance for explanatory purposes. But there seems no reason why, in principle, we should not also have recourse to specific historical or institutional ideal types. (This also, of course, need not involve us in denying that there could be some further explanatory story that serves to explain why there are these differences between different individuals; it is simply the case that this need not matter, when we are faced with a particular explanatory task.) If I am right in this, then those people who have suggested that subjectivism can properly be concerned with the problematic of (if not embrace the explanatory theories of) institutional and historical (and to a degree behavioral) schools of economics were correct, at least in the sense that there is no reason in principle why we may not proceed in such a manner.[24]

The Aim of Economics

The ideas that I expressed in the previous section of this chapter, while perhaps shocking to some, are, in a sense, permissive. For they suggest that economists might take many different paths in explaining things, and this might lead my readers to think that I had become a "relativist" in methodology. (And thus one of those people, the only justification of whose existence is the fact that others are not being permissive or relativistic.)[25] But, as might be suspected by those who know of me as a former assistant of Karl Popper's, this is not the case at all.

Rather, it seems to me that a strange view has developed of what methodology is all about. This, to exaggerate a little, has led to a picture of good, permissive relativists, together with rhetorically and historically-inclined sociologists of economics (all of whom from the point of view of economics itself are pointless, as they are themselves so keen to assure us that their ideas have no normative force, and thus make no difference) and of arrogant, "normative" methodologists, who go around telling others what they can — and, especially, cannot — do. In my view, things are rather different. In the practise of any discipline, we live in various different dimensions. One of these involves issues of method. These can range from fairly practical issues (I do not think that Machlup was right to make a big deal out of the differences between methodology and method)[26] to issues in epistemology and the theory of explanation. There is, in my view, no watertight demarcation between "first order" disciplines and "second order" philosophical reflection upon them. Rather, we are constantly faced with choices and with the possibility of considering whether or not things might better be done differently — whether at the level of the evaluation of hypotheses, or of institutional arrangements. At any one point, we may pause and consider as an object to be investigated what had hitherto been a tacit assumption of how we were conducting ourselves.

In these deliberations, we will need to draw on differing skills. In some cases, it will be the working economist's practical skills and his detailed knowledge of the first-order discipline that is crucial. In other cases, it may be slightly different skills, honed by historical or sociological studies or perspectives. In still others, contributions may be made by those who are interested in more abstract issues, ones which, perhaps, arise in many different areas of human knowledge, or from their comparison.

The concern of the methodologist, in particular, is with the (critical) articulation of our aims and with the discussion of the appropriateness or otherwise of particular means for their pursuit. The reason I above repudiated relativism is that it seems to me that we can make nonarbitrary choices about methodological issues, relative to our choice of aims.

It may seem strange to pose the question: what is economics about? But historically, much of economics was inspired by policy-related concerns (with a concern for the wealth of nations; the appropriate policy for a mint, and so on. One might also tell a rather more sinister story of the problematic of economics in terms of whose interests set its agenda, but this is not my concern here). However, in more recent times, someone looking at economics might well take the view that much that goes on consists of: (1) attempts to explain whatever is taking place in terms of individual maximization, sometimes within the wider constraints of general equilibrium theory; (2) the exploration of technically interesting models, which may have little or no explanatory relation to anything outside themselves; (3) the exploration, by those outside the mainstream, of their own favorite paradigms and assumptions, but usually without much concern for whether the work that they produce, couched in such terms, would be found satisfactory by anybody else.

Now, I make these points not to mock but to suggest that the acceptability, or otherwise, of the suggestion that we may sometimes need to make use of historical or institutional ideal types will depend on what conception of economics is accepted — implicitly or explicitly — by those to whom the suggestion is addressed. I do not, by this, mean to assume a relativistic position. Rather, my point is that it will do little good to address someone whose view of the aims of economics is mainstream neoclassical problem solving on the merits of historical ideal types. With him, rather, one would first have to engage in a discussion about the aims of economics, or even about the sociological organization of academic disciplines and its epistemological consequences, or whether there is any point at all in conscious reflection about the workings of a discipline.

What, No Foundations?

It is possible that my approach may strike the reader as strange. I take methodological issues seriously and suggest that a concern with them is, properly, a continuing part of the pursuit of any discipline. But I place emphasis upon the task of explanation and on our preference for theories upon the basis of what gives us a good explanation, rather than upon some notion of philosophical foundations. My reason for this is that I do not think that the social — or, indeed, other — sciences have or need philosophical foundations. This is not to say that their pursuit does not involve philosophical assumptions, or that philosophers — and practitioners with an interest in such matters — may not say interesting and important things about such issues. Rather, not only are such matters likely to be issues for continuing discussion. But truths about human beings or about the world do not necessarily help us in our explanatory tasks. For what is crucial with respect to explanation is the *level* of explanation that we should use and how different items of our knowledge are to be bundled up together. And this is an issue that is not addressed by the mere fact of our possessing truths about, say, human beings, meaning, and the furniture of the social world. What items of such knowledge we should *select* in order to understand, say, trade cycles; how we should conceptualize such items; and at what level of abstraction we should describe them, are theoretical problems that will still face us, even if we had all the knowledge that we might want about the motivation of individuals in some society. And that is the kind of explanatory task with which economics was, historically, concerned.[27]

But what of explanation — am I not bringing ideas about this in a kind of "rock-bottom" foundation? The answer is: no. I take our ideas about explanation — along with our ideas about epistemology — ideally to rest on a more or less rational consensus; one which, however, can be made the object of criticism and reflection at any time that we may have misgivings about it. In the spirit of the work of Popper and of Bartley, our knowledge rests not upon firm ground, but upon those things that at any one time no one has chosen to contest, or upon those things about which we have (for the time being) been able to agree, in light of argument and discussion that have taken place between people who, initially, were in disagreement. The proper role of methodological discussion is thus the articulation of disagreement and alternatives and argument about them in the hope of reaching consensus.[18] One would not, however, expect that consensus would actually be reached — indeed, one would be suspicious if it were. But at the same time, the contending parties would be engaged in conversation and argument with one another, with the aim of showing that the other is incorrect, not in a kind of live-and-let-live peaceful coexistence. Further, it is not an adequate response to such ideas to suggest that competition can take place simply at the level of success in the production of empirical results, or by who gains the most adherents or even resources. For what constitutes empirical success and an adequate explanation is itself a matter of dispute, and there seems to be no special reason to suppose that power and success in the academic world have any *necessary* connection with truth.[29]

Concluding Remarks

Suppose — unlikely as it may this point seem to the reader — that I am correct in what I say concerning the status of subjectivism, and in my meta-level comments. What, specifically, might *follow* from all this? I conclude this chapter with some more specific comments.

First, my earlier argument has the consequence that it would be perfectly *possible* for someone to take the view that historical or institutional ideal types *could* be used but, nonetheless, to judge that they are best not used in approaching the material with which they are concerned. They might do this, for example, because they are dealing with phenomena that they believe to be generated by the actions of large numbers of people, such that more detailed attention to the individual differences between these people is beside the point. Alternatively, they may argue that the incentives (or the anonymity of the situation) are such that what matters is maximization. They may even argue that, for the particular theoretical purposes that concern them, we may abstract from human ignorance in our models. Such a view is, however, fully compatible with one that says that, for example, when we are dealing with situations in which the decisions of a few people are crucial, we may have to pay attention to their particular and possibly idiosyncratic views.[30]

Second, what of individuals' subjective knowledge, for example, their incorrect theories about the world? When should these be taken into accout (as opposed to our modelling their activity as if they were acting rationally on the basis of a correct knowledge of the situation that faced them)? On the face of it, how we answer this question may depend not only upon the incentives that those individuals face to change their views, but also on the opportunities that they will have to learn that they are wrong. This includes the relative ease with which people can acquire the information in question if they are looking for it, and the frequency with which, as it were, they are confronted with the unpleasant consequences of their having incorrect views.

To put all this in more concrete terms, consider Adam Smith's famous gloss on the debate about the effect of commerce upon manners. He compares the reputations of people of different nationalities in keeping their word. In this, the Dutch, at the time at which he wrote, came out on top, the English in the middle and the Scots at the bottom. He explained these differences as the product of self-interest and the frequency with which they were involved in making contracts:

> A dealer is afraid of losing his character and is scrupulous in observing every engagement. When a person makes perhaps 20 contracts in a day, he cannot gain so much by endeavouring to impose on his neighbours, as the very appearance of a cheat would make him lose. Where people seldom deal with one another, we find they are somewhat disposed to cheat, because they can gain more by a smart trick that they can lose by the injury which it does their characters.[31]

This, clearly, is suggestive of recent work in game theory. But my present point in quoting this passage is that it also suggests an important lesson concerning the relevance of subjectivism. For in cases like that of the Dutch merchant who is frequently involved in deals, his self-interest may insure that we, in modelling his behavior, do not need to bother too much with the more baroque aspects of his subjective understanding of the world, or of his motivation. But in the case of Smith's Scot, who deals only infrequently, we may need to investigate his cultural or his personal world-view very carefully, if we are to be able to understand how he will react to economic incentives. The same would seem to me plausible in respect to the labor market, and indeed, with many of the phenomena with which the economist is concerned, if the people in the consequences of whose actions he is interested are engaged only occasionally in transactions from which they can learn, or where the payoff from different forms of behavior comes only some time after the behavior is undertaken. My suggestion is, thus, that a realistic appraisal of the kinds of situations in which agents are acting may guide us as to the degree to which we should be historical or institutional subjectivists when modelling their actions.

Finally, I referred above to Hayek's departure from Mises, in stressing the significance of institutions and learning. This, and his comments about the study of the dynamics of markets, seem interesting suggestions for research. But how is it, then, that an uncharitable critic of modern Austrian economics might say that it has been stronger in invoking the term "market process" than in saying anything very illuminating about how markets actually function? *If* there is anything in this criticism, I suspect that it is, in fact, an excess of subjectivism that may be at fault. When modeling the processes through which markets adjust, we may at least initially need to work with models that simplify significantly if we are to get a handle upon what plays a key causal role in different types of situation. Too much subjectivist-inspired descriptive realism in our models may prevent us from explaining anything at all.

In addressing these points to my commentator, I am, after all, addressing someone who may feel *some* sympathy for my emphasis upon explanation as a touchstone — as is evidenced by his and Kay's "How Economists Can Accept Shackle's Critique of Economic Doctrines Without Arguing Themselves Out Of Their Jobs."[32] However, rather than attempting further to flatter my discussant, I should stop, and take my medicine.

Acknowledgments

I would like to thank Bruce Caldwell and Roger Koppl for their comments on an earlier version of this chapter. I would also like to thank members of the Center of the Study of Market Processes at George Mason University for their comments when I presented a yet earlier version of the chapter to their colloquium.

Notes

1. It is interesting that Mises' earlier discussion, in "On the Development of the Subjective Theory of Value" (contained in his work of [1981]), is less clear-cut than is his later discussion in (1949, 124ff.)

2. Compare F. A. Hayek (1979, 68).

3. J. H. Runde (1988, 101−20); see p. 101.

4. Karl Popper (1985).

5. My informal account here draws on various of Popper's writings. See, in addition to his work of (1985), and the early discussions in (1966) and (1977), and "The Bucket and the Searchlight" (reprinted in his [1972]), his "On the Theory of the Objective Mind," and "A Realist View of Logic, Physics and History" in (1972), and (1976).

6. Compare, on this aspect of Mises' method, Moss (1990).

7. For some discussion of the first of these issues, see Shearmur (1990).

8. The parallel is closest in some of Weber's methodological writings, notably his work of (1975). For a brief discussion that contrasts these writings with other themes in Weber's work, see Shearmur (1984).

9. For some discussion of their differences on this point, see Mises' "Sociology and History" in (1986). This whole issue is, of course, pursued further in the work of Alfred Schutz. This, however, I cannot discuss on the present occasion, for reasons of space.

10. Runde (1986, 108−9) has suggested that "praxeology differs from the situational

determinism of neoclassical economics only with regard to its information assumptions." This, however, seems to me an overstatement, in the sense that Mises and others in this tradition have suggested that more can be extracted from the formal structure of human action than does neoclassical economics. Compare Di Lorenzo (1990).

11. Kirzner (1986a).

12. Kirzner (1986a, 151).

13. Compare, on this, Yeager (1987). This article raises many other points of great importance concerning subjectivism and the Austrian tradition, many of which I have been unable to take up in the present essay, for reasons of space. Yeager's important essay should be consulted by anyone concerned with these matters.

14. James Buchanan (1991).

15. See Wiseman, "Beyond Positive Economics—Dream and Reality," in Wiseman (1983) or Wiseman (1989, 156—70). The reader might also usefully consult Wiseman (1983) more generally.

16. Wiseman (1989, 159—60).

17. Lachmann (1951); compare Lachmann (1977, 95).

18. R. Ebeling (1986; see 48).

19. Compare O'Driscoll and Rizzo (1985, 6).

20. Compare in this context Etzioni (1988).

21. Compare F. A. Hayek, "Economics and Knowledge," in Hayek (1948, 46—7). Roger Koppl has suggested to me that historical ideal types are implicitly at work in Hayek's theory of business cycles.

22. Compare, for example, Buchanan and Vanberg (1986).

23. Compare Nozick (1974), chapter 1. See also Leland Yeager (1987) for some further problems about a subjectivist approach.

24. Compare Seckler (1975).

25. Their situation reminds me of the old joke about a British philosophy department, heavily influenced by 1950s-style linguistic philosophy and the later Wittgenstein, that supposedly employed a more traditional philosopher to teach first-year courses, so that the rest of the department could then spend their time clarifying the philosophical muddles and confusions that students would subsequently exhibit.

26. Compare Fritz Machlup (1978).

27. For more extensive discussion of this point, compare Shearmur (1983) and (1991a).

28. See also, on this, Shearmur (1991b).

29. Compare Shearmur (1991c) and Bartley (1990).

30. Compare on this some work by Roger Koppl on cases in which the actions of specific individuals may be crucial—as when a government-influenced central bank takes decisions about exchange rates. See Koppl (1990) and (1991) and also Langlois and Koppl (1984).

31. Compare Adam Smith (1978, 538—9).

32. Compare Earl and Kay (1985).

References

Adorno, T. et al. 1976. *The Positivist Dispute in German Sociology*. London: Heinemann Educational.

Barry, Norman et al. 1984. *Hayek's "Serfdom" Revisited*. London: Institute of Economic Affairs.

Bartley, W. W. III 1990. *Unfathomed Knowledge, Unmeasured Wealth*. La Salle, IL: Open Court.

Blaug, M. and de Marchi, N. (eds.) 1991. Appraising Economic Theories. Aldershot, UK: Edward Elgar.

Buchanan, James and Vanberg, Viktor. 1986. "Rational Choice and Moral Order," *Analyse und Kritik* 10: 138–60.

Buchanan, James. 1991. "Jack Wiseman: A Personal Appreciation," *Constitutional Political Economy* 2(1): 1–6.

Butler, E. 1988. *Ludwig von Mises: Fountainhead of the Modern Microeconomic Revolution*. Brookfield, VT: Gower.

Caldwell, B. (ed.) 1990. *Carl Menger and His Legacy in Economics*. Durham, NC: Duke University Press.

Di Lorenzo, T. 1990. "The Subjectivist Roots of James Buchanan's Economics," *Review of Austrian Economics* 4: 180–95.

Earl, P. (ed.) 1988. *Psychological Economics*. Boston: Kluwer.

Earl, P. and Kay, N. M. 1985. "How Economists Can Accept Shackle's Critique of Economic Doctrines Without Arguing Themselves Out of Their Jobs," *Journal of Economic Studies* 12: 34–48.

Ebeling, R. 1986. "Toward a Hermeneutical Economics." In Kirzner (1986a), 39–55.

Etzioni, A. 1988. *The Moral Dimension*. New York: The Free Press.

Hayek, F. A. 1948. *Individualism and Economic Order*. Chicago: University of Chicago Press.

Hayek, F. A. 1979. *The Counter-Revolution of Science*. Indianapolis: Liberty Press.

Kirzner, I. (ed.) 1986a. *Subjectivism, Intelligibility and Economic Understanding*. New York: New York University Press.

Kirzner, I. 1986b. "Another Look at the Subjectivism of Costs." In Kirzner (1986a), 140–56.

Koppl, R. 1990. "Towards an Empirics of Subjectivist Economics." Fairleigh Dickinson University: Center for Economics and Finance, Working Paper 90–8.

Koppl, R. 1991. "Economic Effects of the Choice of Constraints" (unpublished).

Lachmann, Ludwig. 1951. "The Science of Human Action," *Economica* 18 (November 1951): 412–27.

Lachmann, Ludwig. 1977. *Capital, Expectations, and the Market Process*, Walter Grinder, (ed.) Kansas City: Sheed Andrews and McMeel.

Langlois, R. and Koppl, R. 1984. "Fritz Machlup and Marginalism: A Re-evaluation," George Mason University: Center for the Study of Market Processes, Working Paper 1984–14.

Langlois, R. (ed.) 1986. *Economics as a Process: Essays in the New Institutional Economics*. Cambridge: Cambridge University Press.

Lavoie, D. 1986. "Euclideanism versus Hermeneutics: A Reinterpretation of Misesian Apriorism." In Kirzner (1986a), 192–210.

Machlup, Fritz. 1978. *The Methodology of Economics and Other Social Sciences*. New York: Academic Press.

Miller, David (ed.) 1985. *Popper Selections*. Princeton: Princeton University Press.

Mises, Ludwig von 1949. *Human Action*. London: Hodge.

Mises, Ludwig von 1981. *Epistemological Problems of Economics*. New York: New York University Press.

Moss, Laurence. 1990. [Review of Butler (1988)], *Journal of the History of Economic Thought* 12: 236−8.

Nozick, Robert. 1974. *Anarchy, State and Utopia*. Oxford: Blackwell.

O'Driscoll, G. and Rizzo, M. 1985. *The Economics of Time and Ignorance*. Oxford: Blackwell.

Popper, Karl R. 1966. *The Open Society and Its Enemies*. Princeton: Princeton University Press.

Popper, Karl R. 1972. *Objective Knowledge*. New York: Oxford University Press.

Popper, Karl R. 1976. "The Logic of the Social Sciences." In Adorno et al. (1976), 87−104.

Popper, Karl R. 1977. *The Poverty of Historicism*. New York: Harper and Row.

Popper, Karl R. 1985. "The Rationality Principle." In D. Miller (ed.) (1985), 257−65.

Runde, J. H. 1988. "Subjectivism, Psychology and the Modern Austrians." In Earl (ed.) (1988), 101−20.

Seckler, David. 1975. *Thorstein Veblen and the Institutionalists*. London: Macmillan.

Shearmur, J. 1983. "Subjectivism, Falsification and Positive Economics." In Wiseman (ed.) (1983), pp. 65−86.

Shearmur, J. 1984. "Hayek and the Spirit of the Age." In Barry et al (1984), 67−85.

Shearmur, J. 1990. "From Hayek to Menger." In Caldwell (ed.) (1990), 198−212.

Shearmur, J. 1991a. "Common Sense and the Foundations of Economic Theory: Duhem versus Robbins." *Philosophy of the Social Sciences*, 21: 64−71.

Shearmur, J. 1991b. "Popper, Lakatos and Theoretical Progress in Economics." In Blaug and de Marchi (eds.) (1991), 35−52.

Shearmur, J. 1991c. "McCloskey, Dialogue and Spontaneous Order." Paper delivered to History of Economics Society Annual Meeting, College Park, MD.

Smith, Adam. 1978. *Lectures on Jurisprudence*. Oxford: Clarendon Press.

Weber, Max. 1975. *Roscher and Knies: The Logical Problems of Historical Economics*. New York: The Free Press.

Wiseman, Jack (ed.) 1983. *Beyond Positive Economics?* London: Macmillan.

Wiseman, Jack. 1989. *Cost, Choice and Political Economy*. Aldershot, UK: Edward Elgar.

Yeager, Leland. 1987. "Why Subjectivism?," *Review of Austrian Economics* 1: 5−31.

p 103: **COMMENTARY**

Shearmur on Subjectivism: Discussion

Peter E. Earl

The pragmatic tone of Shearmur's conclusion is one that I find highly appealing. Far too often debates about the practical consequences of adopting a subjectivist stance towards economics have proceeded as if all economic problems have similar characteristics. Yet, it would be hard to argue that this assumption is even an approximately accurate representation of the subject matter of economics. In reality, decisions might usefully be classified along a spectrum. At one end would be genuine Shacklean "originative" choices; at the other end would be what Latsis (1972) has called "situational determinism." At the Shacklean extreme the choice problem and the set of constraints both have to be discovered by the chooser; at the other, matters are so fully specified and known to all that there is no room for argument about the need to act and about what the appropriate course of action might be. In the former case economists would be unwise to assume that agents would have the same view of the problem as themselves (the agents might not even recognize they had a problem); in the latter, the tautness of the economic environment might be such that those who did not frame the problem in the same way as the economist would rapidly be forced to adjust their ideas or else be driven from the area in question.

A mistake of Austrians in the past seems to have been to try to find general things to say about human behaviour while placing all choice at the Shacklean end of the spectrum. Here, they have ended up with less to say than they might have because they have distanced themselves from the findings of psychologists on the ways in which people try to cope with ignorance and in the process systematically make errors (a good starting point for reading here would be Hogarth, 1980).[1]

Missing from Shearmur's discussion is a consideration of the question of the economist's expertise or lack of experience with the decision environment in question. If economists were unfamiliar with notions that decision-makers took for granted in a particular area, they would hardly be able to model the situation in a deterministic manner, even though the decision-makers themselves might be so experienced in their task that, to them, it no longer seemed to involve any great creative leaps of imagination. Economists would not be in any position to make pronouncements unless they spent a good deal of time alongside these decision-makers, discussing with them why they were doing what they were doing.

For example, one can well imagine the problems that an Austrian economist might have if asked to write a report on whether, say, those making pricing decisions in the United Kingdom electricity industry were actually following instructions to base their prices on marginal costs (compare Littlechild, 1978, 53–54). Without prior experience in this industry, the economist would by no means be guaranteed to see alternatives in the same way as the specialists whose activities were being audited. Either the price-setters would be using their expertise to make judgments with a view to the opportunity costs of the electricity supply organization (or, if marginal social opportunity cost were the pricing criterion, to society at large, however the latter were defined), or the price-setters would be allowing their judgments to be coloured by personal gains they stood to make by acting opportunistically and breaching the pricing rule. In the latter situation the economist undertaking the audit would then run into the problem that, without some means of making interpersonal comparisons, it would be impossible to say whether opportunistic behaviour was in any case a bad thing for society even were the economist able to detect it (compare Loasby's [1976, 119] comments about problems with X-inefficiency as a concept).

Provided that Austrian economists are prepared to embrace new research methods and abandon tendencies towards a priorism, nihilism need not be implied by the fact that an onlooker can see neither the alternatives nor the evaluative criteria that individuals have on their minds when making choices. In some situations it will be possible to ask decision-makers to reveal their thought processes, for example, via the use of conventional market research techniques or even, during the course of a decision, via the use of "protocol analysis" methods (see Waterman and Newell, 1971). In my own work (Earl, 1986) I have explored at length the potential for economists to uncover opportunity costs with the aid of repertory grid, laddering and implication grid techniques developed by the subjectivist Personal Construct School of psychologists for uncovering in a clinical setting how people see themselves and their problems; some of these methods have already been employed to good effect in practical marketing contexts.

To be sure, there will be some situations in which decision-makers may have self-serving reasons for giving incorrect answers to questions about the alternatives that are being or were considered. In other situations it will simply seem too costly to conduct such research. A case in point may seem to be where we have a large population of decision-makers. However, it may be possible to obtain adequate approximations of the distribution of subjective opportunity costs through sample surveys that uncover relative frequencies of particular broad ways of viewing things. What I am suggesting, then, is that subjectivists should follow marketing scholars and get into the habit of familiarizing themselves with a variety of "ideal types" who may be involved in the particular kind of transaction that they are studying (for example: yuppies, greenies, etc., when modeling consumers); they should not try merely to specify one ideal type for each kind of transaction (a speculator, a worker, etc.). Though subjectivists may thus lump people into different categories, they may unify their view of behaviour by seeing it as emerging from the systematic application of personal sets of judgmental rules.

The explanatory importance of thinking in terms of varieties of decision-makers rather than in terms of a single class of representative agents can easily be illustrated with respect to Keynes' analysis of the determination of interest rates. He portrays relative asset prices as being based at any moment on a mixture of expectations about the future course of their prices. Being mutually exclusive, many of these expectations have to be incorrect. If we are to anticipate the course of events in such markets, we need to be able to anticipate the different ways in which surprising changes in the "state of the news" may be interpreted (for example, by "chartists" or "fundamentalists"); we also need to know the balance of these differing opinions.

Having just myself moved between two superficially similar economies — from Tasmania to New Zealand — I am rapidly amassing experiences that make me most receptive to Shearmur's suggestion that the rules by which people run their lives may be tied up with local and historically specific institutions. For example, such a move really makes transparent the way in which monetary systems function on the basis of conventions that are culturally idiosyncratic. Compared with their United Kingdom counterparts who would accept personal checks up to a relatively modest figure if accompanied by a check guarantee card, Australian businesses seemed to me to have an almost pathological aversion to being paid with personal checks (signs would say "no personal checks except by prior arrangement"). In New Zealand, by contrast, so little thought seems to be given to the possibility of a bouncing check that even very large personal checks (for example, to buy a car) seem to be accepted as if they are cash. Foreigners who do not know the conventions may have many embarrassing moments, as may the natives with whom they interact: what is shocking in one social setting may be quite ordinary behaviour in another. With such surprises may come failures of coordination until new conventions are absorbed.

Episodes of financial history ought to promote an acceptance of the merits of also studying the historical aspect of conventions. Portfolio managers in the financial services industry may build up unsound balance sheets, as may the individuals and corporations from whom they borrow, because they have short memories of how financial disasters of the past came about. The troubles of the late 1980s and early 1990s in banking and property markets should come as no surprise to those who have kept in mind the events of the mid 1970s. Yet, players in these markets appeared to allow their rules for what constitutes safe lending to become slack as memories of the 1970s faded or as senior personnel were replaced by youngsters who had no experience of a downswing. Without tapping into research on how people adjust their perceptions of what constitutes sound financial behaviour (from pessimistic to euphoric), economists and their subjects both risk ending up being unpleasantly surprised by the course of events. Hyman Minsky's (1986) work on financial instability strikes me as an excellent example of what can be done here, and yet, most Austrians seem to have been no keener than mainstream economists to embrace it. Minsky's psychological perspective may enable us to anticipate the direction that events are likely to take if not their precise timing.[2]

To know which alternatives were considered and rejected by an agent is not very helpful for policy purposes if reasons for their rejection cannot be discovered. Unfortunately, it is probably here — in the characteristics space rather than the goods space — that the problem of discovering subjective opportunity costs is most acute. For example, if I ask someone why she has chosen a particular course of action, I may sometimes receive a rather exasperated reply to the effect that, "I can't put it into words, it's just a gut feeling that I had in favour of this one; the others felt wrong." The consumer's position here overlaps to some extent with that of a person trying to enable someone else to set up a factory on the basis of a blueprint that cannot specify the tacit knowledge required to make it function effectively — compare Polanyi's (1958, 52) example of difficulties involved in transferring German lightbulb manufacturing technology to

Hungary. A person who appeals to intuition as a basis for choice may be doing so merely as a cover from some underlying "real reason" that she is to embarrassed to reveal, but she might be perfectly sincere.

But such situations may be the exception rather than the norm; at other times advisors or auditors may be able to improve their insights by asking their subjects/clients for further information to check that they are not misconstruing the latter's view of things. For example, I recall how the most industrious real estate agent I encountered when looking for a house after my arrival in Tasmania failed to direct me to the house I ultimately purchased. He knew of this house and stood to gain commission from introducing me to it. His trouble was that he did not seek sufficient clarification from me about just how fussy I was when it came to wanting a low maintenance house. He later told me that he had thought I would not be keen on the house I purchased, for its decor was no match for the pristine condition of those that he had been showing me. But in fact I was quite prepared to live with such internal decor. What I wanted to avoid were the costs of having to do frequent external painting to preserve the integrity of the materials. Now, as I write this piece in the midst of looking for a house in New Zealand, I am trying to be as clear as possible to estate agents about how I see my opportunity costs, for this will cut down my search costs.

Shearmur's comment that "markets would simply not be able to work unless we were able to anticipate one another's preferences pretty well" is consistent with the example of the Tasmanian estate agent losing his chance to earn commission. So, too, are many classic cases of marketing disasters (see Hartley, 1989); we may learn a lot about resource misallocation from studying them, rather than merely concentrating on situations in which coordination was achieved.

But we should also note that Shearmur's comment implicitly leads us straight to the "transactions cost" literature spawned by the (partly Hayek-inspired) work of Williamson (1975). This analytical foundation for the economics of corporate strategy does not run into difficulties as a result of the existence of agents who may be unwilling to reveal their true positions to other parties with whom they are interacting. On the contrary, this research program focuses on the question of how firms' internalization decisions and hiring contracts may be affected by the difficulty of guessing what others may do, and by fears (whether well founded or not) that they might act in an opportunistic manner. If agents could always "see through" those with whom they were dealing, much of the research on internalization choices would lose its rationale and the world would display a far less rich range of methods of arranging production.[3]

To be sure, the subjectivity of opportunity costs may make it hard for economists to reach deterministic conclusions about the merits of rival forms of industrial organization. But for economists to have to think about a wide range of possibilities that *might* be troubling decision-makers may be no bad thing; if economists' subjects are also having trouble in sizing up their opponents, or are coming to differing conclusions about their likely behaviour, the result may be that a variety of forms of organization is in evidence in the product market in question.

Whether this leaves us unable to "predict" behaviour is debatable. The transaction cost literature might leave us unable to predict which *particular* firm will prefer which strategy if we do not have access to information about the particular fears that loom large in the minds of decision-makers in particular firms. Nonetheless, it does appear to offer explanations of what may be leading one form of strategy to be preferred over another. In so far as such Williamson-inspired scenarios involve plausible explanations that would not have been on the minds of the public at large, the economists responsible for them may justifiably feel that they are practising a constructive form of subjectivism.

Notes

1. I am less convinced than Shearmur seems to be that nihilistic Austrians do acknowledge that decision-makers might be prone to error in their attempts to cope with ignorance and uncertainty; such an acknowledgment would make the typical anti-interventionist stance of Austrians more difficult to uphold.

2. To judge from the scenarios set out in Galbraith's (1990) recent satirical novel about a fictitious Harvard economist who succeeds in devising a very accurate index of euphoric, irrational expectations, it is perhaps no bad thing if economists remain, like their subjects, limited in their capacities for making pinpoint predictions of turning points in markets; their subjects might otherwise start taking them seriously, with the result that their predictions start becoming self-fulfilling.

3. Somehow the focus of Austrians on *market* processes seems to have blinded most of them to the use of internalisation strategies as a way of coping with prospects for market failure. Perhaps libertarian Austrians feel uncomfortable about accepting the suggestion that firms may use internal planning systems owing to inadequacies of the market; it may be too much like the thin end of a wedge towards recognizing possible merits of a mixed economy.

References

Earl, P. E. 1986. *Lifestyle Economics: Consumer Behaviour in a Turbulent World.* New York: St. Martin's Press.

Galbraith, J. K. 1990. *A Tenured Professor.* New York: Houghton Mifflin.

Hartley, R. F. 1989. *Marketing Mistakes* (4th ed). New York: Wiley.

Hogarth, R. M. 1980. *Judgement and Choice: The Psychology of Decision.* New York: Wiley.

Latsis, S. J. 1972. "Situational Determinism in Economics," *British Journal for the Philosophy of Science* 25: 207–45.

Littlechild, S. C. 1978. *The Fallacy of the Mixed Economy.* London: Institute of Economic Affairs.

Loasby, B. J. 1976. *Choice, Complexity and Ignorance.* Cambridge: Cambridge University Press.

Minsky, H. P. 1986. *Stabilizing an Unstable Economy.* New Haven, CT: Yale University Press.

Polanyi, M. 1958. *Personal Knowledge.* London: Routledge and Kegan Paul.

Waterman, D. A. and Newell, A. 1971. "Protocol Analysis as a Task for Artificial Intelligence," *Artificial Intelligence* 2: 285–318.

Williamson, O. E. 1975. *Markets and Hierarchies: Analysis and Antitrust Implications.* New York: Free Press.

5 MARKET CO-ORDINATION

Brian J. Loasby

Equilibrium and Planning

Ludwig von Mises' (1920, 130) claim that "rational economic planning is impossible in a socialist commonwealth" initiated the once-famous planning debate, which was widely thought to have been resolved by Lange (1938) in favour of the planners. Further development of general equilibrium theory apparently strengthened the proposition that, in Frank Hahn's (1984, 347) words, "anything the ideal economy can do the state can also do, but not vice versa since there may be externalities and public goods". Dasgupta (1986, 30–31), having shown how formidable the task is of acquiring the knowledge needed to devise an endowment set that would generate a desired Pareto optimum as a competitive equilibrium, correctly observes that there is no obvious reason why planners who possess such knowledge should not impose that optimum directly. He continues: "The Second Fundamental Theorem of Welfare Economics — which is so often seen by economists as providing a reason why the state ought to rely on markets — holds true only in circumstances where there is no need to rely on markets at all. I have no explanation for this paradox" — which he thereafter ignores, failing to see that the neo-Walrasian models of planning and markets share a basic flaw.

All that has been established is an existence theorem for a perfect planning equilibrium to match the existence theorem for a perfectly competitive equilibrium; and that should be no surprise to anyone who, like Demsetz (1988, 145), recognizes that the appropriate name for what is called perfect competition is perfect decentralization — on the basis

137

of equilibrium prices that are centrally determined. To convert a perfectly decentralized equilibrium into a perfect planning equilibrium all that is necessary is to substitute planners' prices for those called by the auctioneer — for a given specification of the economy, they are, of course, identical — and to substitute an instruction to conform for a market setting in which there is no alternative to conformity. This isomorphism is perfectly exemplified by Coase's (1988a, 8) story of Abba Lerner's visit to Mexico in order to persuade the exiled Trotsky that on his return to power he should simply replicate the results of a perfectly competitive system.

However, as Hayek (1945, 519) pointed out, the logical deduction of an optimal allocation, from an information set that is known to be complete, "is emphatically *not* the economic problem which society faces." The economist's habit of constructing models of equilibrium on the basis of fully-specified data has too easily disguised the problems of discovering, collating, and putting to use the knowledge that is necessary to arrive at a general equilibrium, whether that equilibrium is to be defined as competitive or planned. When these problems are ignored, so are the costs of handling them — the costs, in a market system, of achieving satisfactory transactions. Now as Coase (1988b, 14) has observed, "A world without transactions costs has very peculiar properties." Among these peculiar properties is the impossibility of distinguishing between market processes and planning processes: if both are costless, both can be as elaborate and as rapid as optimality requires.

The Attainment of Equilibrium

Since the calculation of a perfect plan is apparently as simple as the derivation of a perfectly competitive equilibrium, it is fitting that the difficulties of plan making should be matched by the difficulty of explaining precisely how an economy can arrive at a perfectly competitive equilibrium, if no benevolent auctioneer happens to be available. An immediate difficulty is that the economy cannot actually be perfectly competitive while it is still searching for equilibrium; and that opens up an unwelcome range of possibilities. The study of Walrasian tatonnements, to quote Hahn again, has produced "a collection of sufficient conditions, one might almost say anecdotes, and a demonstration by Scarf that not much more could be hoped for" (Hahn, 1984, 89). Franklin Fisher's (1983) skillful, determined, and honest endeavour to establish conditions under which an economy can be relied on to converge asymptotically on some equilibrium produces a specification that requires a complete set of markets at all times, an unchanging set of firms, agents who always have point expectations and unique optimal plans, and no possibility of any favourable surprise arising out of the adjustment process itself. Even if all these requirements are met, Fisher's analysis tells us nothing, as he warns us (1983, 216), about the length of time that an economy will take to approach equilibrium.

It seems that most economists have now lost interest in stability problems, and even with the concept of general equilibrium. (If one surveys the long history of economics, one is tempted to conclude that economists don't solve their major problems; they abandon them. However, sometimes a later generation returns to an abandoned problem.) There does seem to be a fundamental difficulty in handling disequilibrium by the currently approved methods of analysis, which require us to consider only optimizing behaviour; for disequilibrium implies, in Barro's (1979) words, as quoted by Gordon (1990, 1136), "a failure of agents to realize perceived gains from trade." That only equilibrium is compatible with optimization has been argued by Boland (1986), and recently by Huw Dixon (1990); both believe that this "puts a great constraint on economics" (Dixon, 1990, 392). Hey (1981) has argued the need for economists to develop systematic theories of disequilibrium processes, and to recognize (p. 243) that "[t]rue disequilibrium analysis requires us to abandon optimality." Most economists, it seems, take the opposite view: that all economic phenomena can be interpreted, and indeed must be interpreted, as equilibrium phenomena. The boldest go on to claim that real economies are always in equilibrium; this is but a small step away from arguing that all situations — including those characterised by extensive government intervention — are optimal, when the opportunity sets are correctly defined, and therefore that economics exists solely for the amusement of economists.

We can take our first step back from nirvana by recognizing that an equilibrium of optimizing agents does not necessarily imply market clearing. In fact, if there are costs of realizing perceived gains from trade, then the opposite is more nearly true, for optimization requires the marginal gain from trade to be set equal to the marginal cost of achieving it — which is the marginal cost of transacting. It is even likely that some perceived gains from trade will not cover the costs of bringing the relevant markets into existence. If we are prepared to assume that transactions costs are an increasing function of the magnitude and speed of the adjustment desired — which seems plausible in at least some circumstances — then we may be able to perform the approved trick of converting a disequilibrium process into an equilibrium adjustment path.

We can now take a further step. Coase (1937) included in his specification of transactions costs the costs of gaining the information that is needed before any optimum can be calculated; so we might expect that some gains from trade might not even be worth perceiving. (Within this information, we should note, Coase included knowledge of "the relevant prices". Whether these should be correct or equilibrium prices, and how people are to decide which prices are general equilibrium prices, are awkward questions for anyone who wishes to interpret Coase as a refiner of general equilibrium theory.) Having got this far, we might be prepared to abandon the assumption that knowledge is always readily available, even if sometimes expensive. In its place we may provisionally adopt Hayek's central contention in 1937: knowledge is incomplete and scattered among economic agents, and equilibrium must be attained by a process of integrating, communicating, and extending this knowledge.

In his opening paragraph, Hayek (1937, 33) makes what is probably the first reference in English-language economics to Popper's logic of falsification; but he applies this only to "propositions about the acquisition of knowledge," not to the status of the knowledge which is acquired. Austrians have been reluctant to give full scope to Popperian and post-Popperian conceptions of knowledge, and have therefore missed opportunities both for incisive criticism of neoclassical theories of rational equilibrium and for the construction of alternative kinds of theory. The construction of theories which recognise that knowledge is problematic is a primary motivation of this chapter.

Hayek's Concept of Equilibrium

Hayek's proposal to replace price and quantity in the definition of equilibrium by the plans of economic agents anticipated Hahn's (1973) scheme — with a subtle difference to be exploited later. It brings knowledge to the focus of attention. Agents make optimal plans on the basis of their current subjective knowledge, and equilibrium exists when each agent's plan is compatible both with the plans of all other agents and with the relevant external phenomena (Hayek, 1937, 41). If the plans are not compatible, then some of them will prove impossible to carry out, in full or in part, and the recognition of this failure changes the knowledge of the disappointed agents, causing them to revise their plans. When failures no longer occur, the economy is in equilibrium.

Hayek (1937, 53) is careful to point out that this equilibrium is relative to the sum of the original knowledge of agents and that which they necessarily gain as a result of the market process itself. All perceived gains from trade are realized; but there may be gains that are not perceived, simply because the attempts to carry out plans do not bring them to anyone's attention. Prices may remain different (even allowing for transport costs) in different markets, if the market process does not lead anyone to make a comparison of those prices. The economy might be represented by the metaphor of an island archipelago, as in some more recent macro-economic models. In general, there will be many possible Hayekian equilibria, and which of these (if any) is attained will depend on the particular path which is followed.

Hayek (1937, 44) argues, as did Fisher much later, that good reasons for believing in a strong and reliable tendency to equilibrium are needed to justify faith in equilibrium models, and he observes that "we are still pretty much in the dark about (1) the conditions under which this tendency is supposed to exist and (2) the nature of the process by which individual knowledge is changed" (Hayek, 1937, 45). However, he directs attention away from the study of this process towards the question of "how much knowledge and what sort of knowledge the different individuals must possess in order that we may be able to speak of equilibrium" (Hayek, 1937; 1948, 50). He does not enquire how agents set about revising their plans, nor how the revisions of many agents may interact. We shall make such enquiries shortly.

The Entrepreneur

First, however, we should distinguish Hayek's problem of equilibrium, in its simplest form, from Kirzner's concept of entrepreneurship. The problem with the planned economy, as Mises and Hayek clearly recognized, is the absence of any adequate means for mobilising the dispersed and differen-tiated knowledge on which continued economic progress depends and getting it into the hands of the planners. Hayek's (1940, 188) insistence on the need for continual updating (implying a search for a new equilib-rium), which Lange never managed to cope with, can now be seen to have been especially perceptive; for the evidence from Eastern Europe suggests that although planners may be able initially to install the latest technology (especially if it can be bought in), they are liable to be extremely bad at replacing or even improving it. It was Mises above all who emphasized the virtues of a market system in channeling human self-interest in socially desirable directions (though the idea, of course, per-meates Adam Smith's theory of progress). The market solution to the problem of dispersed knowledge is that individuals make it available by selling it — usually in the form of products or services.

This idea can be traced back to the foundations of Menger's (1871) analysis: it is knowledge of its power to meet some human need that makes an object a good, and this knowledge is typically dispersed, incomplete, and sometimes problematic, especially as methods of production become increasingly roundabout. (The knowledge that transistors could be used in radio receivers originated in Sony, not among the inventors of the transistor in Bell Labs, who doubted their suitability for the high frequencies required.) All goods and services are solutions, or projected solutions, to human problems; that is not just a marketing view, but also implicit in Menger's conception of economics. The discovery and effective use of new goods or services that provide better solutions are primary functions of any economic system; Mises argued that for these purposes a system of free markets far surpassed any rival.

Kirzner's theory of market coordination owes much more to Mises than to Hayek: its focus is not on agents' plans but on entrepreneurial action to secure gains from trade which no-one has previously noticed. Kirzner claims that such action, in a competitive setting, drives the economy towards equilibrium. This is a stability theory, which explains how initial disorder provides both the scope and the incentive for private profit that brings with it the public benefit of greater allocative efficiency. Kirzner (1985, 14, 160–161) is keen to point out that it provides a better justification for what he regards as the basic truths that are represented by neoclassical equilibrium analysis than neoclassical economists themselves have been able to provide.

Kirzner's (1973, 9) first description of the initial state of the market is a misleading introduction to his theory, for it combines decisions that cannot be carried out because they depend on expectations that are falsified, and decisions that can be carried out but which might have been better. However, he does not wish to discuss the response to plan failure; his concern is with the entrepreneurial opportunities created by inconsistency between exchanges which embody successful plans. It is, therefore, a Hayekian equilibrium with which Kirzner's analysis starts, and the process of equilibration that he describes is set in motion by the entrepreneurial disruption of that equilibrium. Kirzner's entrepreneur, therefore, engages in creative destruction in his own small way — and so we return to the problem of plan revision.

Now, in order to make the strongest case for entrepreneurial competition as a solution to the problem of equilibration which has defied the efforts of neoclassical economists, Kirzner keeps very close to the standard neoclassical definition of a fully defined possibility set. Many of these possibilities are hidden, but once perceived they are unmistakable: the ten-dollar bill is discovered to be lying in one's hand. However, in accepting the neoclassical definition of the problem, Kirzner has also accepted the neoclassical view of knowledge as "information," which is not merely inadequate but false. For many simple entrepreneurial perceptions, the falsity of this view does not matter, but for more complex opportunities of arbitrage — for example between output prices and a set of input prices, linked by a technology which is not currently in use — it may be important. As Menger reminds us, there can be imaginary goods.

As Kirzner (1985, 84−86) extends his analysis, the factual basis of entrepreneurial perception becomes steadily less secure. Intertemporal arbitrage requires the perception of future facts, and although these may perhaps be deduced from present information, any such deduction may be invalidated by actions or events which are not, and perhaps cannot be, foreseen. Indeed, Cantillon's definition of entrepreneurship as speculation was explicitly based on the uncertainty of future prices; Cantillon's entrepreneur never found free ten-dollar bills within his grasp, but made fixed present commitments in the hope of future gain. Nor should we forget that production, unless to firm order, entails such speculation. Finally, Kirzner (1985, 56) implicitly abandons the sharp distinction that he originally drew between his conception of entrepreneurship and that of Schumpeter, and extends entrepreneurial alertness to include "imaginative, bold leaps of faith, and determination," which enable the entrepreneur to "*create* the future for which his present acts are designed."

Kirzner would no doubt agree with Casson (1982, 14) that the entrepreneur is in the business of being "right, while everyone else is wrong," or even with Schumpeter (1934, 85) that the entrepreneur has "the capacity of seeing things in a way which afterwards proves to be true". But is it reasonable to assume that entrepreneurs will usually succeed in being right — or, as a second-best argument, cause little damage if they are wrong? Casson, Kirzner, and Schumpeter all have vanishingly little to say about either the causes or the consequences of entrepreneurial failure. There is, of course, nothing wrong with proposing a theory that accounts for the successes of those who succeed — as Mrs. Penrose (1959) quite explicitly did in her theory of firms that grow, but that cannot serve as a general theory of market coordination or economic development. If the entrepreneur's plans are always securely based, why do they need to be "tested in the market" (Kirzner, 1973, 10)? If they do need to be tested, what happens if they fail the test?

Kirzner's (1985, 55) claim that "man is motivated to *formulate* the future, as he envisages it, as accurately as possible" may be derived from Mises' basic axiom of human action, but it does not dispose of the objections by Shackle, Lachmann, and Popper to the possibility of foreknowledge. It is certainly reasonable to argue that this motivation is likely to be strongly reinforced by the profit incentives that are inherent in market processes; but, we should recognise, with Keynes (1936, 154–158), that sometimes the most attractive route to profit lies in forecasting other people's expectations, or perhaps by creating false expectations. More fundamentally, we can observe many entrepreneurial mistakes, some of them very expensive. The real problems of entrepreneurial knowledge are not in motivation but epistemology.

Explaining Entrepreneurship

Austrian economists typically take the initial distribution of knowledge as the starting point for an analysis of market process and consider the explanation of this distribution as unnecessary, or even impossible, because every person's knowledge is subjective. However, there is scope for investigating the causes of systematic differences between groups — most obviously between equivalent industries in different countries — in the content and quality of the knowledge that they seem to possess, and the use that they make of it. There are often visible differences both in the degree of market coordination and in the level of performance that is coordinated.

Austrians should have no difficulty in accepting the concept of multiple equilibria (though they might prefer to think of multiple patterns) or of making comparisons between them. Mark Casson's studies of international business have convinced him — as many noneconomists have been convinced — that differences in resource endowment provide a very inadequate explanation of international differences in economic performance, and he is seeking a better explanation in factors that tend to produce systematic differences in entrepreneurship (Casson, 1982; 1990). Here is both a challenge and an opportunity.

We might begin by applying Casson's distinction between high-level and low-level entrepreneurship to Kirzner's classification of entrepreneurial activities. In distinguishing entrepreneurship from Robbinsian economising, Kirzner draws attention to the importance of frameworks. He insists, quite correctly, that the adoption of a framework is logically prior to efficient allocation (Kirzner, 1985, 46), but does not observe that it is also logically prior to perception — even though he points out how effective the concept of allocative efficiency has been in directing, and also diverting, the perceptions of economists (Kirzner, 1985, 152–153). Though distinguishing between the coordination of dispersed but existing information and the creation of new information that "represents an *escape* from the limits imposed by the finite and scattered information possessed at earlier dates," Kirzner (1985, 162–163) wishes to attribute all entrepreneurial initiatives to a single faculty of alertness. I believe, however, that this attempt at assimilation is less helpful than a distinction between the continued use of a familiar framework to focus thought and perception and the creation or adoption of a different framework. We may then interpret alertness as the ability to make effective use of an interpretative framework and imagination as the ability to create a new framework.

This is a distinction between incremental and discontinuous change, which can never be precise, but is particularly relevant to the problems of coordination. It is not, however, equivalent to a distinction between learning from plan failure and entrepreneurial alertness to new opportunities. What we call learning always requires events to be interpreted within a framework, and there are very few frameworks which do not allow scope for a variety of interpretations. Moreover, it is perfectly possible that a plan failure may lead to a questioning of the assumptions on which the plan was based and the adoption of different assumptions that lead to the perception—or even creation—of opportunities that Kirzner might wish to call entrepreneurial. If, as Casson (1982, 146–148) argues, the entrepreneur synthesises information from various sources, may not the perceived consequences of action make a critical contribution to the perception of new opportunities?

Austrians can outflank neoclassical economists by insisting that all expectations, and all plans that are based on them, are necessarily conjectures, any of which may be refuted when exposed to test. The market process is then to be considered as a method of testing conjectures and rejecting those that do not fit comfortably into the environment to which they are exposed.

Austrians can then exploit their advantage by emphasizing that refutations do not lead in any simple way to new conjectures. Instead, we should think of opportunities in the same way as scientific hypotheses: they are not discovered but invented. This, as is well known, is Shackle's view; it was also set out very clearly thirty years ago by G. B. Richardson (1960, 105):

> Imagination, rather than information in any ordinary sense, is what entrepreneurs require in order to discover new ways of combining resources so as to meet consumers' desires; production functions exist unknown to entrepreneurs only in the sense that musical tunes await discovery; in either case originality, rather than the possession of "information", as considered exclusively hitherto, is what is required for successful new combinations to be produced.

Rizzo (1989, 23−24) points out that the prospect of profits that encourages people to be alert to the possibility of exploiting change also encourages the origination of change; although he does not give due weight to the creative element in all responses, he does draw attention to the significance of market systems in promoting innovations of many kinds. There seems to be no reason why Austrians should not extend the scope of their analysis to include the generation, as well as the unveiling of knowledge, and, in particular, the development of new technology. To do so, as we shall see, involves an extension of their theoretical structure; however, it does not need any new foundations. Such an extension is, by contrast, beyond the reach of any analytical system that requires fully specified models, even if the analyst requires his subjects to uncover some of the data through optimal search.

The Problem of Convergence

We now turn to the standard question about stability analysis: will the process converge? The Austrian theory of market processes deduces convergence from a combination of motivation and increasing knowledge. Everyone has a prospect of bettering his or her condition by putting private knowledge to use; further, the act of putting it to use makes it available to other people and allows them, at the least, to adjust their behaviour accordingly and, at the most, to combine it with their own private knowledge and thereby generate new opportunities for profitable initiatives. This argument is sometimes reinforced by appeals either to evidence that activities do seem to become fairly well coordinated, or to an axiom (which is supposed to encapsulate experience) that "the only way we can conceive of markets is to conceive of a tendency towards equilibrium" (Garrison, 1982, 133). That may satisfy committed Austrians, but it will not satisfy many economists who find many Austrian concepts and attitudes attractive. It is my view that no definitive proof is attainable on this, as on many other fundamental issues; however, I believe that we can get further, and without violating any Austrian principles.

Let us allow an entrepreneur to make the first move and consider what may happen next. The immediate effect of the entrepreneur's action, as was noted earlier, is the disruption of some previously satisfactory plan. "No agent can enter a market, or extend his range of activity within one by making offers to other agents, without disrupting some market relationship presently existing between them and others" (Lachmann, 1986, 5). Even in the simplest case of arbitrage, sellers in the higher priced market can no longer do as well as before, and buyers now have a chance to do better, while in the lower priced market the reverse is true. How will these people respond?

The first possibility that we should consider is that they will simply attempt to continue as before. They may expect — and they may have good reason to expect — that there are many disturbing factors at work, and therefore are not surprised if sometimes their plans cannot be carried out. The difficulty that is well known to scientists, of deciding exactly what is wrong when an experiment fails to produce the predicted result, applies to everyday human activity too. Like scientists, we can choose to reject the evidence, and, like scientists, we would often be right to do so. Such behaviour is very useful in damping down oscillations, but it obviously does not help when some genuine adjustment is required.

How ready people are to contemplate changing their plans depends on two factors that deserve investigation. The first is the magnitude of plan failure that is judged to be acceptable. In the language of behavioural economists, what are the relevant aspiration levels? People, businesses, and nations who set high standards of performance may be expected to respond more quickly and more strongly to both threats and opportunities; systematic differences of this kind are a proper subject for economists — including Austrian economists — to investigate. Casson (1990, 96) argues that high performance norms, which encourage recognition of a need for improvement, are a major factor in driving people to make more of the situation. "She'll be right, mate" is hardly an entrepreneurial manifesto. We should not, however, immediately conclude that high standards promote coordination. To examine that question we must turn to the second factor.

It is not enough to recognize that one has a problem; it is also necessary to envisage some way of reaching an acceptable solution. By "acceptable" I mean not only a solution that seems likely to resolve, at least in part, the original difficulty — though even that may not be easy to find — but one that does not threaten the coherence of a person's interpretative framework and moral sentiments, by which that person makes sense of what is going on and acts on consistent principles. Many options are rejected, often without a moment's consideration, because they threaten one's view of the world or of oneself. The greater the disruption, the greater the difficulties on either score. Furthermore, sharp differences between the frameworks employed by the participants in a market are a major obstacle to coordination — as they are in international relations. A homogeneous culture, by contrast, prevents such differences, and favours coordination.

Plans and Policies

We can make this analysis a little more precise if we can suppose, with
Hahn (1973), that people have policies that guide them in making plans.
Unlike Hahn (1973, 56), however, I do not propose to define a policy as a
"mapping from messages to acts," which could be described by "structurally
stable equations." Austrians would, very properly, decline to interpret a
policy as a set of contingent plans, or as a Bayesian structure for plan
revision; it is to be thought of as a set of heuristics. A natural comparison
is with the concept of a scientific research programe, though we might
normally expect an agent's policy to be much more limited in its scope.
What that scope may be, in relation to the stream of events against which
it is tested, is a matter for empirical (perhaps mainly historical) study.
We can think of two ways in which an agent may acquire a policy. It may
be gradually developed as an unintended consequence of the natural
human tendency to impose patterns on events, or it might be deliberately
created, as Menger (1871, 82) suggests people create a stock of medicines,
as a reserve of useful remedies against an uncertain future.

Coordination in a Single Market

Entrepreneurs forming their judgements about opportunities and agents
seeking to find better plans will need to take similar account of the
possible actions of other people that may affect the outcome of their own
decisions. Interdependence is the norm, even when considering adjustment processes in what appear to be perfectly competitive industries,
as Richardson (1960) has shown. The study of essential imperfections
that make coordination possible is a long-signalled but little-perceived
opportunity for Austrian economists. The contribution of other people's
ignorance to entrepreneurial confidence in the reality of the apparent
opportunity is built in to the Austrian conception of the problem, and the
constraints of other people's commitments, to capital structures and interpretative frameworks, also lie ready to hand. Nor is there any reason
why purposeful human action should exclude various kinds of communication, understandings or even agreements.

If the people interacting in a market follow compatible policies, then
we have good reason for thinking it likely that a sequence of plans will
converge towards what might be called an equilibrium. We can even
suggest a way of interpreting Hayek's claim, which is discussed by Rizzo
(1989, 14), that the tendency to equilibrium will be strongest if we are
already close to equilibrium; for we can construct a concept of equilibrium

that rests on the compatibility, not of plans, but of policies — in our sense, of course, not Hahn's. We can then consider a process in which plans are disrupted and replaced, while policies remain intact; if the policies do remain intact, then it seems reasonable to make at least the weak causal claim that the process will terminate only when plans as well as policies are compatible. It should be obvious that the attainment of an equilibrium set of plans will be continually frustrated by changes in the underlying conditions, and also that there will normally be multiple equilibria, some of which might be judged better than others. We can also agree with Rizzo that it is illegitimate to assume a tendency to equilibrium at a crisis point of a business cycle — or at any other point of crisis.

An alternative way of studying the coordination of agents' policies is to think of each market as governed by a set of conventions. In an organized market, such as those for basic materials or financial securities, some of these conventions are formalized; but in all markets, many of them rest on what is sometimes called custom and practice. The evolution of such institutions, as the largely undesigned result of a long sequence of (mostly) purposeful human actions, was identified by Menger (1883) as a very important field of study; it is time that it received more attention. There are often major differences between countries in the way that markets for similar goods operate; these differences may be expected to influence the direction, speed, and even the possibility of coordination. We should not overlook the possibility that a particularly powerful set of institutions may coordinate the members of a market so effectively that they all decline together. It is not difficult for anyone who has lived for years in Britain to think of examples, such as cotton textiles, shipbuilding, motor cycles and machine tools.

Such an introspectively coordinated market is particularly vulnerable to the kind of radical change on which Schumpeter focussed his analysis, or even to the entrepreneurial activities which Kirzner describes as creating the future. By transcending the currently accepted framework (Kirzner, 1985, 7), such an entrepreneur is challenging the institutions of the market and adopting a policy which is at odds with those of the other market participants.

Schumpeter's claim that such creativity is necessarily destructive of existing patterns of coordination is not obviously less persuasive than Kirzner's belief that the forces of equilibration will be strong enough to cope. Those forces are the minds of people, and in particular, their ability to create (or for the less agile, to adopt) a new policy that entails changes in the way that they interpret and respond to information. The replacement of familiar and long-serviceable routines is a major problem. Economists, and others who are trained in intellectual exercises (which are rarely embodied in expensive and highly specific physical capital), do not often find these changes easy — indeed, they can be found denying the need for anything more than minor adjustments perhaps as readily as businessmen. Neither human psychology nor the history of science suggests that adjustment to this kind of change will usually be either quick or comfortable. If the adjustment has to be agreed upon, perhaps tacitly, among the members of a large group, it may be very slow, and perhaps even impossible.

Intermarket Coordination

So far we have been considering coordination within a single market and attempting to find a way of distinguishing between circumstances in which the market process will work smoothly and those in which there may be serious failures of coordination that may last for some time (perhaps years). But, as Lachmann (1986, 9–11) has warned us, we must also consider intermarket processes. Even if all those interacting within a single market are relying on compatible policies, it is possible that well-coordinated adjustment in that market — especially if it produces substantial change in price or quantity — will spill over to cause problems in other markets, as the growth of intercontinental air travel posed insurmountable problems for shipyards that specialized in building ocean liners. Major coordination failures in a single market are potentially much more dangerous. I wish to suggest a two-stage procedure for analyzing such effects.

The first stage is to examine the decomposability of the relevant parts of the economic system. Is the changing or disrupted market more or less isolated from all, or most, other markets? Herbert Simon (1969) has emphasized the importance of decomposability in helping to stabilize both natural and social systems and suggested that a process of natural selection has ensured that most surviving systems are highly decomposable. (One might, of course, note that recently constructed systems that are not decomposable may have rather poor chances of survival.) This is very different from the general equilibrium approach, which insists on handling every element in the system simultaneously; that insistence has contributed substantially to the unsurmounted problems of explaining how a general equilibrium might be achieved.

Menger's reserves (of which liquidity is an important special case), organizational slack, the creation of flexible structures and versatile resources in organizations, all help to decouple the fortunes of one person, firm, or industry from those of another. Where this decoupling is effective, local difficulties remain local, and local convergence contributes to global convergence. Low-level entrepreneurs can do their work in a single market with no fear of being overwhelmed by forces beyond the range of their perception.

Complementarity and Coordination Failure

However, as Simon warns us, decomposability is never complete; in some parts of the system, the protection may be very limited. Where decomposability cannot be presumed, we must proceed to the second stage of analysis, which turns on the distinction between substitution and complementarity.

Most of our thinking about the economy is dominated by the concept of substitution. Our whole theory of resource allocation depends on it. When Herbert Simon (1982, 1, 325−353) was asked in the late 1940s to assess the likely impact of nuclear power on U.S. national income, he concluded that the effects were likely to be small — for precisely the same reason that Fogel (1964) later argued that America would have been little worse off if its railroads had never been developed. Where there are plenty of alternatives, no single alternative matters very much. Where there is a "diversity of imaginations and actions" (Fehl, 1986, 80), the system is likely to be well supplied with reserves. This may easily be true even if each alternative, taken singly, is heavily dependent on a chain of complementarities — provided that these chains do not have particular vulnerable links in common. Such a situation, in which there are alternative projects, each of which has its own critical interdependencies, is quite common in science-based industries. But do not the factors that help to explain which alternatives are created, and why some societies fail to create them, deserve some study?

The principal exception to economists' emphasis on substitution — and therefore on successful coordination — is to be found in Keynes' theory of unemployment and other work, such as the Harrod-Domar growth model, which is related to it. In Keynes' theory there are very few categories of goods, which severely restricts the scope for substitution at the outset; then the standard relation of substitution between investment and consumption is replaced by complementarity, and other substitution possibilities are blocked by removing every price apart from the rate of interest and constraining that by the effects of liquidity preference.

Lachmann (personal communication) has commented that the Austrians' quarrel with Keynes was quite unnecessary. Indeed, it is possible to develop from Austrian components a theory of general unemployment that has some striking similarities to that of Keynes. These similarities derive from a combination of two Austrian principles: that knowledge is dispersed, incomplete, and sometimes wrong, and that complex roundabout structures of production are often the most productive. Hayek (1931) used false knowledge and closely complementary structures of production to explain how an economy could become committed to plans that could neither be carried out nor adapted in any useful way; however, the false knowledge was attributed entirely to misleading interest rates, which were the responsibility of the banking system or the government. Schumpeter explained how existing knowledge structures are falsified by innovations, which however offer no clear guidance on how to replace shattered routines. In terms of the distinction made earlier, both causes leave economic agents without policies — let alone coordinated policies — on which to start the process of developing compatible plans.

The depression stories told by Hayek and Schumpeter resemble that told by Keynes in explaining that people and physical resources are unemployed because no one can think of any sensible way of employing them: the knowledge (whether true or false depends on the theory) that had conferred on them their status as goods has been destroyed, and they can become goods (or employable people) once more only when relevant new knowledge has been discovered. Indeed, some ex-resources may never regain their status. It is a great mistake to assume that a new theory and a new policy are always at hand. This is a crucial failing of the new classical macroeconomics; it is a mistake that Austrians ought to find it rather easy to avoid. But some of them apparently do not.

The twin problems of knowledge and unemployment come to a natural focus in the Austrians' praiseworthy insistence on examining capital structures. Here close complementarity is evident, together with its power to propagate movement — either towards prosperity, if the structures are aligned with the environment, or towards depression, if the alignment is, or becomes, awry. This has been a major contribution of Lachmann; since he, like Shackle, has no great hopes of our ability to make correct forecasts, he expects coordination failure to be endemic. Since capital structures embody structures of knowledge, it should be a natural extension to think of the possibilities of substitution and complementarity between frameworks of knowledge and to examine the implications for coordination.

Markets and Management

A distinguishing characteristic of Austrian economics is its concern with problems of knowledge. But this concern needs to be extended beyond the pioneering analyses of the relationship between knowledge and equilibrium by Hayek and by Kirzner. As Lachmann has insisted, knowledge inevitably changes with time; furthermore, much of it is created within, and indeed, through the working of the economic process that is to be analyzed. The central problem is not the perpetual search for an ever-changing equilibrium that is dictated by external forces, but the creation, maintenance, and if possible, improvement of a coherent system for generating and using knowledge. This is a conception that links Adam Smith, Menger, and Marshall. But it is Marshall who provides the clearest guidance to new endeavours by Austrian economists in his analysis of the forms of organisation which aid knowledge. (For an exposition, see Loasby, 1990.)

The first form that Marshall identifies fills the uncharted territory of Austrian economics that lies between the individual and the market: the firm and its management.

Austrians have not been noted for their interest in management — though one Austrian-born (but not Austrian-trained) economist, Peter Drucker, has demonstrated what can be done. They have something to contribute to the current work on markets and hierarchies. Coase's (1937) explanation of the firm as a coordinating mechanism that could achieve lower costs for particular kinds of transactions than were possible in the market (and also, one might suggest, more effective localized planning than central planners could achieve) implies a need to compare the efficiency of market processes with those carried on by the firm. Williamson's (1985, 1986) extension of Coase's argument shows that particular kinds of market transactions are vulnerable to opportunism, which he believes is a natural corollary of self-interest. Perhaps it is in the United States; and perhaps Williamson's analysis is a product of American culture. Casson (1990, 105–124) adapts Williamson's argument to explain why the Japanese, who he claims are much less prone to opportunism, organize their affairs differently and often enjoy lower transactions costs. The American tendency to opportunism was perceived by Marshall on his American tour of 1875 and explained by a combination of American self-reliance and mobility. "Money is a more portable commodity than a high moral reputation" (Whitaker, 1975, 2, 364).

However, there is much more to management than the reduction of transactions costs. As that noted sympathiser with Austrian economics, Harold Demsetz, has correctly observed, the transactions cost approach to the firm does not pay enough attention to the firm's role in "the acquisition and use of knowledge" (Demsetz, 1988, 157). Indeed, the "real tasks of management" are "to devise or discover markets, products, and production techniques" (Demsetz, 1988, 146).

Though Austrians can make selective use of Herbert Simon's work, they would probably be most comfortable with Penrose's approach to the firm, with its central subjective concept of a "productive opportunity, which comprises all of the productive possibilities that its 'entrepreneurs' see and can take advantage of" (Penrose, 1959, 31). This productive opportunity changes both with perceptions of the firm's environment and with the growth in its knowledge and capabilities, which "will change even in the absence of any change in external circumstances or in fundamental technological knowledge" (Penrose, 1959, 56). Such a firm is well designed to operate in a continuous market.

What is missing from Penrose's analysis is any treatment of interfirm relationships, which Marshall identified as another form of organization which aids knowledge. Here Austrians may find their principal guidance in the work of Richardson, who in addition to his study (1960) of the imperfections that help to provide a framework for action, has developed (1972) the theme of affiliation and cooperation between firms whose activities are closely complementary, but too dissimilar to be comfortably managed within a single business. Marshall (1920, 271−4) argued that continuing relationships between rival firms, especially within an industrial district, could help them to learn from each other, although it might confirm them in their belief that no change was called for. Continuing relationships with suppliers and customers, which could be built up into a capital structure of complementary knowledge, provided the basis for the synthesis of information that has been emphasized by Casson. But might Austrians not investigate the reliability of the sources, the selection of information, and the framing of the synthesis?

The economics profession, and not only Austrian economics, needs a much more thorough analysis of the relationship between management and markets, and an analysis, which at present hardly exists, of management in markets. Though this analysis poses problems for Austrian economists, they have an important comparative advantage in their long-established interest in problems of knowledge. The coordination of the growth of knowledge is both a market and a management process. Menger's exposition identified the growth of knowledge as the principal source of economic progress; modern Austrian economists, I suggest, should extend the scope of their analysis the better to realize Menger's vision.

References

Barro, R. J. 1979. "Second thoughts on Keynesian Economics," *American Economic Review* 69(2): 54−9.

Boland, L. A. 1986. *Methodology for a New Microeconomics: The Critical Foundations*. Boston: Allen and Unwin.

Casson, M. 1982. *The Entrepreneur: An Economic Theory*. Oxford: Martin Robertson.

Casson, M. 1990. *Enterprise and Competitiveness: A Systems View of International Business*. Oxford: Clarendon Press.

Coase, R. H. 1937. "The Nature of the Firm," *Economica*, NS 4: 386–405. Reprinted in Coase (1988b), 33–55.

Coase, R. H. 1988a. "The Nature of the Firm: Origin," *Journal of Law, Economics, and Organization* 4: 3–17.

Coase, R. H. 1988b. *The Firm, the Market, and the Law*. Chicago: University of Chicago Press.

Dasgupta, P. 1986. "Positive Freedom, Markets and the Welfare State," *Oxford Review of Economic Policy* 2(2): 25–36.

Demsetz, H. 1988. *The Organization of Economic Activity*, Volume I: *Ownership, Control and the Firm*. Oxford: Basil Blackwell.

Dixon, H. 1990. "Equilibrium and Explanation." In *Foundations of Economic Thought*, Creedy, J. (ed.) Oxford: Basil Blackwell, 356–93.

Fehl, U. 1986. "Spontaneous Order and the Subjectivity of Expectations: A Contribution to the Lachmann-O'Driscoll Problem." In *Subjectivism, Intelligibility and Economic Understanding*, Kirzner, I. M. (ed.) Basingstoke and London: Macmillan.

Fisher, F. M. 1983. *Disequilibrium Foundations of Equilibrium Economics*. Cambridge: Cambridge University Press.

Fogel, R. W. 1964. *Railroads and American Economic Growth: Essays in Econometric History*. Baltimore and London: Johns Hopkins Press.

Garrison, R. W. 1982. "Austrian Economics as the Middle Ground: Comment on Loasby." In *Method, Process, and Austrian Economics: Essays in Honor of Ludwig von Mises*, Kirzner, I. M. (ed.) Lexington, MA: D.C. Heath, 131–8.

Gordon, R. J. 1990. "What is new-Keynesian Economics?" *Journal of Economic Literature* XXVIII: 1115–71.

Hahn, F. H. 1973. *On the Notion of Equilibrium in Economics*. Cambridge: Cambridge University Press. Reprinted in Hahn (1984), 43–71.

Hahn, F. H. 1984. *Equilibrium and Macroeconomics*. Oxford: Basil Blackwell.

Hayek, F. A. 1931. *Prices and Production*. London: Routledge.

Hayek, F. A. 1937. "Economics and Knowledge," *Economica*, NS 4: 33–54. Reprinted in Hayek (1948), 33–56. Page references are to this reprint.

Hayek, F. A. 1940. "Socialist Calculation: The Competitive 'Solution'", *Economica*, NS 8: 125–49. Reprinted in Hayek (1948), 181–208.

Hayek, F. A. 1945. "The Use of Knowledge in Society," *American Economic Review* XXXV: 519–30.

Hayek, F. A. 1948. *Individualism and Economic Order*. Chicago: University of Chicago Press.

Hey, J. D. 1981. *Economics in Disequilibrium*. Oxford: Martin Robertson.

Keynes, J. M. 1936. *The General Theory of Employment, Interest and Money*. London: Macmillan.

Kirzner, I. M. 1973. *Competition and Entrepreneurship*. Chicago: University of Chicago Press.

Kirzner, I. M. 1985. *Discovery and the Capitalist Process*. Chicago: University of Chicago Press.

Lachmann, L. M. 1986. *The Market as an Economic Process*. Oxford: Basil Blackwell.

Lange, O. and Taylor, F. M. 1938. *On the Economic Theory of Socialism*. New York: McGraw-Hill.

Loasby, B. J. 1990. "Firms, Markets and the Principle of Continuity." In *Centenary Essays on Alfred Marshall*, Whitaker, J. K. (ed.) Cambridge: Cambridge University Press.

Marshall, A. 1920. *Principles of Economics*. London: Macmillan.

Menger, C. 1871 [1950]. *Principles of Economics*. Translated and edited by James Dingwall and Bert F. Hoselitz. Glencoe, IL: Free Press.

Menger, C. 1883 [1963]. *Problems of Economics and Sociology*. Edited by L. Schneider and translated by F. J. Knock. Urbana, IL: University of Illinois Press.

Mises, L. von. 1920. "Economic Calculation in the Socialist Commonwealth." (translated). In *Collectivist Economic Planning* (1935), Hayek, F. A. (ed.) London: Routledge, 87–130.

Penrose, E. T. 1959. *The Theory of the Growth of the Firm*. Oxford: Oxford University Press.

Richardson, G. B. 1960. *Information and Investment*. Oxford: Oxford University Press.

Richardson, G. B. 1972. "The Organization of Industry," *Economic Journal* 82: 883–96.

Rizzo, M. 1989. "Hayek's Four Tendencies Toward Equilibrium," C.V. Starr Center for Applied Economics Research Report, 89–32.

Schumpeter, J. A. 1934. *The Theory of Economic Development*. Cambridge, MA: Harvard University Press.

Simon, H. A. 1969. *The Sciences of the Artificial*. Cambridge, MA: MIT Press.

Simon, H. A. 1982. *Models of Bounded Rationality*. Volumes 1 and 2. Cambridge, MA: MIT Press.

Whitaker, J. K. 1975. *The Early Economic Writings of Alfred Marshall 1867– 1890*. Volumes 1 and 2. London and Basingstoke: Macmillan.

Williamson, O. E. 1985. *The Economic Institutions of Capitalism*. New York: Free Press.

Williamson, O. E. 1986. *Economic Organization: Firms, Markets and Policy Controls*. Brighton: Wheatsheaf.

p13?: **COMMENTARY**

Christopher Torr

The word *coordinate* conjures up images of movement and rest. The solution to a jigsaw puzzle represents a coordinated state arising from the process of bringing the pieces into a certain relation with each other. A distinction should thus be made between a *state* of coordination and a *process* of coordination (see Kirzner, 1988, 87).

One does not have to search far in the modern Austrian literature to find a close link between equilibrium and the state of coordination, and between the coordinating process and out-of-equilibrium events. Kirzner (1973, 218), for example, notes that "the movement from disequilibrium to equilibrium is at once a movement from imperfect knowledge to perfect knowledge and from uncoordination to coordination." O'Driscoll and Rizzo (1985, 99) also associate coordination with equilibrium, and refer to the entrepreneur as the coordinating agent. Although they explicitly state that plan coordination serves as their equilibrium concept (116), they attach different shades of meaning to coordination and argue that equilibrium is not synonymous with exact coordination (85).

In his illuminating chapter on market coordination, Brian Loasby refers time and time again to equilibrium. The word equilibrium appears in the headings of the first three sections. In the following two sections he investigates whether the entrepreneur plays an equilibrating role (as in Kirzner) or a disequilibrating role (as in Schumpeter and Kirzner). In the next section he asks whether the market process will converge on an equilibrium or not. In fact, in the first half of the chapter, the word equilibrium and its variants appear fifty times, whereas coordination is

157

mentioned six times. In the second half coordination improves its score, but the final result is 63−26 in favour of equilibrium.

If a coordinated state represents an equilibrium state, the coordinating process amounts to the equilibrating process. Hence, Loasby intimates that the market coordination process is stability analysis by another name. He points out that Kirzner's theory of the market coordination process deals with "entrepreneurial action to secure gains from trade which no one has previously noticed. Kirzner claims that such action, in a competitive setting, drives the economy towards equilibrium. This is stability theory . . . ." In a narrow sense, Loasby's remarks might be taken to mean that Austrian work on the coordination process is Walrasian stability analysis in disguise. After all, much of received stability analysis has taken place on Walrasian playing fields.

His remarks may, however, be interpreted in a broader sense. In a moment, the reader will be introduced to eight types of equilibria (states of coordination). If stability analysis is concerned with what might happen when equilibrium does not obtain, one can envisage at least eight types of stability analyzes. Somebody interested in stability analysis around equilibrium of the eighth kind is not necessarily doing the same kind of stability analysis as somebody investigating stability problems of the second kind. In this broad interpretation, Loasby is saying that modern Austrians are engaged in stability analysis, but he is not (necessarily) saying that they are doing Walrasian stability analysis.

The broad interpretation of Loasby's remarks seems to be the correct one. Certain Austrian economists such as O'Driscoll and Rizzo (1985, 71) are not in favour of deposing king equilibrium. But even if Austrian economists were to say, "The king is dead, long live coordination," they would still have to consider whether or not the coordinating queen dominates the discoordinating forces in her realm. Such considerations would amount to stability analysis. Loasby's chapter is entitled "Market Coordination." The epithet "market" can indicate either the singular or the plural and he subsequently distinguishes between "coordination in a single market" and "inter-market coordination." The number of markets involved is of key importance in understanding the Austrian debate on coordination. There are economists who would not object to the idea of coordination in a single market, or even coordination among a few markets, but for whom the very idea of general equilibrium is anathema

> Marshallian markets for individual goods may for a time find their respective equilibria. The economic system never does. What emerges from our reflections is an image of the market as a particular kind of process, a continuous process

without beginning or end, propelled by the interaction between the forces of equilibrium and the forces of change. General equilibrium theory only knows interaction between the former (Lachmann, 1976, 61).

If, in the above quotation, one replaces general equilibrium with general coordination, one starts to get an idea of the tensions within the Austrian approach on the issue of coordination (equilibration).

From an Austrian point of view, the question of stability is logically prior to the issue of the existence of an equilibrium (Loasby, 1989, 172). Kirzner (1973, ch. 6) and Hayek (1937) argue that we should direct our attention to the process of market coordination before we talk about the existence of equilibrium. If one proceeds the other way round (as in Walrasian theory), the danger exists that the equilibrium position will dictate the way stability is treated.

If stability analysis is given pride of place, however, one is led to wonder what type of equilibrium (if any) is dictated by the coordination process. In examining this issue, O'Driscoll and Rizzo (1985, ch. 5) come to a conclusion at odds with the Hayek-Kirzner view that equilibrium should be viewed as a limiting position in which perfect foresight obtains. Perfect foresight may, in fact, prevent equilibrium from ever being obtained, in which case imperfect foresight emerges as a necessary (but not sufficient) condition for equilibrium to be obtained (O'Driscoll and Rizzo, 85).

Loasby confronts the issue of what state of coordination is dictated by the coordinating process when he remarks: "We now turn to the standard question about stability analysis: will the process converge?" If Jill announces to Jack that she will be converging next weekend, he will want to know on what she is converging. If she says she is converging on the seaside, he will presumably want to know whether she is converging on her great aunt's seaside cottage or whether she is converging on her ex-lover's cottage at Dover. (Although Jack may refuse to concede that there is a difference between a lover and an ex-lover.) So when Loasby raises the question of whether the market process will converge, the reader starts wondering what kind of cottage he has in mind.

One can hardly expect the author of *Choice, Complexity and Ignorance* to have a Walrasian model in mind. He comes close to suggesting, however, that Kirzner might have:

Kirzner ... is keen to point out that ... [his approach] ... provides a better justification for what he regards as the basic truths which are represented by neoclassical equilibrium analysis than neoclassical economists themselves have been able to provide (Loasby, 1991, 10).

Of course, neoclassical theory can mean different things. Some might associate neoclassical theory with Walrasian theory, while others might regard Marshall as the epitome of a neoclassical economist. Whether Kirzner's Austrian heart beats in France or England, however, it sends out equilibrating pulses. In a similar vein, Boehm (1986) denies that Hayek is a Walrasian, but grants that Hayek employs an equilibrium approach.

Equilibrium analysis proceeds on the assumption that equilibrating factors are stronger than disequilibrating factors. On a single market such presumptions may be no cause for alarm. What is equilibrating in one market, however, may be disequilibrating in another market. Walrasian analysis is predicated on the understanding that, in general, the equilibrating forces will win the day. One suspects, therefore, that those Austrians who pin their hopes on the coordinating process are presuming that, *in general*, the coordinating forces dominate the discoordinating forces. In other words, the notion of general coordination is at the back — if not at the front — of their minds. In Lachmann's (1979, 6) view, the notion of general coordination should be in neither the front nor the back of an Austrian mind:

> Outside the text-book industry general equilibrium has few defenders these days, and the more thoughtful among them now readily admit that it has little to do with the real world. It puzzles me that some Austrians seem ready to die in the last ditch for a cause that is not theirs ....

The reader is once again invited to replace general equilibrium with general coordination in the above quotation.

In his early writings on the market process Kirzner (1973, 127) was keen to point out that the entrepreneur plays an equilibrating role, as opposed to the disequilibrating role put forward by Schumpeter. As Loasby indicates, Kirzner has subsequently admitted that the entrepreneur plays both an equilibrating and a disequilibrating role. Nevertheless, the impression one gains from Kirzner's writings is that the coordinating tendencies have the upper hand. (Lachmann, 1979, 7) argues that we have no guarantee that the coordinating forces will always predominate:

> General demand and supply equilibrium cannot serve as a "centre of gravity," a source of permanent forces of constant strength as, under the impact of innovation, technical progress and simple changes of taste, relative demand and supply of various commodities are continuously changing. A planet whose composition and mass are undergoing continuous transformation could not exert a gravitational force of constant strength. If so, how can it be asserted that economic equilibrium forces, necessarily of varying strength over time, will always overwhelm and outlast all other forces?

Loasby is looking at a section of the economic landscape when he notes: "We should not overlook the possibility that a particularly powerful set of institutions may coordinate the members of a market so effectively that they all decline together." The car and the tire market could be coordinated in a recession. They could also be coordinated in a boom. From this it seems a short step to argue that since all markets declined together in the Great Depression, the mid-1930s could be characterized as a state of market coordination. If we find such a brutal conclusion strange, we must ask ourselves if we are not associating market coordination with market clearing.

At this stage of the argument a Walrasian economist is sure to cry foul and bring the labour market into the discussion. A Walrasian would argue that if the nth market (the labour market) is not clearing, the other n-1 markets cannot be in a state of coordination. Suppose, however, that we superimpose rational expectations on to a Walrasian model, as modern classical economists insist that we should. Modern classicists are fond of pointing out that there is no such thing as involuntary unemployment and that the labour market always clears. Those who are unemployed are voluntarily unemployed. From this point of view the Great Depression provides an example of a system in which all markets — the labour market included — are perfectly coordinated.

Clower (1965) and Leijonhufvud (1968) argue that the *notional* supply and demand curves of Walrasian analysis are not applicable in analysing the type of problems that exercised Keynes's mind. They indicate that an economic system can get locked into a situation of less than full employment in terms of *effective* demand and supply curves. It can then be argued that the markets are perfectly coordinated in terms of the effective supply and demand curves. If we insist that markets are not coordinated in the Clower-Leijonhufvud approach, we must ask ourselves if we have a Walrasian cottage at the back of our minds.

Kirzner points out that entrepreneurs operate in a fog of uncertainty, if not total ignorance. As they ply their trade, some of the mist rolls back, and in the limit, if there were no more uncertainty, all markets would be fully coordinated. In much the same way Hayek (1976, 42) notes that "Correct foresight is then not, as it has sometimes been understood, a precondition which must exist in order that equilibrium may be arrived at. It is rather the defining characteristic of a state of equlibrium." As pointed out earlier, O'Driscoll and Rizzo (1985, 85) disagree — equilibrium may not exist in the presence of perfect foresight.

The impression one thus gains from the writings of Kirzner and Hayek is that ignorance stands in the way of final coordination. Leinjonhufvud (1986, 48) argues that general equilibrium theory without the auctioneer (the personification of perfect knowledge) gives you the *General Theory*. Kirzner and Hayek would not argue that a path called ignorance leads to a Keynesian cottage. This, of course, does not prevent Kirzner (1988, 85) from distinguishing — in Keynesian fashion — between ignorance and utter ignorance. In the presence of utter ignorance, Kirzner would presumably also say: "We simply do not know" (Keynes, 1973, 114).

The equilibrium position in a Walrasian model is dictated by supply and demand forces. The equilibrium position in Keynes's *General Theory* is dictated by the principle of effective demand. So what represents a state of coordination in a Keynesian framework does not necessarily represent a state of coordination in a Walrasian setup, for the equilibrium concepts employed are different.

Ricardian economists consider that the only state of rest worth considering is the long-run centre of gravitation, in which all industries are earning a uniform rate of profit. If there is a uniform rate of profit across industry, one could say that the different markets are coordinated, but a uniform rate of profit is no guarantee that the system is at full employment (Garegnani, 1976, 42–43; Roncaglia, 1978, 16). For a Ricardian, a Walrasian equilibrium cannot serve as a long-run centre of gravitation (Eatwell, 1982, 226). Walrasian coordination is not the same as Ricardian coordination.

Eight different types of coordination have been mentioned, namely:

1. The state of coordination dictated by a uniform rate of profit,
2. Walrasian general coordination (notional supply and demand curves),
3. Marshallian coordination,
4. Hayekian coordination,
5. The state of coordination dictated by the principle of effective demand,
6. The state of coordination dictated by effective supply and demand curves,
7. Walrasian general coordination (notional supply and demand curves plus rational expectations),
8. Kirznerite coordination.

The order is chronological. The coordination process is bound up with the state one has in mind.

Although Loasby does not provide much information on what a state of coordination might look like, his remarks on what it might *not* look like are revealing, for he suggests that, "We can take our first step back from nirvana by recognizing that an equilibrium of optimizing agents does not necessarily imply market clearing" — in other words market coordination is not synonymous with market clearing. If market coordination is synonymous with market clearing, Loasby's remarks come across as a contradiction in terms, for he would then be saying that markets are coordinated when they are not coordinated.

Loasby is prepared to concede that the market process can lead to coordination in Marshallian fields, but he is as reluctant as Lachmann to entertain the notion of general coordination. In suggesting that the market coordination process is stability analysis in disguise, Loasby is asking Austrian economists whether they have any right to believe that the coordinating forces inevitably dominate the discoordinating forces. In the process he leaves the reader wondering anew whether Kirzner is a General or a Field Marshall.

The impression created by Loasby is that the economic system should not be viewed as some sort of gigantic puzzle that has a final solution. For a while, some parts of the puzzle may fit quite nicely, but the very process of interlocking may disturb other pieces on the board.

Acknowledgment

I should like to thank Stephan Boehm for his constructive comments on an earlier draft.

References

Boehm, S. 1986. "Time and Equilibrium: Hayek's Notion of Intertemporal Equilibrium Reconsidered." In *Subjectivism, Intelligibility and Economic Understanding: Essays in Honor of Ludwig M. Lachmann on His Eightieth Birthday*," Kirzner, I. M. (ed.). New York: New York University Press, 16–29.

Clower, R. W. 1965. "The Keynesian Counterrevolution: A Theoretical Appraisal." In *The Theory of Interest Rates*, Hahn, F. H. and Brechling, F. P. R. (eds.). London: Macmillan, 103–25.

Eatwell, I. 1982. "Competition." In *Essays in Honour of Ronald L. Meek*, Bradley, J. and Howard, M. (eds.). London: Macmillan, 203–28.

Garegnani, P. 1976. "On a Change in the Notion of Equilibrium in Recent Work on Value and Distribution." In *Essays in modern capital theory*, Brown, M., Sato, K. and Zarembka, P. (eds.). Amsterdam: North-Holland, 25–45.

Hayek, F. A. 1937. "Economics and Knowledge," *Economica*, NS, vol. 4. Reprinted in Hayek, F. A. (1976) *Individualism and Economic Order*. London and

Henley: Routledge & Kegan Paul, 33−56.

Keynes, J. M. 1936. *The General Theory of Employment, Interest and Money.* Reprinted as Vol. VII of *The Collected Writings of John Maynard Keynes.* London: Macmillan.

Keynes, J. M. 1937. "The General Theory of Employment," *Quarterly Journal of Economics*, February 1937. Reprinted in *The Collected Writings of John Maynard Keynes*, Vol. XIV. London: Macmillan (1973), 109−123.

Kirzner, I. M. 1973. *Competition and Entrepreneurship.* Chicago: University of Chicago Press.

Kirzner, I. M. 1988. "Welfare Economics: A Modern Austrian Perspective." In *Man, Economy and Liberty: Essays in Honor of Murray Rothbard.* Block, W. & Rockwell, L. H. (eds.). Auburn: The Ludwig von Mises Institute, 77−88.

Lachmann, L. M. 1976. "From Mises to Shackle: An Essay on Austrian Economics and the Kaleidic Society," *Journal of Economic Literature*, 14: 54−62.

Lachmann, L. M. 1979. "On the Recent Controversy Concerning Equilibration," *Austrian Economics Newsletter* 2(2): 6−7.

Leijonhufvud, A. 1968. *On Keynesian Economics and the Economics of Keynes.* New York: Oxford University Press.

Loasby, B. J. 1976. *Choice, Complexity and Ignorance.* Cambridge: Cambridge University Press.

Loasby, B. J. 1989. *The Mind and Method of the Economist.* Aldershot: Edward Elgar.

O'Driscoll, G. P. Jr & Rizzo, M. J. 1985. *The Economics of Time and Ignorance.* Oxford: Blackwell.

Roncaglia, A. 1978. *Sraffa and the Theory of Prices.* Chichester: John Wiley and Sons.

B29 B25

A13

6 ORDERS AND ORGANIZATIONS: TOWARD AN AUSTRIAN THEORY OF SOCIAL INSTITUTIONS

Richard N. Langlois

Introduction

That the Austrian school of economics is and has been fundamentally concerned with the theory of social institutions is a proposition gaining wide acceptance today — by critics of this school as well as by its adherents. This is a rather striking development. Not too many years ago, the prevailing wisdom was that the American Institutionalist school (of Thorstein Veblen, John R. Commons, and Wesley C. Mitchell) was the sole repository of thinking about social institutions and that, moreover, Institutionalist approaches and beliefs were strongly at odds with everything Austrian.[1] But a recent spate of articles, including a couple of symposia in the journals, has highlighted the Austrian approach to institutions and brought it into contact — albeit sometimes violent contact — with the Institutionalist school (Boettke, 1989; Hodgson, 1989; Langlois, 1989; Perlman, 1986; Rutherford, 1989a, 1989b; Samuels, 1989; Vanberg, 1989).

One result of this flurry of interest in Austrian institutionalism[2] is that the methodological issues and controversies have been well aired. This in turn leaves me free to engage in synthesis and extension without too much attention to the doctrinal niceties.

This essay proceeds in three parts. The first part looks into the concept of an institution itself. What exactly *is* an institution? How do we think about institutions in general and within the framework of Austrian economics as broadly understood? One of the important distinctions to emerge from this enquiry is F. A. Hayek's dichotomy between (spontaneous)

165

orders and organizations. The remaining two sections will examine in turn the theory of these two classes of institutions. The discussion of spontaneous orders will be largely a matter of synthesis and exposition, but the discussion of organizations will, I hope, point to new directions. Indeed, the analysis of organizations — notably the business firm — is a much-neglected area in Austrian economics. It is also an area in which there is a good deal of exciting theoretical work today that draws on many of the Austrian's favorite insights.

What are Social Institutions?

At the base of virtually all formulations of the concept of a social institution lies the notion of rule-following behavior. Institutions reflect behavior that is highly organized, in the sense that the behavior represents a relatively predictable or non-random pattern.[3] And such patterns emerge as the result of the following of rules; they are, as Hayek (1967) puts it, systems of rules of conduct.

Sometimes the rules seem to be a property of the human agents themselves. Agents follow rules unconsciously as if, in effect, programmed to do so. Writers who take an evolutionary perspective on social institutions often incline to this interpretation, even though most are aware that rules have other meanings as well (Hayek, 1967, 1973; Nelson and Winter, 1982). These writers stress the skill-like nature of behavior, which implies that the rules guiding behavior are often necessarily inexplicit or tacit (Polanyi, 1958). Sometimes, however, social institutions seem to consist of rules external to individuals. Such rules are more in the nature of side-constraints (Nozick, 1974) that channel the behavior of individuals whose operating principles may not be the following of rules in the first sense. For example, the agents may be consciously maximizing their utility within a framework (like private property rights) that constrains their choices. In both cases, the rules generate an orderly pattern of behavior.[4]

There is not necessarily a conflict between these two meanings of rule following, and one can imagine both types to be operating, to varying degrees, in a system of social institutions. For example, consider what is probably the canonical example of a social institution in the modern literature: the convention that one drive on the right-hand side of the road in North America and Continental Europe. This institution is an explicit rule of law that one can be punished for violating; but it is also an unconscious predisposition of native drivers. Indeed, as Hayek and others would point out, the following of unconscious rules obviates attention to many of the details of behavior, which frees up attention and thus actually facilitates conscious action (constrained or otherwise).

Another important aspect of social institutions, one closely related to their order-producing and rule-like aspects, is their capacity to economize on knowledge or information. The late Ludwig Lachmann put it this way:

> An institution provides a means of orientation to a large number of actors. It enables them to coordinate their actions by means of orientation to a common signpost. ... The existence of such institutions is fundamental to civilized society. They enable each of us to rely on the actions of thousands of anonymous others about whose individual purposes and plans we can know nothing. They are nodal points of society, co-ordinating the actions of millions whom they relieve of the need to acquire and digest detailed knowledge about others and form detailed expectations about their future action. (Lachmann, 1971, 49–50)

Thus, by making the behavior of others more predictable, institutions reduce the amount of information we need to behave effectively in society. To make this point clearer, consider again our canonical example. Because of the convention that everyone drive on the right, I do not need information about the lane preference of each driver who confronts me head on. This is related to the point I made above. Institutions — viewed as rules, customs, routines, habits, or conventions[5] — contain or embody knowledge about effective behavior. This economizes on the explicit knowledge one must have to behave effectively. Knowledge and the following of rules are strongly intertwined.

Another important aspect of institutions is their hierarchical nature. This is an aspect that has received too little attention in the literature. Again, institutions are *systems* of rules of conduct. Theory here is not well developed; but it is probably not too much of an oversimplification to say that institutions — systems of rules — operate at many different levels, each level affecting the operation of the rules at the level below. For example, Lachmann distinguishes between external and internal institutions.

> [I]t might be said that the undesigned institutions which evolve gradually as the unintended or unforeseeable result of the pursuit of individual interests accumulate in the *interstices* of the legal order. ... In a society of this type we might then distinguish between the *external* institutions which constitute, as it were, the outer framework of society, the legal order, and the *internal* institutions which gradually evolve as a result of market processes and other forms of spontaneous individual action. (Lachmann, 1971, 81; emphasis original.)

This captures some flavor of the hierarchical structure of institutions.[6]

It may be helpful here to reassert a distinction that cuts across the one Lachmann suggests. Carl Menger long ago distinguished between institutions that are of *pragmatic* origin and those that are of *organic* origin. The former are the result of "socially teleological causes," that is, they arise because of a common will directed toward their creation. By contrast, organic institutions are "the unintended result of innumerable efforts of economic subjects pursuing individual interests" (Menger, 1963, 158). Menger was primarily concerned with the *origin* of institutions. And, as Viktor Vanberg (1889, 338) reminds us, the question of the origin of an institution is logically distinct from the question of its social functionality, that is, of its principles of operation once created. Hayek makes a distinction about rules of operation that is analogous to Menger's distinction about origins. We can divide institutions into *orders*[7] and *organizations*. Although Hayek is not always clear on this point, what distinguishes the two classes is not so much their origins as the nature of the rules they comprise. The rules of an order are abstract and independent of purpose, whereas the rules of an organization are concrete and directed toward a common purpose or purposes (Hayek, 1973, 38).

These distinctions leave us with a matrix of intersecting possibilities. (See figure 6–1.) One class of institutions comprises systems of rules that are independent of purpose and are of organic origin. These are what Hayek calls *spontaneous* orders. Examples include: various kinds of social

	ORDERS	ORGANIZATIONS
ORGANIC	Common Law Social conventions (Spontaneous Orders)	Public Choice view of government Evolutionary view of the firm
PRAGMATIC	Constitutional design	GM/Toyota joint venture NASA manned space-flight program

Figure 6–1. Matrix of explanatory possibilities. Modified from Vanberg (1989).

conventions; the common law, language, money. At least in principle, however, not all orders need be organic. Writers of a constitutionalist bent (Buchanan, 1990) would insist that systems of rules can be both independent of purpose and pragmatic, at least in the sense that one can consciously design a constitutional framework. The proper domain of the spontaneous and the planned is a matter of running controversy between the followers of Hayek and the constitutionalists.

What has been less often noticed is that organizations can also be of organic origin. It is tempting to assume that, since organizations comprise rules directed toward specific ends, and since attention to goals is a feature of human rationality, all such institutions must have been consciously created. In fact, however, one finds the same sorts of unintended consequences and unplanned outcomes in the realm of organizations that one finds in spontaneous orders. The goals framing the rules of operation of, say, a government regulatory commission may be quite different from the goals envisaged by those who set the commission up (Edelman, 1964). Indeed, one might easily portray the entire Public Choice theory of politics as undermining a conception of government as a pragmatic institution. As I will suggest later, one can also see the evolution of another type of organization — the firm — as organic in character.

Conscious intention certainly does play a role in the formation of organizations; but it is a role fully analogous to the one it plays in the formation of a spontaneous order. That is to say, the explanation for the existence of an organization as we observe it today is not the conscious intention of any single individual or unified group but rather the diverse intentions of many individuals and groups interacting with one another and with external circumstance over time. For an organization to be genuinely of pragmatic origin, then, unintended consequences must not intrude to alter the intentions of the founders. This may occur when the organization is not very complex. It may also happen when we examine a short-lived organization or limit our time perspective to a short period. Examples of such pragmatic organizations might include a joint venture between GM and Toyota to produce cars in California, or perhaps the American manned spaceflight program of the 1960s.

How do these distinctions square with Lachmann's distinction between external and internal institutions? Not perfectly, I think. All external institutions are orders rather than organizations. They are general and abstract rules, facilitating many different concrete purposes. But some internal institutions may also be abstract. A constitution establishing the rights of property is internal to the institutions of language; the common law of contracts is internal to the system of property rights, and so on. In some ways, of course, the distinction between an order and an organization is also a matter of degree, with orders shading off into organizations as the rules become more particular and concrete. And, in the end, it may well be that the externalness of an institution is tied up with the generality and abstractness of its rules. But I'm not sure how to prove this.

In the remainder of this chapter I will put aside pragmatic orders in the strict sense and consider in turn spontaneous orders and — if the reader will forgive the expression — organic organizations.

The Theory of Institutional Evolution

Following Menger's lead, a modern Austrian theory of social institutions would necessarily be a causal-genetic or process theory. By that I mean a theory in which explanation involves tracing out a sequence of events rather than merely constructing the conditions for an equilibrium. The exemplar of this approach is Carl Menger's theory of the institution of money (O'Driscoll, 1986).

To put it another way, Austrian theories of social institutions rely on Invisible Hand explanations. Such explanations describe the development of institutions as a sequence of the actions of individuals aggregated by some compositional principle (Langlois, 1986c). The compositional principle need not be merely "adding up" the behavior of the individuals (whatever that means), but would typically involve filtering or selection mechanisms. There is in my view no fundamental distinction between Invisible Hand explanations and evolutionary explanations, except to the extent that one takes the biological analogy to restrict the latter to particular types of selection principles. Indeed, it is now well understood that Menger's approach to social institutions and Darwin's theory of biological evolution have a common ancestor in the writings of the Scottish Enlightenment (Schweber, 1977; Jones, 1986).

With this said, it may seem paradoxical for me now to suggest that a useful place to begin a theory of institutions is with the theory of games. In its pure form, game theory is an equilibrium theory and certainly not a process theory. But there is ultimately no paradox. I will argue that game theory in its simpler manifestations can be a valuable complement to a causal-genetic or evolutionary theory of social institutions. Building on the work of philosophers David Lewis (1969) and Edna Ullmann-Margalit (1977), economists like Andrew Schotter (1981, 1986), Jack Hirshleifer (1982), Robert Sugden (1986), and Nicholas Rowe (1989) have looked at social institutions instructively from within the framework of game theory.

I particularly recommend Sugden's book as a starting place for those interested in this area.

In order to simplify the exposition, let me restrict myself to the two most important canonical games that appear in this work. The first of these is the *coordination game*, of which the automobile example is an instance. (See figure 6−2.) If I choose to drive on the left-hand side of the road and an oncoming motorist chooses the right (or vice-versa), the "payoffs" to both of us will likely be negative. If, however, we both choose the same side of the road—either side—we will not incur these penalties. With repeated play of this game, one would expect drivers to keep to one particular side as a matter of *convention*. Notice that such a convention is self-enforcing: anyone who consistently drives on the left in the United States will be punished by negative payoffs quite apart from any penalties invoked by the courts. Notice also that, while far superior to discoordination, a convention solution need not be optimal. In figure 6-2, driving on the right has a higher payoff than driving on the left, perhaps, we might imagine, because automobiles are cheaper when one conforms to the standard that is more popular around the world. But historical accident may lead a region to the opposite standard. Such conventions are path-dependent processes of the sort Paul David (1985) has popularized. It is typically costly to alter a convention once established, and it may take some kind of centralized coordination to do so—as when Sweden and Okinawa changed their side-of-the-road driving conventions.

In a coordination game, the incentives of both players are aligned; their common objective is facilitated by the reduction in information costs

Player 1

		Right	Left
Player 2	Right	2 / 2	-10 / -10
	Left	-10 / -10	0 / 0

Figure 6−2. A coordination game.

a convention achieves. By contrast, what characterizes a *prisoners' dilemma* is a divergence of incentives. The parable commonly attached to the game is as follows. Two suspects are hauled in by the police for a bank robbery. Without a confession, the authorities have insufficient evidence to convict the two, although they could convict them of a lesser crime. The police interrogate the criminals in separate rooms and propose a deal to each: if you turn state's evidence and testify against your cohort, you go free, and we throw the book at him. The resulting matrix looks like figure 6–3. In this case, each prisoner has a private incentive to confess, whereas the "social optimum" is for both to hold firm, in the sense that such steadfastness minimizes the total number of years in prison. Because of the private incentive to confess—both to lower one's own sentence and to insure against confession by one's compatriot—the solution of such a game played once is for both to confess,[8] a result that maximizes total years in prison. If, however, the game is played repeatedly, and neither of the players knows when the game will end, there may emerge a *norm* of reciprocity, according to which the players refrain from confessing despite the private incentive to do so.

Like a convention, a prisoners' dilemma norm is an institution with an information function. It substitutes for the costly direct communication and negotiation between the players that might otherwise facilitate agreement on the joint-miximizing solution. Unlike a coordination convention, however, a norm of this sort is not completely self-enforcing. Whenever the players face an end-game, the discipline of repeated play evaporates, and the private incentives loom large.

Player 1

		Hold firm	Confess
Player 2	Hold firm	-2 / -2	0 / -10
	Confess	-10 / 0	-7 / -7

Figure 6–3. A prisoners' dilemma game.

Thus, prisoners' dilemma situations often call for some sort of external policing mechanism. For example, businesses can usually be expected to adhere to their contracts out of fear of harming their reputations and losing future business (Klein and Leffler, 1983); but if the private incentive for breach of contract becomes great enough, the contract leaves the "self-enforcing range," and the parties may find themselves in court. We should distinguish, however, between privately rational reciprocity enforced by repeated play and the idea of a norm proper. In many situations, people follow norms of behavior — like honesty — even in end-game situations. One often tells the truth even when lying would be costless and privately beneficial. The reason is that norms of this sort are often internalized to form a part of culture. They are, in effect, instances of the tacit rule following I mentioned earlier. After repeated play of a prisoners' dillemma game by many different individuals, the original game situation and the sanctions of repeated play are forgotten. Only the norm remains. In this sense, the norm is *itself* an enforcement mechanism. This is not to say that a norm must always emerge or that the mechanism of repeated play must always solve the prisoners' dilemma in happy fashion. There are far too many examples of social situations in which norms have collapsed or failed to emerge and in which the dilemma of this game is all too real. It is a major task of research in this area to understand the circumstances under which efficiency-enhancing norms will in fact emerge.

By now it should be obvious why a game-theoretic approach is not at all incompatible with a causal-genetic approach. The idea of repeated play of the game implies a process over time. And, although formal game theory in its resplendent glory treats repeated games in an equilibrium framework, the theory of social institutions need not. What substitutes for the idea of an equilibrium strategy is the notion of an evolutionarily stable strategy, a concept borrowed from biologists who have adapted game-theoretic models to natural evolution (Maynard Smith, 1982).

Perhaps the best example of evolutionary game-theory modeling is the much-discussed work of Robert Axelrod (1984). Axelrod invited prominent game theorists to submit algorithms for solving the repeated prisoners' dilemma game. These he tested by a computer tournament in which the algorithms were pitted against one another. The frequent winner was one of the simplest: the tit-for-tat strategy. Under this strategy, a player initially cooperates (doesn't confess); however, whenever the other player fails to cooperate (confesses) in any period, the first player "punishes" the rival by also failing to cooperate for one period. One can think of this strategy as a kind of norm.

This discussion has merely scratched the surface, of course. Many important issues remain. When will efficient strategies emerge that are evolutionarily stable? What is the precise nature of the selection process? What are the respective roles of imitation and selection? To what extent does group selection operate? What is the cultural analogue of genetic memory? Addressing these and similar issues forms a large part of the ongoing research program of a theory of institutional evolution. But the details of evolutionary theory are the subject of another chapter in this volume.

The Evolution of Organizations

With its roots in Menger and its more recent elaboration by Hayek, the theory of spontaneous orders is relatively well known within Austrian economics. By contrast, there has been remarkably little work within the Austrian tradition on the theory of organizations. One class of organizations comprises the institutions of government. This area of inquiry has fallen to the Public Choice theorists, with whom many Austrians are broadly sympathetic. James Buchanan, the father of Public Choice theory, is in many ways a bridge between the Public Choice school and the Austrian tradition. Nonetheless, Public Choice theory has always stood within the boundaries of neoclassical theory (especially the Chicago School variant), and has availed itself little of those insights one would consider distinctively Austrian. The same may be said of another sort of organization to which Austrians have paid comparatively little attention: the business firm. I want to examine this second case in some detail and to argue that, although there is really no Austrian theory of the firm, a number of strands now developing should be attractive to writers in the Austrian tradition. Moreover, this developing theory of the firm would benefit greatly from a more explicit admixture of characteristic Austrian insights and perspectives.

In many respects, one can think of the theory of the firm — or of any organization — as an extension of the theory of social institutions outlined above. An organization is also a system of rules of conduct. In comparison with the rules of an order, the rules of an organization are concrete: rather than facilitating many different purposes, they are focused on achieving certain specific goals. Yet, the rules of an organization are similar to those of a more abstract institution in the sense that we can view them as evolving in much the same way and as having many of the same informational benefits.

The seminal work in the modern theory of the firm as organization — as

distinct from the neoclassical portrayal of the firm as production function —
is that of Ronald Coase (1937).[9] Coase begins by considering a more
abstract institution: the spontaneous order of the price system. As many
writers before and since have argued, the price system is a set of conventions that provides rather marvelous information and coordination
functions. In view of the remarkable qualities of this institution, Coase
wonders, why do we observe some transactions to be removed from the
price system and carried out within the business firm?[10] The answer:
there must be a cost to using the price system. Since a cost is a foregone
benefit, this implies that there is a benefit to using an institution alternative
to — or, at any rate, additional to — the price system at its most abstract.
Wherein lie the benefits of such institutions? Although I cannot make the
case here, it is arguable that Coase saw the benefits in terms of improved
coordination and flexibility in the face of changing circumstances.[11]

The Coase-inspired literature that has blossomed since the 1970s casts
these benefits in a rather different light, however. Rather than seeing the
firm as a coordinating institution, theorists have focused on the role of the
firm in solving prisoners' dilemma-like problems. As Alchian and Woodward (1989) have pointed out, the modern transaction-cost theory of the
firm, as this literature is called, feeds from two different but related
streams. One is the moral hazard or measurement cost approach (Alchian
and Demsetz, 1972; Cheung, 1983; Barzel, 1982, 1987); the other is the
asset specificity approach (Klein, Crawford, and Alchian, 1978; Williamson,
1985). In the first case, the abstract institution of the market generates
transaction costs in situations in which the incentives of the cooperating
parties diverge and monitoring is costly. In the second case, the market
can lead to transaction costs when, in the presence of highly specific
assets, one of the parties might threaten the other with noncooperation in
order to extract a larger share of the quasirents of cooperation. In both
cases, common ownership of the cooperating assets — that is to say, a
firm — may avoid these transaction costs. Such extra-market arrangements
would be most common when transactions are infrequent, since repetition
and norms of reciprocity are then less able to support market exchange.

This body of theory has vastly enriched our understanding of the
nature of and rationale for extra-market organization. It is my contention,
however, that, by focusing on the prisoners' dilemma-like problems of
markets, this theory has ignored a large, and perhaps even more important,
set of institution-shaping forces. In other words, there is much to be
gained by looking at organizations as responses to coordination problems.

Let us begin by returning to the observation that, like a more abstract
institution, an organization is a system of rules of conduct. In the work of

Edith Penrose (1959) and G. B. Richardson (1972), and more recently of Nelson and Winter (1982) and David Teece (1980, 1982, 1986), one gets a picture of the firm as possessing certain "capabilities." That firms differ in their capabilities helps explain, as Coase once put it, "why General Motors was not a dominant factor in the coal industry, and why A&P did not manufacture airplanes" (Coase, 1972, 67). This is a way of looking at the firm that should appeal to writers in the Austrian tradition,[12] since it rejects the neoclassical portrayal of the firm's knowledge as explicit and easily transferable, a matter of "blueprints." To see firms as possessing limited and distinctive capabilities accords well with Hayek's (1945) insights about the decentralized nature of knowledge. Indeed, it is a vision of the evolution of the firm that also accords well with Hayek's writings on cultural evolution. Nelson and Winter (1982, chs. 4 and 5) are explicit in seeing capabilities as a matter of rules. The machines and personnel of a firm follow, invent, learn, and imitate routines that persist over time. As in Hayek's theory of culture, the routines are often tacit and skill-like, followed unconsciously because they produced success in the past. And it is these routines upon which the mechanism of selection operates.

As in the case of rules in abstract institutions, the rules in an organization serve a coordinating function. This may at first seem at odds with the thesis of Hayek (1945). Isn't the point of decentralized knowledge and the coordinating virtues of the price system that such a system is superior to central planning, especially in situations of economic change? There is no contradiction.[13] First of all, the capabilities view suggests that the internal workings of the firm are far less in the nature of conscious planning than popular accounts (e.g., Galbraith, 1968) would have it. Moreover, Hayek's argument is about the ability of the price system to coordinate multifarious plans. It is not an argument that the price system must always be a superior way to coordinate specific plans at what we may think of as a "lower" or more concrete level of the hierarchy.[14]

In arguing for the coordinating benefits of the price system, Hayek (1945, 523) pointed out that "economic problems arise always and only in consequence of change." And, indeed, the respective merits of firm and market as institutions of coordination appear most clearly when we consider economic change and the response to it.[15] Just as firms possess capabilities, so also can we think of markets as possessing capabilities, in the sense that one can choose to produce a good or service using one's internal capabilities or one can use the capabilities of others by acquiring the good or service on the market. When will internal organization prove superior to market procurement in a world of economic change? The answer depends (1) on the existing level of capabilities in the market and (2) on the nature of the innovation involved.

Situations in which existing market capabilities are limited, or in which those capabilities are ill-adapted to the innovation, would tend to favor internal organization, *ceteris paribus*. This effect would be more significant in the case of a systemic innovation, that is, an innovation that involves coordinating change in many different routines. Consider the case of the American automobile industry (Langlois and Robertson, 1989). In the early days of that industry, automobile makers were all assemblers, that is, they contracted for almost all the parts that went into the cars, reserving only the assembly stage for themselves. They could do this because the American economy — and the Detroit region in particular — possessed a high level of general-purpose machining and metal-working capabilities available in the market. The innovation of the moving assembly line at Ford, however, rendered these capabilities obsolete, in that Ford could mass-produce parts much less expensively than it could buy them on the market. Because Ford could not quickly and cheaply convey to suppliers the (partly tacit) nature of the innovation — which was in any case a slowly unfolding process — it was forced to integrate vertically into parts manufacture. It is in this sense, then, that an organization can be a coordinating institution: it can sometimes avoid the coordinating costs of informing, negotiating with, and persuading potential contracting parties who may not share one's faith in the proposed innovation or even, in a fundamental sense, one's view of the world (Silver, 1984; Langlois, 1988).[16] This suggests the importance of a neglected set of "transaction" costs in explaining the firm: the costs of changing one's capabilities, or to put it another way, the costs of not having the capabilities you need when you need them.

Economic change may also favor the market over internal organization. This might be the case when the existing level of capabilities is high in the market relative to those within the organization proposing to innovate. The market would also gain advantages when the innovation involved is largely autonomous, that is, when the innovation does not require change in many different routines. Consider the example of the IBM personal computer (Langlois, 1990b). In entering the PC market in the early 1980s, IBM understood both (1) that the market possessed a high level of capabilities and (2) that IBM's own capabilities were severely lacking. This latter was the case partly because the company had focused on larger computers and didn't possess all the capabilities necessary for smaller machines. But it was also and more importantly because the company's hierarchical structure, internal sourcing procedures, and elaborate system of controls made it too inflexible to respond well to a rapidly changing market. As a result, IBM chose in effect to disintegrate vertically into the production of PCs. They spun off a small group of executives and engineers, exempted them from IBM internal sourcing and other procedures, and treated them as, in effect, a venture-capital investment. The original IBM PC was in fact almost completely assembled from parts available in the market, very few of which were produced in IBM plants. IBM's motives for *disintegration* were in this regard strikingly similar to Henry Ford's motives for *integration*: the need to access quickly capabilities that would not otherwise have been available in time. The coordinating virtues of the market here are very much those Hayek praised.

Summary

I have tried in this chapter to outline what an Austrian theory of social institutions would look like. My objective, however, has not been to be definitive; quite the opposite, I have tried to be suggestive and to point to new directions and to useful ideas from outside the areas of traditional Austrian interest.

At the center of this theory of social institutions is the notion of rule-following behavior. Institutions are systems of (often tacit) rules that provide information useful to behavior. Sometimes the rules a social institution embodies are quite general and abstract. Such institutions are social "orders." In other cases, the rules are concrete and directed toward more-or-less specific goals. Such institutions are "organizations."

The Austrian theory of social institutions — from Menger to Hayek — has focused primarily on social orders like language and law, money and morals. At the base of all these institutions are the fundamental phenomena of social conventions and social norms. I have argued that the modern game-theoretic approach to explaining conventions and norms is both consistent with and helpful to the Austrian theory.

Austrian theory has been almost entirely silent, however, on the subject of organizations. It is my contention that such organizations — like government and the business firm — can be understood in the same evolutionary terms as social orders. A useful starting point for an Austrian theory of the firm would be the transaction-cost approach of Ronald Coase and his followers, leavened with a number of Austrian insights, for example, notions of radical uncertainty and the decentralized character of knowledge. In particular, the existing literature focuses to its detriment on issues of incentives and neglects issues of coordination in explaining the evolution of organization.

Notes

1. Veblen (1898) set the tone by singling out Carl Menger for attack as his representative marginalist revolutionary.

2. Some of the discussion, I should note, is in terms not of Austrian institutionalism specifically but in terms of the New Institutional Economics (NIE). In my view (Langlois (1986b), these two approaches are — or at least ought to be — closely related. In what follows I will draw on insights from the NIE, but I will stress the Austrian aspects and influences. For an excellent survey of the NIE from a more neoclassical perspective, see Eggertsson (1990) I should also mention the important work of Douglas North, which has broadened considerably away from the strict neoclassical perspective in recent years (see, for example, North, 1990).

3. "By 'order' we shall throughout describe a state of affairs in which a multiplicity of elements of various kinds are so related to each other that we may learn from our acquaintance with some spatial or temporal part of the whole to form correct expectations concerning the rest, or at least expectation which have a good chance of proving correct." (Hayek [1973, 36], emphasis deleted.)

4. For a discussion of rule following and situation-constrained behavior as alternate modeling strategies, see Langlois and Csontos (1992) and Langlois (1990a).

5. These are all arguably quite different things, of course, and a full-blown theory of social institutions would have to account for the differences among them.

6. The notion of a hierarchy in the narrow sense may prove too rudimentary and confining a concept for capturing the interaction among systems of institutions, but it is a convenient starting point. (See, for example, Langlois, 1986a.)

7. The term Hayek uses, of course, is actually *spontaneous* order. I will restrict this term to a particular class of orders, namely those of organic origin.

8. Assuming the so-called Nash conjecture.

9. Coase came out of the London School of Economics in the 1930s, locus of a tradition with a number of Austrian influences and affinities. The often misunderstood writings of Frank Knight (1921) on this subject (Langlois and Cosgel, 1990) are also relevant.

10. In Coase's original formulation, he conceived of the dichotomy between firm and market in simple terms. A transaction uses the price system if the cooperating capital is separately owned and the intermediate product or service exchanged in an arm's-length arrangement. A transaction is carried out within a firm when the relevant cooperating capital is commonly owned and the operative contract is a more open-ended employment contract. However, it is clear that the categories are more complicated. On the one hand, separate capital owners might cooperate using an open-ended or "relational" contract; and, on the other hand, transactions within the domain of commonly owned capital — as between the divisions of a large firm — might be carried out using prices and simple arm's-length contracts. Those who look only at the contractual aspects are thus led to a kind of agnosticism about the very definition of the firm, a position we might call the nexus-of-contracts view (e.g., Cheung, 1983). Looking at ownership gives a clearer — and to the present author more appealing — definition of the firm. (On the latter view, see Hart, 1989.)

11. On Coase's own interpretation of his 1937 paper, and his criticisms of present-day theory, see Coase (1988).

12. In another sense, of course, the idea of a firm as a system of rules would not appeal to those modern Austrian writers who take their inspiration more from Ludwig von Mises than from Hayek. These writers, who tend to be more rationalist and who prefer to see economics in light of what Hayek called the Pure Logic of Choice, would tend to be suspicious of the very idea of rule-following behavior. (On these issues see Langlois, 1985.) Perhaps this helps explain the reluctance of Austrians as a group to take Hayekian insights into the theory of the firm.

13. For a contrary argument, see Minkler (1991).

14. On the hierarchical nature of plans, see Langlois (1986a).

15. This discussion follows Langlois (1992).

16. Notice that such coordination costs must be related to uncertainty and, in fact, to the kind of radical uncertainty one often reads about in the Austrian literature (Langlois, 1984).

References

Alchian, Armen, and Demsetz, Harold. 1972. "Production, Information Costs, and Economic Organization," *American Economic Review* 62(5): 772–795.

Alchian, Armen, and Woodward, Susan. 1988. "The Firm Is Dead; Long Live the Firm: A Review of Oliver E. Williamson's *The Economic Institutions of Capitalism*," *Journal of Economic Literature* 26(1): 65–79.

Axelrod, Robert. 1984. *The Evolution of Cooperation*. New York: Basic Books.

Barzel, Yoram. 1982. "Measurement Costs and the Organization of Markets," *Journal of Law and Economics* 25: 27–48.

Barzel, Yoram. 1987. "The Entrepreneur's Reward for Self-Policing," *Economic Inquiry* 25: 103–116.

Boettke, Peter J. 1989. "Evolution and Economics: Austrians as Institutionalists," *Research in the History of Economic Thought and Methodology* 6: 73–89.

Buchanan, James M. 1990. "The Domain of Constitutional Economics," *Constitutional Political Economy* 1(1): 1–18.

Cheung, Steven N. S. 1983. "The Contractual Nature of the Firm," *Journal of Law and Economics* 26: 1–22.

Coase, Ronald H. 1937. "The Nature of the Firm," *Economica* (N.S.) 4: 386–405.

Coase, Ronald H. 1972. "Industrial Organization: A Proposal for Research." In *Policy Issues and Research Opportunities in Industrial Organization*, V. R. Fuchs, (ed.). New York: National Bureau of Economic Research.

Coase, Ronald H. 1988. "The Nature of the Firm: Origin, Influence, Meaning," *Journal of Law, Economics, and Organization* 4(1): 3–47.

David, Paul. 1985. "Clio and the Economics of QWERTY," *American Economic Review* 75(2): 332–337.

Edelman, Jacob Murray. 1964. *The Symbolic Uses of Politics*. Urbana: University of Illinois Press.

Eggertsson, Thrainn. 1990. *Economic Behavior and Institutions: Principles of*

Neoinstitutional Economics. New York: Cambridge University Press.

Galbraith, John Kenneth. 1968. *The New Industrial State*. Boston: Houghton Mifflin.

Hart, Oliver D. 1989. "An Economist's Perspective on the Theory of the Firm," *Columbia Law Review* 89(7): 1757–1774.

Hayek, F. A. 1945. "The Use of Knowledge in Society," *American Economic Review* 35(4): 519–530.

Hayek, F. A. 1967. *Studies in Philosophy, Politics, and Economics*. Chicago: University of Chicago Press.

Hayek, F. A. 1973. *Law, Legislation and Liberty*. (Volume I: *Rules and Order*). Chicago: University of Chicago Press.

Hirshleifer, Jack. 1982. "Evolutionary Models in Economics and Law: Cooperation versus Conflict Strategies," *Research in Law and Economics* 4: 1–60.

Hodgson, Geoffrey M. 1989. "Institutional Economic Theory: The Old versus the New," *Review of Political Economy* 1(3): 249–269.

Jones, Lamar. 1986. "The Institutionalists and *On the Origin of Species*: A Case of Mistaken Identity," *Southern Economic Journal* 52: 1043–55.

Klein, Benjamin, Crawford, Robert G., and Alchian, Armen. 1978. "Vertical Integration, Appropriable Rents, and the Competitive Contracting Process," *Journal of Law and Economics* 21(2): 297–326.

Klein, Benjamin, and Leffler, Keith. 1983. "The Role of Market Forces in Assuring Contractual Performance," *Journal of Political Economy* 89: 615–41.

Knight, Frank H. 1921. *Risk, Uncertainty, and Profit*. Boston: Houghton Mifflin.

Lachmann, Ludwig M. 1971. *The Legacy of Max Weber*. Berkeley: The Glendessary Press.

Langlois, Richard N. 1984. "Internal Organization in a Dynamic Context: Some Theoretical Considerations." In *Communication and Information Economics: New Perspectives*, M. Jussawalla and H. Ebenfield, (eds.) Amsterdam: North-Holland, 23–49.

———. 1985. "Knowledge and Rationality in the Austrian School: An Analytical Survey," *Eastern Economic Journal* 9(4): 309–330.

———. 1986a. "Coherence and Flexibility: Social Institutions in a World of Radical Uncertainty." In *Subjectivism, Intelligibility, and Economic Understanding: Essays in Honor of the Eightieth Birthday of Ludwig Lachmann*, Israel Kirzner, (ed.). New York: New York University Press, 171–191.

———. 1986b. "The New Institutional Economics: An Introductory Essay." In *Economics as a Process: Essays in the New Institutional Economics*, R. N. Langlois, (ed.). New York: Cambridge University Press.

———. 1986c. "Rationality, Institutions, and Explanation." In *Economics as a Process: Essays in the New Institutional Economics*, R. N. Langlois, (ed.). New York: Cambridge University Press.

———. 1988. "Economic Change and the Boundaries of the Firm," *Journal of Institutional and Theoretical Economics* 144(4): 635–657.

———. 1989. "What Was Wrong with the 'Old' Institutional Economics (And

What Is Still Wrong with the 'New')?" *Review of Political Economy* 1(3): 271−298.

———. 1990a. "Bounded Rationality and Behavioralism: A Clarification and Critique," *Journal of Institutional and Theoretical Economics* 146(4): 691−695.

———. 1990b. "Creating External Capabilities: Innovation and Vertical Disintegration in the Microcomputer Industry," *Business and Economic History*, Second Series, 19: 93−102.

———. 1992. "Transaction-Cost Economics in Real Time." *Industrial and Corporate Change* 1(1): 99−127.

Langlois, Richard N., and Robertson, Paul L. 1989. "Explaining Vertical Integration: Lessons from the American Automobile Industry," *Journal of Economic History* 49(2): 361−375.

Langlois, Richard N., and Cosgel, Metin M. 1993. "Knight on Risk, Uncertainty, and the Firm: A New Interpretation," *Economic Inquiry* (forthcoming).

Langlois, Richard N., and Csontos, Laszlo. 1992. "Optimization, Rule Following, and the Methodology of Situational Analysis." In *Rationality, Institutions, and Economic Methodology*, Uskali Mäki, Bo Gustafsson, and Christian Knudsen, (eds.). London: Routledge (forthcoming).

Lewis, David K. 1969. *Convention: A Philosophical Study*. Cambridge: Harvard University Press.

Maynard Smith, John. 1982. *Evolution and the Theory of Games*. Cambridge: Cambridge University Press.

Menger, Carl. 1963. *Problems of Economics and Sociology*. Trans. F. J. Nock. Urbana: University of Illinois Press. (First published in 1883.)

Minkler, Alanson P. 1991. "The Problem with Knowledge: An Essay on the Theory of the Firm." Working Paper No. 91−2102. Department of Economics, University of Connecticut.

Nelson, Richard R., and Winter, Sidney G. 1982. *An Evolutionary Theory of Economic Change*. Cambridge: Harvard University Press.

North, Douglass C. 1990. *Institutions, Institutional Change and Economic Performance*. New York: Cambridge University Press.

Nozick, Robert. 1974. *Anarchy, State, and Utopia*. New York: Basic Books.

O'Driscoll, Gerald P. 1986. "Money: Menger's Evolutionary Theory," *History of Political Economy* 18(4): 601−616.

Penrose, Edith T. 1959. *The Theory of the Growth of the Firm*. Oxford: Basil Blackwell.

Perlman, Mark. 1986. "Subjectivism and American Institutionalism." In *Subjectivism, Intelligibility, and Economic Understanding: Essays in Honor of the Eightieth Birthday of Ludwig Lachmann*, Israel Kirzner, (ed.). New York: New York University Press.

Polanyi, Michael. 1958. *Personal Knowledge*. Chicago: University of Chicago Press.

Richardson, G. B. 1972. "The Organisation of Industry," *Economic Journal* 82(327): 883−896.

Rowe, Nicholas. 1989. *Rules and Institutions*. Ann Arbor: University of Michigan Press.

Rutherford, Malcolm. 1989a. "Some Issues in the Comparison of Austrian and Institutional Economics," *Research in the History of Economic Thought and Methodology* 6: 159–172.

Rutherford, Malcolm. 1989b. "What Is Wrong with the New Institutional Economics (And What Is Still Wrong with the Old)?" *Review of Political Economy* 1(3): 301–320.

Samuels, Warren J. 1989. "Austrian and Institutional Economics: Some Common Elements," *Research in the History of Economic Thought and Methodology* 6: 53–71.

Schotter, Andrew. 1981. *The Economic Theory of Social Institutions*. New York: Cambridge University Press.

Schotter, Andrew. 1986. "The Evolution of Rules." In *Economics as a Process: Essays in the New Institutional Economics*, R. N. Langlois, (ed.). New York: Cambridge University Press.

Schweber, S. 1977. "The Origin of the *Origin* Revisited," *Journal of the History of Biology* 10: 229–316.

Silver, Morris. 1984. *Enterprise and the Scope of the Firm*. London: Martin Robertson.

Sugden, Robert. 1986. *The Economics of Rights, Cooperation, and Welfare*. Oxford: Basil Blackwell.

Teece, David J. 1980. "Economies of Scope and the Scope of the Enterprise," *Journal of Economic Behavior and Organization* 1(3): 223–247.

Teece, David J. 1982. "Towards an Economic Theory of the Multiproduct Firm," *Journal of Economic Behavior and Organization* 3: 39–63.

Teece, David J. 1986. "Profiting from Technological Innovation: Implications for Integration, Collaboration, Licensing, and Public Policy," *Research Policy* 15: 285–305.

Ullmann-Margalit, Edna. 1977. *The Emergence of Norms*. Oxford: Clarendon Press.

Vanberg, Viktor. 1986. "Spontaneous Market Order and Social Rules: A Critical Examination of F. A. Hayek's Theory of Cultural Evolution," *Economics and Philosophy* 2(1): 75–100.

Vanberg, Viktor. 1989. "Carl Menger's Evolutionary and John R. Commons' Collective Action Approach to Institutions: A Comparison," *Review of Political Economy* 1(3): 334–360.

Veblen, Thorstein. 1898. "Why Is Economics Not an Evolutionary Science?" *Quarterly Journal of Economics* 12: 373–397.

Williamson, Oliver E. 1985. *The Economic Institutions of Capitalism*. New York: The Free Press.

COMMENTARY
Institutional Evolution and Methodological Individualism
Geoffrey M. Hodgson

Richard Langlois has provided a perceptive and stimulating chapter on the contribution of the Austrian School to the theory of institutions. The distinction between order and organization is particularly valuable. Although it is not really developed in the works of Hayek, it leads to some important questions concerning the nature and evolution of socio-economic institutions. I found particularly suggestive the recommendation by Langlois that "the externalness of an institution is tied up with the generality and abstractness of its rules" (170).

Langlois's research strategy is to combine the insights of the Austrian School with the transaction-costs economics of Coase and Williamson. This is a very interesting and illuminating project, but I am personally skeptical as to the ability of the transaction-costs approach to withstand the test of time. The idea has been subject to some recent criticism, and may well prove untenable (Dietrich, 1991; Dow, 1987; Hodgson, 1988). I do not have here the space to discuss this issue further, but it does relate to some of the questions, such as that of methodological individualism, and the nature of economic evolution, which I do raise below.

My commentary covers a major issue and some relatively minor points of criticism. Fortunately the major issue and the minor points are connected, so one of the latter can be used as a means of introducing the major theme.

The relatively minor but symptomatic point is that in an early footnote Thorstein Veblen is accused by Langlois of "singling out for attack Carl Menger as his representative marginalist revolutionary," in his essay

"Why is Economics Not an Evolutionary Science?". This is not strictly true. While completely dismissing the "old" institutionalism in a single footnote — unfortunately a wider habit — Langlois is trying to give the impression that Veblen had picked the wrong target in Menger.

In fact, in the aforementioned essay, Veblen (1919, 72–73) sees Menger as the "spokesman" of the Austrian School, and not of "marginalism" as a whole. Menger receives only a brief mention in the identification of the "Austrian failure" as deriving from a "hedonistic" and "faulty conception of human nature — faulty for the present purpose, however adequate it may be for any other" (73).

Incidentally, for Veblen, the "present purpose" is to turn economics into an "evolutionary" science. Some inadequacies of methodological individualism and a "hedonistic" conception of human nature, in relation to conceptions of socioeconomic evolution, are discussed below.

On the very same page of Veblen's text we find the beginning of the famous passage where he criticizes orthodox economics for its conception of the actor as a "lightning calculator of pleasures and pains." However, Veblen makes it clear that his criticisms apply not to the Austrian School alone, but to "all received formulations of economic theory, whether at the hands of English economists or those of the Continent" (73).

William Jaffé (1976) has pointed out that in this famous passage Veblen does not give due credit to the different conception of rationality in Menger's theory. This criticism is valid, but it does not support the erroneous view that Menger was the main target of Veblen's article. Furthermore, the charge that both Austrian and neoclassical theorists proceed from a "hedonistic" and "given" idea of human nature remains accurate, even if the adjectives "inert" and "passive" should not have been applied to the Austrian conception.

Veblen also briefly mentions Adam Smith and Alfred Marshall in the same essay. But, contrary to the impression of an Austrian primary target, he reserves by far the greatest amount of criticism for the German Historical School — notable victims of Menger and the Austrians.[1]

In referring to a recent debate between "old" institutionalists and Austrian theorists as "violent," Langlois may give the impression that it was entirely a matter of controversy. In fact, two of the more important contributions to that debate — one from each side of this "battle" — were primarily concerned to establish *common ground* between Austrian and "old" institutionalist theory.[2]

To illustrate the potential fruitfulness of Austrian-institutionalist collaboration, consider Langlois's definition of an "institution." There is the problem whether the weight of the definition should be in terms of "rule following" as Langlois suggests, or in terms of "settled habits of thought common to the generality of men" (Veblen, 1919, 239) or "a way of thought or action of some prevalence and permanence, which is embedded in the habits of a group or the customs of a people" (Hamilton, 1963, 84). Although Langlois rightly points out that rule-following behavior can be habitual and based on tacit knowledge, the Veblen-Hamilton definitions leave open the possibility that the perception and interpretation of a rule is itself subject to cognitive factors. Rule following implies the preexistence of the rule, whereas a "habit of thought or action" may be prior to the rule itself. In fact, the Veblen-Hamilton definition could be regarded as more subjectivist than the one provided by Langlois.

It is true, as Langlois suggests, that "Menger's approach to social institutions and Darwin's theory of biological evolution have a common ancestor in the writings of the Scottish enlightenment." However, it is notable that Langlois follows Friedrich Hayek (1967, 1978, 1982, 1988) in putting emphasis on the inspiration that Darwin obtained from the Scottish School, to the total neglect of several other key figures including Thomas Robert Malthus.

Langlois supports his statement with two references to works by Lamar Jones and Silvan Schweber. Although Schweber (1977, 1980) gives due prominence to the influence of the Scottish School, his work is not one-sided. In fact, Schweber (1977, 232) argues that the Malthusian principle of population became in Darwin's theory "the *force* behind the selection process. In that sense the Malthusian statement was critical." Furthermore, in a later essay Jones (1989) sees Malthus as being a crucial inspiration for Darwin, contrary to the Hayek-Langlois account.[3] Although the nature and precise extent of Malthus's influence is open to dispute, it cannot be sensibly denied or ignored.

Unfortunately, this is not simply a question of minor historical in-accuracy. One possible clue to the Hayek-Langlois lapse is that the conceptions of evolution in the works of Malthus and Smith are quite different.

The object of evolutionary analysis for Mandeville and the Scottish School is the socioeconomic system. In accordance with the stance that we now describe as "methodological individualism," the elements driving such a development are individuals with preferences and purposes. Thus, it is appropriate to assume that the socioeconomic system is analogous to a given organism, and the individuals within it are analogous to the genes.[4]

Mandeville and the Scottish School typically write as if this "genetic" material—that is the set of individuals themselves, not the biological genes — were given, and they are examining the development of the socioeconomic structure as it emerges unintentionally from the combined actions of all the individual "genes." This is analogous to the biological notion of ontogeny — the development of a particular organism from the coding in its given genetic material.

In pursuing their objectives, and in relation to their general environment, individuals develop habits, dispositions or behavioral rules. This is analogous to the emergence of the phenotype from the genotype. Note that ontogeny does pay due regard to the environment of the organism, as the same genotype may have different phenotypical results in different environments. However, the key point is that the genetic material remains constant. When Mandeville writes of the development of social order from the interaction of greedy individuals, and Smith claims to expose the origin of economic order and the mechanisms of growth, they are both taking, for the purposes of their analyses, the population of individuals with their various propensities as given.

The above arguments have their place and may go some way to help explain the origins of social order and the springs of economic growth. However, a broader conception of socioeconomic evolution is possible. For the Scottish School, habits and rules may change, but changes in individual preferences and propensities are not crucial for their argument. Accordingly, what methodological individualists do not contemplate is the development of different individual preferences and purposes, or even a different population of individuals through some cumulative process of feedback.

Consequently, an analogue to phylogeny is not considered: the evolutionary processes of selection and development among a whole population of individuals. If individuals and their propensities are analogous to the biological genes, then the arguments of Mandeville and the Scottish School are confined to ontogeny. If phylogeny was to be studied, then changes in the pool of individual propensities would be considered. This could occur either through the Darwinian "natural selection" of different individuals, or through a quasi-Lamarckian process in which the characteristics of individuals may change.[6]

While for Mandeville and the Scottish School the population is taken as given, Malthus considers a changing population of individuals. He goes further to study the complete evolutionary process of selection within, and development of, such a population. Although Malthus also is a nineteenth century individualist and still tends to take individual preferences as given, the "genetic material" may nevertheless change through the operation of selection, that is, differential birth and death. In addition,

Malthus was primarily concerned with overall numbers and not the selection of different individuals. Nevertheless, his idea of change resulting from contest and struggle, which inspired Darwin, is phylogenetic — albeit in a limited sense — rather than simply ontogenetic.

In contrast, another example of evolution of the "ontogenetic" type is Menger's account of the evolution of money. Clearly, the object of evolutionary analysis is an emerging monetary unit, and the focus is on the cumulative reinforcement of a given unit through the actions of individual traders. The genetic material is the individuals with their given preferences. There need not be even evolutionary selection between rival monetary units, nor is there a consideration of the changes in individual preferences, nor of the population of individuals themselves. We are thus again confined to ontogeny.[6]

Clearly all this has relevance for Veblen's critique of both neoclassical economics and the Austrian School for presuming an "immutably given human nature." For Veblen, Darwinian evolution was "cumulative" in character. The cumulative quality of evolutionary thinking rests precisely on the fact that it does not take human nature or preferences as given or for granted. Both the circumstances and temperament of an individual are part of the cumulative processes of change:

> They are the products of his hereditary traits and his past experience, cumu-
> latively wrought out under a given body of traditions, conventionalities, and
> material circumstances; and they afford the point of departure for the next step
> in the process. (Veblen, 1919, 74)

For Veblen, the objects of economic evolution are institutions and routines. Their genetic component is habits and instincts. The nature of the evolutionary process governing these elements is selective rather than purely developmental, and phylogenetic rather than simply ontogenetic. Veblenian economic evolution, in other words, is not confined to the development of the organism from its genetic rules. It is phylogenetic in that the ongoing processes of selection and development of the whole population of institutions is considered. His evolutionary theory is thus more extensive than that of Smith or Menger and has the same phylogenetic quality as that of Malthus. That is one reason why Veblen wanted a "post-Darwinian" economics.

In his discussion of the evolution of institutions, Langlois does not mention the fact that, for Hayek, selection operates on groups rather than individuals. This has led to a controversy where Viktor Vanberg (1986) has used the arguments of "genetic reductionists," such as Richard Dawkins, against cultural group selection, and in favour of methodological individualism. However, I show elsewhere (Hodgson, 1991) that Vanberg was wrong to suggest that biologists now eschew group selection. The idea of group and even higher levels of selection is now advanced by a number of biological theorists. Whether they are right or wrong in the biotic context, the idea of levels of selection higher than the gene or the individual has even more credence in economic evolution, where information is clearly stored and transmitted at a number of different levels, not simply the genes.

Given this point, Hayek should be criticized, not for embracing group selection and eschewing a consistent individualism, but for failing to incorporate additional processes of selection above the group level, involving the selection of different types of institution, including both market and nonmarket forms.

The connecting thread and major theme of all the points made above is the question of methodological individualism and the disposition to take individual preferences and purposes as given.[7] In my view, these two elements are closely connected (Hodgson, 1988, ch. 3; Hodgson, 1993b), and I have suggested above that methodologically individualist approaches are typically connected with ontogeny.

This leads to a tension in Hayek's work. On the one hand he proclaims "methodological individualism," in which case it would seem that we are confined to the discussion of the emergence of rules, institutions and socioeconomic systems from a given population of individuals with given preferences and purposes. On the other hand we could take Hayek as suggesting that rules and norms are the "genetic elements" driving the system, and that a selection process is going on upon those elements. The difference depends upon whether we take the individual or the rules as the elemental unit and driving force. In the former case we are confined to ontogeny. In the latter case we may embrace a version of phylogentic evolution, but methodological individualism is no longer the centrepiece. Hayek has clearly moved towards the latter alternatives.

The next logical step is not simply to consider the phylogeny of rules but also changes in the whole human population and its individual preferences. After embracing the idea of socioeconomic evolution, it is thus reasonable to suggest, to use Stephan Böhm's (1989, 211) words, that "Hayek is by no means the champion of methodological individualism that he claims to be."

If Hayek is to be regarded as a phylogenetic evolutionist, then he leaves the ontogenetic camp of Smith, Menger and Schotter, and joins that of Malthus and Veblen to embrace "cumulative causation." In any case, the comparison of the institutionalism of both the Austrian and the "old" institutionalist schools should be made with due regard to what is of value in both.[8]

Acknowledgments

In writing this comment, the author is grateful for the supportive facilities of the Swedish Collegium for Advanced Study in the Social Sciences. He also wishes to thank the editors of this volume for their helpful criticisms and encouraging comments.

Notes

1. Note that in his introduction to *Capitalism and the Historians*, Hayek (1954) states that the American institutionalists were the spiritual successors of the German Historical School. While there is indeed some spiritual connection, neither the differences with Thorstein Veblen in particular, nor the *similarities* between Veblen and Hayek, should be ignored.

2. Notably, Boettke (1989) and Samuels (1989). See also the excellent essay by Rutherford (1989). Also, contrary to the more adversarial viewpoints from both sides, Charles Leathers (1990) rightly takes the view that the theoretical positions of Hayek and Veblen are much closer than either Hayek or Langlois suggest. See also Wynarczyk (1992).

3. It is curious also that Joseph Schumpeter (1954, 445–6) simply denies that Malthus had a significant influence on Darwin. This error is the focus of Jones's (1989) excellent essay.

4. It should be emphasized that we are using an analogy here and not proposing that human behavior is programmed by biological genes. For excellent criticisms of biological reductionism and Social Darwinism see Hayek (1982, vol. 1, 23–4; 1982, vol. 3, 154–6).

5. The use of the distinction between ontogeny and phylogeny to categorize economic theories was suggested to the author by Pavel Pelikan. The author is also grateful to Hilary Rose and Steven Rose for discussions on this point.

6. A similar case of ontogeny is Andrew Schotter's analysis of the emergence of institutions, as discussed by Langlois.

7. In the light of this I very much welcome Langlois's (1990, 363) statement that "the issue of endogenous preferences is a most important one, to which institutionalists of all stripe ought to be paying more attention."

8. Several of the main points in this comment, including the relationship between economic and biology, the distinction between ontogeny and phylogeny, and the role of variety in the evolutionary process, are discussed in more detail in Hodgson (1993a).

References

Boettke, P. 1989. "Evolution and Economics: Austrians as Institutionalists," *Research in the History of Economic Thought and Methodology* 6: 73–89.

Böhm, S. 1989. "Hayek on Knowledge, Equilibrium and Prices: Context and Impact," *Wirtschaftspolitische Blätter* 36(2): 201−13.

Dietrich, M. 1991. "Firms, Markets and Transaction Cost Economics," *Scottish Journal of Political Economy* 38(1) February: 41−57.

Dow, G. K. 1987. "The Function of Authority in Transaction Cost Economics," *Journal of Economic Behavior and Organization* 8(1), March: 13−38.

Hamilton, W. H. 1963. "Institution." In *Encyclopaedia of the Social Sciences*, E. R. A. Seligman and A. Johnson (eds.). Vol. 7, 84−89.

Hayek, F. A. (ed.) 1954. *Capitalism and the Historians*. London and Chicago: Routledge and Kegan Paul and University of Chicago Press.

Hayek, F. A. 1967. *Studies in Philosophy, Politics and Economics*. London: Routledge and Kegan Paul.

Hayek, F. A. 1978. *New Studies in Philosophy, Politics, Economics and the History of Ideas*. London: Routledge and Kegan Paul.

Hayek, F. A. 1982. *Law, Legislation and Liberty*. (Three-volume combined edn.). London: Routledge and Kegan Paul.

Hayek, F. A. 1988. *The Fatal Conceit: The Errors of Socialism, Collected Works of F. A. Hayek*, Vol. 1. London: Routledge.

Hodgson, G. M. 1988. *Economics and Institutions: A Manifesto for a Modern Institutional Economics*. Cambridge: Polity Press.

Hodgson, G. M. 1989. "Institutional Economic Theory: The Old Versus the New," *Review of Political Economy* 1(3), November: 249−69. Reprinted in G. M. Hodgson, *After Marx and Sraffa: Essays in Political Economy*, London: Macmillan (1991).

Hodgson, G. M. 1991. "Hayek's Theory of Cultural Evolution: An Evaluation in the Light of Vanberg's Critique," *Economics and Philosophy* 7(1), March: 67−82.

Hodgson, G. M. 1993a. *Economics and Evolution*. Cambridge: Polity Press (forthcoming)

Hodgson, G. M. 1993b. "Methodological Individualism." In *Handbook of Institutional and Evolutionary Economics*, W. J. Samuels, G. M. Hodgson and M. Tool (eds.). Aldershot: Edward Elgar (forthcoming).

Jaffé, W. 1976. "Menger, Jevons and Walras De-homogenized," *Economic Inquiry* 14: 511−24.

Jones, L. B. 1989. "Schumpeter versus Darwin: In re Malthus," *Southern Economic Journal* 56(2), October: 410−22.

Langlois, R. N. 1990. Review of Geoffrey M. Hodgson, *Economics and Institutions*. In the *Journal of Institutional and Theoretical Economics* 146(2), June: 363.

Leathers, C. G. 1990. "Veblen and Hayek on Instincts and Evolution," *Journal of the History of Economic Thought* 12(2), June: 162−78.

Rutherford, M. C. 1989. "Some Issues in the Comparison of Austrian and Institutional Economics," *Research in the History of Economic Thought and Methodology* 6: 159−71.

Samuels, W. J. 1989. "Austrian and Institutional Economics: Some Common

Elements," *Research in the History of Economic Thought and Methodology* 6: 53–71.

Schweber, S. S. 1977. "The Origin of the *Origin* Revisited," *Journal of the History of Biology* 10(2), Fall: 229–316.

Schweber, S. S. 1980. "Darwin and the Political Economists: Divergence of Character," *Journal of the History of Biology* 13(2), Fall: 195–289.

Vanberg, V. 1986. "Spontaneous Market Order and Social Rules: A Critique of F. A. Hayek's Theory of Cultural Evolution," *Economics and Philosophy* 2(2), June: 75–100.

Veblen, T. B. 1919. *The Place of Science in Modern Civilization and Other Essays*. New York: Huebsch. Reprinted 1990 with a new introduction by W. J. Samuels, New Brunswick: Transaction Publishers.

Wynarczyk, P. 1992. "Comparing Alleged Incommensurables: Institutional and Austrian Economics as Rivals and Possible Complements?" *Review of Political Economy* 4(1), January: 18–36.

7 ON THE POSSIBILITY OF AUSTRIAN WELFARE ECONOMICS

Alan P. Hamlin

Introduction

Austrian economics is sometimes accused of inconsistency with respect to welfare economics. On the one hand, it is critical of the structure and practice of mainstream welfare economics with its flavor of social engineering; while on the other hand it is seen to be keen to propose particular policies in certain circumstances and to argue that these policies are justified economically. In short, Austrians are charged with allowing themselves access to the levers of social control that they would deny to others. While this statement of the charge of inconsistency is brief and sketchy, the charge is familiar enough.

My intentions in this chapter are first to analyze the sources of the tension between Austrian economics and mainstream welfare economics and then to suggest a resolution of that tension. This resolution will involve the characterization of an Austrian welfare economics and the discussion of the linkages between this conception of welfare economics and the constitutionalism associated with James Buchanan and others.

The chapter is divided into six further sections. Sections two and three sketch out the characteristics of mainstream welfare economics and Austrian economics that are of importance to the debate. Section four brings these two sets of characteristics together to identify the nature and extent of the tension between them. Section five contains an argument toward the resolution of the tension by means of identifying an Austrian approach to welfare economics that stands in clear contrast with mainstream welfare economics. Section six argues that the Austrian welfare economics identified is essentially similar to the position normally associated with constitutional political economy. Essentially, I will suggest that these are two lines of argument that lead to substantially the same conclusions. Finally, section seven offers some brief concluding comments.

Mainstream Welfare Economics

A detailed review of the structure and content of welfare economics is well beyond the scope of this section.[1] I shall attempt only to provide an overview and some more detailed comments on a few selected points.

At the theoretical level, a central organizing idea of welfare economics is the social welfare function (SWF), which represents a social ordering over possible states of the world. This ordering is required to satisfy restrictions that generally include: *individualism*, *welfarism*, and the *Pareto principle*. Individualism in this context refers to the assumption that a social ordering should be based on individual orderings over states of the world. Welfarism refers to the assumption that individual orderings are themselves represented by individual utility functions, so that the "utilities" or "welfares" achieved by each individual in each state of the world can be thought of as the (only) arguments of the SWF. The Pareto principle (in its strong form) states that if state α is ranked above state β by one person, and is not ranked below state β by anyone, then α should rank above β in the social ordering.

At this level of abstraction we should notice an ambiguity in the use of "utility".[2] In the context of an individual utility function, utility is normally taken to index preference. An individual's utility of state α is greater than her utility of state β, if and only if, she prefers state α to state β. But by the time we get to the social welfare function, we are typically told that if social welfare is higher in state α than in state β, then state α is *better* than state β. It is the ambiguity of utility as between an index of preference and an index of good that allows of this slippage, and this slippage is characteristic of much of welfare economics.

At the formal level we may go either one of two ways: we may either eliminate the slippage by adopting a preference satisfaction theory of good, so that what is good for an individual is defined in terms of the satisfaction of her preferences; or we must choose between preferences and good as the basic ingredient of welfare economics. The first route involves a thorough subjectivism in which an individual's actual preferences, whatever their origin, are the only relevant criterion. The second route leaves open the possibility of some objective element in the criterion of good.

Taking the second route and working with preferences raises some concerns. First, the concern that we lose normative significance by ignoring aspects of good that are not directly included in preference; for example, the assumption of "welfarism" lacks normative appeal when interpreted in terms of preferences alone. Second, it is by no means obvious what the result of the aggregation of preferences gives rise to (even if it is possible). The notion of a preference is intimately tied up with the notion of choice: to prefer α to β is to say that α would be chosen over β in relevant circumstances. This is unexceptional at the level of individual preference and individual choice, but problematic at the social level since society is not the sort of thing that can make choices or have preferences in a direct and uncomplicated way. We use the language of collective preferences expressed via collective choices, but we always mean to identify the outcome of a specified institutional process, rather than some simple choice. If Jane and Julia prefer α to β and would choose accordingly, while John prefers β to α and would choose accordingly, there is no unambiguous way of identifying the preference or choice of the society made up of Jane, Julia and John, although we might speak loosely of society "preferring" or "choosing" α under the institutional arrangement of majoritarianism. Of course, one might argue that a SWF indicates that which *should* be chosen at the social level, but this requires a normative interpretation which is somewhat undermined by the adoption of the preference interpretation of utility.

For these reasons, I will assume — somewhat controversially — that the real spirit of welfare economics lies in the interpretation of utility as good;[3] although I shall leave open the question of whether this arises from a preference satisfaction theory of good or from some other theory. On this interpretation a SWF is intended to indicate the aggregate good of each state of the world, and so to provide a straightforwardly normative criterion. Of course, there are many problems surrounding such a view; but this is not the place to raise them.[4] Instead, I will simply note the key aspects of the practical application of welfare economics.

At the level of application, welfare economics is concerned with the operationalization of the notion of a SWF as a mechanism for the evaluation of alternative actions or policies. This requires three steps: the identification of the effects of alternative policies; the measurement of the impact of these effects on the utility of each individual; and, finally, the aggregation of individual utilities. The practical usefulness of the welfare economics approach depends, then, on the ability to take these three steps. More detailed discussion is postponed until the section entitled "Tension in Theory and Practice."

Austrian Economics

Once again, a detailed review of Austrian economics is beyond the scope of this section — and particularly so in a volume of this type — and I will simply sketch three aspects of the Austrian approach that will be important in what follows. These are: the Austrian theory of value, individualism and the treatment of uncertainty.

It is uncontroversial to identify the dominant theme within Austrian value theory with the subjectivist school deriving from Menger. We may crudely characterize this position in two steps. First, it is a preference based theory of good; but second, it views individual preference as being formed in actions of choice, rather than logically prior to those actions. This point may be expressed differently by saying that Austrians would deny the existence of a well-defined preference ordering that characterizes an individual and is, in principle, knowable. In place of such a construct, the Austrian would emphasize two points: that preferences derive from a process of learning from past choices, and that preferences are therefore, in principle, unknowable by anyone other than the individual herself; and, in particular, cannot be recovered from the study of past choices that reflect all kinds of mistakes and experiments as well as the evolution of preferences.[5] In short, choice does not *reveal* preference, if by reveal we mean the unveiling of a preexisting and well-defined preference ordering. Choice certainly results from an interaction between an individual's instantaneous preference, her imagining of the future (see below) and a variety of other factors, but this interaction is sufficiently complex that it is not possible for preferences to be identified (or *revealed*); and, given that preferences may evolve in ways that depend upon the actual choice situations encountered, no preexisting, or well defined preference ordering, may be relevant. I will refer to this unknowability as the inscrutability of individual preferences.

But this account of value is not the only one available within the Austrian tradition. This second theory of value[6] is more objectivist in character and defines value in terms of individuals' *right* preferences, rather than simply their actual preference. That is, value is determined by that which individuals *ought* to prefer. Of course, the objectivist element here does not completely swamp the subjectivist, and it is possible for the Austrian to combine, to some extent, this second theory of value with the views on the evolution and inscrutability of preference sketched above.

But nevertheless, the foothold of objectivity introduced here must set some limits to the evolution and unknowability of value.

The individualism within the Austrian position is both methodological and moral, but it is the moral individualism that concerns us here.[7] Moral individualism forms the background against which the particular theories of value mentioned above are drawn. It tells us, loosely, that in the first instance we must be concerned with the good of individuals. We might say that the preference (or *right* preference) theory of value is a further specification of Austrian moral individualism. But it is only a partial further specification. Moral individualism comes in a variety of forms and may make further requirements.

A further requirement of particular relevance to Austrians (although not necessarily endorsed by all Austrians) is that good is essentially individuated, so that the notion of "good" only makes sense in relation to an individual. Such a view implies that there can be no such thing as the collective or social good, although it does not totally rule out the possibility of aggregating good interpersonally. An analogy may help here. An uncle is an essentially individuated role. An uncle is an uncle only in view of a specified relationship with a particular individual (or individuals). We may each have uncles, and have different numbers of uncles, and we might aggregate the total number of uncle relationships in any given society in a variety of ways, but it makes no sense to speak of a collective or social uncle.

The final aspect of the Austrian position to be mentioned here is the approach to uncertainty. The inscrutability of preferences mentioned above represents one form of unknowability within the Austrian tradition, but Austrians also typically hold that the future is essentially unknowable, rather than known with an error in the fashion of more mainstream models of uncertainty. This unknowability is in part a rejection of the idea that the essence of uncertainty can be captured by attaching probabilities to alternative future states, but equally a rejection of the idea that a complete or coherent list of possible future states could be drawn up in principle. Considering the future, on the Austrian model, is an act of individual imagination and not something that can be modeled in an impersonal manner; just as good is essentially individuated, so visions of the future are essentially individuated.

Tension in Theory and Practice

The caricatures of welfare economics and Austrian economics sketched in the preceding sections are, I hope, sufficient to identify the source of the tension between the two positions. I will argue that this source is not to be found in the deep theoretical structure of the two positions, but rather in the commitments that characterize the translation of theory into practice. Thus, although the tension is real and significant, it is sufficiently superficial to leave the door open to resolution, or in the words of my title, to admit the possibility of Austrian welfare economics.

One view of the tension between Austrian and mainstream welfare economics is that it arises from the alternative theories of value embedded in the two traditions — but as my caricatures indicate, this is an untenable view. Both theories of value face the same internal tension between the purely subjective and the partly objective theories of good, and it is clear that *some* Austrians will differ from *some* mainstream welfare economist on these issues. But there is no deep or foundational distinction between the two schools in this area. One could hold a radically subjectivist preference theory of good within either tradition; one can be a welfarist within either tradition; one could hold objective theories of the good within either tradition, and so on.

A second view might locate the source of the tension in attitudes to individualism and, in particular, in the lack of a commitment to the essentially individuated nature of good in the mainstream welfare economics tradition, which is essentially aggregative or synoptic in character. While the argument between individuation and aggregation is familiar enough, it again fails to distinguish between the two traditions. It is perfectly possible (even if it is unfashionable) within the welfare economics tradition, to maintain the impossibility of interpersonal comparisons of "utility" and so restrict the form of the SWF. Just as it is possible with the Austrian tradition (and particularly if a more objectivist theory of value is held) to allow of at least some element of interpersonal comparison.

So far, while the two traditions have distinctly different flavors, there is nothing sufficiently distinctive to ground the observed tension. To locate the source of this tension we must move away from the foundations and toward more practical issues. The practical aspect of the welfare economics tradition was sketched above in three parts: the identification of policy effects, the measurement of those effects on individuals, and the aggregation across individuals. The question of the individuation of good bears on the third and final stage of this process, but, as I have already suggested, this logically only concerns the *form* of the SWF. Of course the form of the SWF may impose considerable limits on the practical value of the welfare economics approach. If interpersonal incommensurability is maintained, the SWF will support only the Pareto partial ordering, and this implies that the welfare economics approach will be silent on most issues. But the real tension between the welfare economics approach and the

Austrian lies in the other two stages of the process.

The identification of the effects of alternative policies or actions presumes something that Austrians deny, namely the knowability of the future. The Austrian would argue that the required task of identification was infeasible. Of course each individual could imagine a future, but these imaginings might be very different and there would be no sense in combining them. Certainly, no one imagining (the "official" imagining) should be given precedence over others in the way that is required by the practice of welfare economic policy evaluation.

Even if some particular version of the future could be established, the Austrian would have a separate objection to the second stage of the process — the evaluation stage. The objection here relates not to the unknowability of the future but to the inscrutability of individual preferences, and particularly preferences relating to the future. Again, the Austrian would claim that the practice of welfare economic evaluation is infeasible.

In summary, the Austrian objection to mainstream welfare economics is not, at root, an objection to the logical construct of the SWF, but a deep objection to the effect that the operation of welfare economic policy evaluation is infeasible once the Austrian view of uncertainty and inscrutability is accepted.[8] It is the claim that the SWF is a practically useful construct to which the Austrian must object.

This account of the tension makes plain the difficulty in communication between the two sides of the debate. To the welfare economist, the Austrian position sounds like a rejection of attempts at measurement on the grounds that measurement is imprecise. And this gives rise to the reaction that imprecise measurement is surely better than no measurement at all. And of course this is true within the mainstream view of "imprecision" (uncertainty) as an essentially quantitative problem. But from the Austrian perspective, the "imprecision" involved in the attempted measurement is not a matter of simple quantitative error, but a matter of qualitative or categorical error. The difference between "uncertain" and "unknowable" is profound, but at the same time, it is a difference that is apparently difficult for someone deeply immersed in one tradition or the other to understand fully.

An Austrian Welfare Economics

Given this diagnosis of the tension between the Austrian tradition and the welfare economics tradition, what are the prospects for an Austrian welfare economics? The key to answering this question may be found by

considering another aspect of the difference between Austrian and mainstream approaches to economics—their respective treatments of markets.

The relevant distinction here is that between the mainstream concentration on market equilibrium and the Austrian concentration on the
market as process. This distinction is familiar,[9] and I will not pursue the
topic in detail here beyond noting that this distinction also arises as a
result of the Austrian commitments to the unknowability of the future
and inscrutability of individual preferences. The basic shift in emphasis
from the mainstream to the Austrian is clear. Both value markets instru-
mentally, but mainstream economics values the market to the extent that
it gives rise to an allocation of resources which satisfies certain efficiency
criteria, while Austrian economics values the market because it involves a
procedure that operates without making impossible demands. That is, while
mainstream economics emphasizes the desirability of market outcomes,
Austrian economics emphasizes the feasibility of market processes.[10]

This Austrian concern with the operating characteristics of processes,
rather than their particular outcomes, provides the basis for an Austrian
welfare economics. The central point here is that while a genuinely
Austrian welfare economics cannot set out to evaluate states of the world
seen as outcomes, it could set out to evaluate alternative institutional and
procedural structures in terms of their feasibility and general operating
properties. There seems to be no good reasons why the Austrian's praise
for the institutional and procedural aspects of markets should be their
only foray into institutional evaluation. An Austrian welfare economics,
conceived in this manner, could not make detailed or precise policy
recommendations, but could make recommendations for institutional and
procedural reform. If we return to the charge of inconsistency referred to
in the opening paragraph of this essay, we can now see that the Austrian
grants (or *should* grant) herself access to only a small subset of the levers
of social control that are claimed by the mainstream welfare economist.

Before looking in slightly more detail at the possible content of an
Austrian welfare economics, it is necessary to defend the idea against the
obvious charge of "constructivism" from within the Austrian ranks. In its
most extreme form, anticonstructivism is the view that social institutions—
market based and otherwise—evolve in ways that are mysterious to
individuals and embody wisdom that is not understood consciously. Such
a view would imply that any conscious intervention in the structure of
institutions would fall foul of the same argument employed against
conscious intervention on detailed policies. If the operating characteristics
of alternative institutions are held to be unknowable, then any intervention
will be essentially arbitrary. And in these circumstances one should avoid

the dangers associated with tampering with those institutions that have arisen.

Such an extreme anticonstructivism certainly amounts to a denial of the possibility of an Austrian welfare economics, but would equally deny the possibility of Austrian approval of the market process. The only statement allowed would be that what exists should be allowed to continue to evolve without conscious control or intervention. But such an extreme anticonstructivism is also very implausible. As indicated by the Austrian analysis of the market process, the requirements for the evaluation of an institutional process do not necessarily extend beyond the resources available to Austrians. The analyst is not required to know or forecast the future, nor is she required to know individual preferences; she is required to think through the ways in which a given institutional structure impinged on human action; this may be a complex task, but it is not an infeasible one.

In sketching the framework of an Austrian welfare economics, I have so far emphasized only that it would take institutional structures and procedures — rather than particular policy actions — as its domain. But the other vital ingredient is a specification of the criterion against which it evaluates these structures and procedures. Clearly, this criterion cannot be constructed directly from the Austrian theory of value, since any attempt in this direction would involve the same problems of unknowability and inscrutability as the Austrian claims to be fatal to the mainstream welfare economics enterprise. Rather, the criterion has to reflect the Austrian theory of value indirectly. The first aspect of such a criterion has already been mentioned — feasibility: where feasibility refers, not to technical feasibility, but social feasibility — the idea that an institution or procedure can actually operate in a society of individuals. The second aspect of the criterion must reflect the institution's ability to coordinate or resolve conflict in human action. These two aspects of an Austrian welfare criterion are, again, familiar from the discussion of the market process.

It may be helpful at this stage to consider an example of the application of such an Austrian welfare economics and the contrast with more mainstream welfare economics. Consider the case of global warming. Here we have an issue that is widely regarded as of major significance but is shrouded in uncertainties of all kinds. The mainstream welfare economics approach is first to reduce the various aspects of technical or scientific uncertainty to a "manageable" set of probability distributions over outcomes. So, for example, the sea level is "expected" to rise by around two feet by the year 2025 in the absence of any new policy intervention. Next, targets for the key control variables are considered. So, for example, the costs of reducing emissions of greenhouse gases are considered alongside the costs of abating the damage caused by a rise in sea levels to arrive at a target level of emission reduction that minimizes total expected cost. Next, alternative means of achieving this target are considered, and a particular policy chosen.[11]

How might an Austrian welfare economist approach this area? I suggest that first she would disavow any attempt to forecast or measure the detailed consequences of global warming in terms of its impact on societies. Rather, she would address the question of how individual concerns about global warming might be coordinated, and any resulting conflicts resolved. That is, what structure of institutional forum might best act to respond to those individual concerns. There may be good reasons in the general nature of the problem (rather than the specific outcomes that may be forecast) to suppose that a market may not be a feasible or an effective institution; there may also be good reasons to suppose that national governments will not provide the most effective institution. Whatever the detailed arguments may be, the Austrian's conclusion will take the form of an institutional procedure for addressing the substantive problem rather than particular actions or policies. There is no guarantee that the actual policies that emerge from this procedure will be the policies that would be recommended by the mainstream welfare economist, nor is there any claim that these policies are "better" than some other policies. The claim is simply that they have been generated by a process that is appropriate to the general structure of the problem.

How should we compare these two approaches? On one level this question is unanswerable. The basis of the Austrian argument against mainstream welfare economics, as we have argued above, is that it attempts the infeasible. Austrians do not (or should not) claim that their approach gives "better" answers, since they lack the basis for any judgment of "betterness." Rather, they should claim that their approach recognizes the severe restrictions imposed by the nature of the subject matter and works within them, while the mainstream welfare economist attempts too much and risks too much.

Of course, if we disagree with the Austrian concerning the unknowability of the future and the inscrutability of individual preferences, then we will also disagree with the claim that the mainstream welfare economist's project is infeasible. The question of which of the two approaches is to be preferred is then an open one. The major advantage to be claimed by the mainstream welfare economist is that her policy recommendation maximizes ex ante expected welfare, while the major advantage to be claimed by the Austrian is that her approach recognizes that, in the real world, decisions are made by particular institutional procedures and analyses those procedures directly. Of course, ex post either approach might give rise to the "better" outcome in any particular case.

Constitutionalism

This sketch of an Austrian welfare economics brings out the similarity with the constitutional perspective advocated in the public choice tradition associated with James Buchanan and others, which I shall term Constitutional Political Economy (CPE). This is no accident. I want to argue that these two approaches share the same basic commitments and may be seen as two slightly different lines of argument that arrive at essentially the same position.

We may sketch the CPE position in the following way. Individuals act within a framework of institutions and rules. Once the rules are set, the complex interactions between individuals will determine particular outcomes. But we must also recognize that the rules and institutions are, at least to a considerable extent, chosen or capable of being modified by choice. Now, within this general structure we may inquire as to the role of the economist. Clearly, one role is the study of individual action within a particular set of rules. Indeed, such analysis must form the basic subject matter of economics. But the debate concerns the normative role of economics. Here there are two major possibilities. On the one hand the economist could operate within the institutions offering policy advice to those in positions of authority; on the other hand, the economist could take a step back to the constitutional level and advise on the choice or reform of institutions. This then is the tension between, on the one hand, the mainstream welfare economist and, on the other hand, the CPE analyst. And it mirrors the tension already discussed between the welfare economist and the Austrian.

But the CPE and the Austrian arguments are not identical in form, and it is instructive to note the differences since this throws another light onto the Austrian approach. I have emphasized the idea that the Austrian would deny the feasibility of the welfare economists project; that is, in the context of the last paragraph, she would deny the feasibility of generating meaningful advice to those in positions of authority that lives up to the claims of welfare economics. The CPE analyst, by contrast, argues that the offering of such advice — even if feasible — is pointless, since the actions of those in positions of power will not be influenced by such advice. This criticism of mainstream welfare economics is encapsulated in the comment that welfare economics mistakenly assumes that it is offering advice to a benign despot. This criticism in turn derives from a basic commitment to modeling individuals consistently, regardless of the roles they may be playing. Thus, for example, an individual does not become public spirited simply by taking public office.

We can understand this criticism of welfare economics with the aid of a simple illustration. Imagine the standard prisoners' dilemma, in which each prisoner is faced with the decision between informing and remaining silent in the absence of information on the decision of the other prisoner. Now imagine a prison advisor, well versed in game theory and with the ability to explain the situation fully to each prisoner. A moment's thought tells us that such an advisor can make no difference to the situation. Formally, this is because we typically assume that the prisoners are fully informed and fully rational, but more generally, it is because each players' action will be determined by the various structural aspects of the game — its rules and institutional framework — in conjunction with motivational and other considerations internal to the individual. Unless the advisor actually changes one or more of these factors, she can have no impact on the course of the game. Her advice for both prisoners to remain silent may be good advice (from the point of view of the prisoners) but she is wasting her breath. By contrast, we may imagine reforming the criminal justice procedure in a variety of ways that might transform the prisoners' dilemma and so affect the behavior of the prisoners and the outcome. But such reform will not simply involve giving advice.

The CPE analyst sees normative analysis operating at the level of institutions and conceives of the analysis in terms of a generalized principal agent problem. Institutions of all sorts define agency relations, and the general problem is to write institutional rules in such a way as to ensure that the incentives faced by the agents are appropriate from the perspective of the principals. This raises the question of how to conceptualize "appropriateness" from the perspective of the principals, and the approach adopted within CPE is the generally contractarian one. Institutions are to be judged by the criterion of whether they would be chosen unanimously in certain circumstances or whether any individual could reasonably object to them in those circumstances.[12]

This contractarian criterion of eligibility replaces the Austrian emphasis on feasibility and accounts for the apparent differences between the two approaches, but inspection of the content of the two lines of argument make it clear that their convergence is no accident. Each line of argument emphasizes individuality — the Austrian via the inscrutability of preference, the CPE analyst via the commitment to contractarianism; and each emphasizes uncertainty — the Austrian via the unknowability of the future, the CPE analyst via the general structure of the principal agent problem. In truth, the distinction between the feasibility-based approach taken by Austrians and the eligibility-based approach taken within CPE represents a difference of emphasis rather than basic substance; and both stand in sharp contrast with the pure desirability approach of mainstream welfare economics.

Concluding Comments

I have argued that the tension between Austrian economics and mainstream welfare economics does not derive from deep theoretical differences in either the respective theories of value or on the question of the individuation of good. Rather, the tension arises from the different treatments of individual preference and uncertainty that must form a basic ingredient of the practice of any welfare economics.

The Austrian critique of welfare economics cannot ultimately be that it is constructivist (since such a criticism is both implausible and would be fatal to much of concern to Austrians), but must be that it is too ambitious and attempts the conceptually infeasible. In turn, the emphasis on feasibility must be a central characteristic of any Austrian welfare economics, and I have argued that this implies that Austrian welfare economics should be based on the normative evaluation of institutional procedures (on the model of the Austrian analysis of the market process), rather than on the direct evaluation of detailed policy proposals. Such an Austrian welfare economics would be very similar to the normative analysis within the Constitutional Political Economy School, which arrives at a similar position by a different line of argument.

The arguments sketched here suggest that — despite the identified tensions — there is perhaps more common ground in the general area of welfare economics than might have been supposed by those who see the various schools of thought as being in basic conflict. The prospects for progress in the normative analysis of institutional structures that draw on the resources of each school are considerable.

Notes

1. See, for example, Boadway and Bruce (1984). Discussion of the ethical evaluation of alternative economic systems can be found in Hamlin (1992).
2. For an excellent discussion of this ambiguity and its dangers, see Broome (1991b).
3. This is controversial in several respects, not least because the real spirit of consumer

choice theory clearly lies in the interpretation of utility as an index of preference, so that the link between consumer theory and welfare economics is threatened.

4. See Broome (1991a).

5. See, for example, Wiseman (1989).

6. See, for example, Fabian and Simons (1986) and Chisholm (1986).

7. For a discussion of methodological and moral individualism see Hamlin and Pettit (1989).

8. This criticism from "infeasibility" is clearly distinct from, and I would argue, more fundamental than the line of criticism that objects to "the communist fiction" or "synoptic viewpoint" involved in most mainstream welfare economics. This second line of criticism argues against interpersonal aggregation and in favor of subjective conceptions of welfare, but these criticisms can be accommodated, in principle, within the SWF tradition. The SWF tradition does not logically require the adoption of an integrated framework of means and ends, even if such a framework is normally adopted in practice.

9. See, for example, Lachmann (1986).

10. For lengthier discussion of the distinction between "desirability" and "feasibility"-based approaches (and the discussion of "eligibility"-based approaches relevant to the section below entitled "Constitutionalism") see Hamlin and Pettit (1989) and Hamlin (1992).

11. Of course, the analysis is much more complex than this in practice and there are feedbacks between the various steps identified here, but the essential structure of the argument is not particularly controversial.

12. This is an example of the eligibility approach referred to in note 10 and discussed in Hamlin and Pettit (1989). A contractarian approach is contrasted with the mainstream welfare economics approach in more detail in Sugden (1989).

References

Boadway, Robin and Bruce, Neil. 1984. *Welfare Economics*. Oxford: Blackwell.

Broome, John. 1991a. *Weighing Goods*. Oxford: Blackwell.

Broome, John. 1991b. "Utility," *Economics and Philosophy* 7: 1–12.

Chisholm, Roderick. 1986. "Brentano on Preference, Desire and Intrinsic Value." In *Austrian Economics*, Grassl, W. and Smith, B. (eds.). London: Croom Helm.

Fabian, Reinhard and Simons, Peter. 1986. "The Second Austrian School of Value Theory." In *Austrian Economics*, Grassl, W. and Smith, B. (eds.). London: Croom Helm.

Hamlin, Alan. 1992. "Economic Systems." In *Encyclopedia of Ethics*, Becker, L. and Becker, C. (eds.). New York: Garland.

Hamlin, Alan and Pettit, Philip. 1989. "The Normative Analysis of the State: Some Preliminaries." In *The Good Polity*, Hamlin, A. and Pettit, P. (eds.). Oxford: Blackwell.

Lachmann, Ludwig. 1986. *The Market as an Economic Process*. Oxford: Blackwell.

Sugden, Robert. 1989. "Maximizing Social Welfare." In *The Good Polity*, Hamlin, A. and Pettit, P. (eds.). Oxford: Blackwell.

Wiseman, Jack. 1989. *Cost, Choice and Political Economy*. Aldershot: Edward Elgar.

p 193 / COMMENTARY

Austrian Prescriptive Economics

Robert Sugden

There can be no doubt that much of Austrian economics is prescriptive in character: it is concerned with recommending the institutions of the market. This is particularly true of the work of Friedrich Hayek, on which I will focus in this commentary. Despite the strong evolutionary themes in his work, despite his insistence on the limitations of human knowledge and of human reason, and despite his rejection of the concepts of social welfare and social justice as meaningless, Hayek repeatedly makes certain specific prescriptions: we are advised to maintain and strengthen market institutions and to reject the models of economic organization offered by socialism. To give just one example from *The Constitution of Liberty*: after describing his own position as liberalism, Hayek tells us that liberalism looks forward to the "improvement of institutions." And this is not just a matter of passively waiting for improvements to occur spontaneously. Liberals should seek to reverse the growth of government control over the economy: "what is most urgently needed is a thorough sweeping-away of the obstacles to free growth" (1960, 399). Many commentators have pointed to the tension between Austrian advocacy of the market and Austrian subjectivism. Is there a framework of analysis within which Austrian prescriptions can coherently be made, but which is not vulnerable to the same methodological criticisms as Austrians direct against neoclassical welfare economics? Or, as Alan Hamlin puts it, can there be an Austrian welfare economics?

I agree with Hamlin that an Austrian form of prescriptive eocnomics *is* possible — although I wonder if it should be called *welfare* economics. I will argue that in Hayek's work we can find the outlines of a system of prescriptive economics, within which he can coherently generate recommendations. However, I must concede straight away that there are some strands in Hayek's thinking which, if pursued to their logical conclusions, might undermine this system.

The concept of spontaneous order is central to Hayek's work. Spontaneous orders emerge from the workings of general rules or principles in an environment of unpredictable contingencies. The formation of crystals, and the evolution of biological organisms, are example of spontaneous order in the natural world. We may be able to understand the general principles at work in these processes but we can never know all the circumstances bearing on a particular case; so "our knowledge will be restricted to the general character of the order which will form itself" (1973, 41). In Hayek's early work, the market is seen as a system of rules *within which* a spontaneous order forms. Although we cannot predict the detailed workings of the market system, we can understand how its rules work, and in this way say something about the general properties of its outcomes. Thus, we can make general comparisons between the likely outcomes of market and centrally planned economies (Hayek, 1948). This leaves room for normative economics.

Hayek also argues that the market is the undesigned result of a process of evolution: it is a method of economic organization on which man "happened to stumble" (1948, 88−89). Merely to say this is not to rule out the possibility of normative appraisal. There is a sense in which socialism is also a method of economic organization on which the human race has stumbled. Give that these systems exist, we may hope to understand the rules by which they operate and compare the general properties of the orders they tend to generate. But a difficulty arises when, in Hayek's later work, he develops the idea that the rules of the market are themselves *part of* a spontaneous order, within which the rules governing human societies evolve by a process of group selection.

For Hayek, the individual steps by which a spontaneous order forms itself are not susceptible to normative appraisal, since they depend on particular circumstances which are unknowable. For this reason, we cannot hope to fully understand individual events within a market system:

A complex civilization like ours is necessarily based on the individual adjusting himself to changes whose cause and nature he cannot understand: why he should have more or less, why he should have to move to another occupation, why some things he wants should become more difficult to get than others, will always be connected with such a multitude of circumstances that no single mind will be able to grasp them .... (1944, 151)

Since we cannot understand why such events occur, or know how they affect different individuals, it is pointless to ask whether their effects are good or bad. This is why Hayek regards the concept of social justice as "strictly empty and meaningless" within a free society (1976, 68). But if the rules of the market are understood, not as defining a process within which a spontaneous order is formed, but as steps in the formation of some wider order, then they too may be beyond normative appraisal. Thus, in one of his later works, Hayek can argue that social organization depends on our following rules "whose purpose . . . we often do not know and of whose very existence we are often unaware"; man does not "know why he ought to observe the rules which he does observe, [nor] is even capable of stating all these rules in words" (1973, 11). If we were to say this of the rules of the market, we would seem to have no basis for recommending them. In what follows, I will take the approach of the early rather than the late Hayek.

If there is to be a Hayekian prescriptive economics, it must be compatible with Hayek's consistent rejection of the idea that society has goals. A free and progressive society, he argues, cannot be directed by a common purpose (e.g., 1976, 109–111). Thus, Hayek rejects the kind of welfare economics that starts from a conception of the social good. For example, he rejects utilitarianism because of its attempt to find a "measurable common attribute" of people's separate ends. He sees this as a kind of anthropomorphism, in which a society of distinct individuals is treated as if it were a single person (1976, 17–23).

Hamlin puts this point clearly when he says that Austrians see the concept of good as "essentially individuated": we can speak of each person's good, as he or she perceives it, but we cannot meaningfully speak of the collective good of a group of people. However, Hamlin perhaps underplays the significance of this point of difference between Austrian and neoclassical approaches to normative economics. As Hamlin says, the concept of a social welfare function is central to mainstream normative economics. A social welfare function is a specification of a set of social ends, or of judgements about the overall good of society. To think that normative economics can be written in terms of properties of a social welfare function is to presuppose that normative economics should be about the welfare of society—that normative economics should be coextensive with welfare economics. The welfare economist's role, on the conventional account, is to take a synoptic view of society—to look on it from some external and neutral position—and make judgements about its overall good. The implication is that the appropriate way to recommend any policy or process is to show that it will tend to increase the overall good of society. This is a view that Hayek rejects.

Hayek's objection to utilitarianism is similar to John Rawls's (1971, 27): it does not take seriously the distinction between persons. Rawls presents the contractarian approach as a way of taking this distinction seriously. In the contractarian approach, recommendations are addressed separately to individuals, the object being to show that a particular policy or process will tend to promote each person's interests, as he or she perceives them (see Sugden, 1989). Hamlin sees the contractarian approach as offering the most promising prospects for an Austrian form of prescriptive economics. I agree; and I suggest that Hayek's prescriptions are often contractarian in structure.

Consider three quotations from Hayek, in which he argues for the market order and for the liberties on which it rests:

> ... while agreement is not possible on most of the particular ends which will not be known except to those who pursue them (and would be even less possible if the ultimate effects of the decision on particular interests were known), agreement on means can to a great extent be achieved precisely because it is not known which particular ends they will serve. ... What makes agreement and peace in [a free] society possible is that the individuals are not required to agree on ends but only on means which are capable of serving a great variety of purposes and which each hopes will assist him in the pursuit of his own purposes. (1976, 3)

> It was the discovery that an order definable only by certain abstract character- istics would assist in the pursuit of a great multiplicity of different ends which persuaded people pursuing wholly different ends to agree on certain multi- purpose instruments which were likely to assist everybody. Such agreement became possible not only in spite of but also because of the fact that the particular results it would produce could not be foreseen. It is only because we cannot predict the actual result of the adaptation of a particular rule, that we can assume it to increase everyone's chances equally. (1976, 4)

> A policy making use of the spontaneously ordering forces therefore cannot aim at a known maximum of particular results, but must aim at increasing, for any person picked out at random, the prospects that the overall effect of all changes required by that order will be to increase his chances of attaining his ends. ... The aim will have to be an order which will increase everybody's chances as much as possible — not at every moment, but only "on the whole" and in the long run. (1976, 114–115)

In these passages, Hayek is recommending the market as a procedure which maximizes every individual's long-run expectation of benefit. And each person's benefit is being understood in terms of his own perception of his interests. Thus, the rules of the market are rules on which everyone could agree, with each person evaluating alternative sets of rules in terms of his own aims. *Whatever your aims*, Hayek is saying to each of us, you can expect to be better able to achieve them in a market economy than under any other known system of economic organization. Whether this claim is true or false, it does not rely on any overarching conception of the social good. Hayek's argument here is contractarian.

In this respect, as Hamlin points out, there is a close similarity with the contractarian arguments of James Buchanan and the Virginia School of constitutional political economy. However, there is also an important difference. The Virginia School has been much less concerned with methodological questions than has Hayek and has tended to use the theoretical tools of neoclassical economics. The pathbreaking nature of such works as Buchanan and Tullock's *Calculus of Consent* (1962) lies in the application of conventional economic modes of reasoning to constitutional issues. In contrast, Hayek (1948) is the author of powerful and fundamental critiques of neoclassical equilibrium analysis. We may ask what kind of analysis Hayek would expect us to use to establish the truth of such claims as that the market system maximizes the long-run expectation of each individual. Is there a theoretical framework within which such claims can be formulated and evaluated, which is not subject to the same objections as neoclassical equilibrium analysis?

I suggest that such a framework is possible, and that we need not make a radical break with conventional forms of economic analysis. As a starting point, it is useful to consider what neoclassical economics can say about the market system. Hamlin's distinction between mainstream welfare economics, which evaluates "policy actions," and constitutional political economy, which evaluates "institutional structures and procedures", seems too sharp. One of the main results of mainstream welfare economics — indeed, it is often called the First Fundamental Theorem of Welfare Economics — is that, in general equilibrium, a perfectly competitive market will produce a Pareto-efficient allocation of resources. This is a theorem about the results that would be generated by a particular institutional structure or procedure: the competitive market.

Whatever its limitations (about which more will be said later), this is a theorem about spontaneous order. Imagine an exchange economy in which a finite number of homogeneous goods are traded by auction. Prices are adjusted by an auctioneer following the Walrasian *tâtonnement* process. Each trader knows his own preferences and knows the prices that are being called out by the auctioneer. The auctioneer knows the total quantities of each good demanded and supplied at each list of prices that she calls out. Given certain stability assumptions, it can be proved that such an economy would reach a Pareto-efficient equilibrium. The defining characteristic of Pareto efficiency in an exchange economy is that, for each pair of goods, marginal rates of substitution are equal for all individuals. In this model, each trader's preferences are known only to him. (Notice that they are not known to the auctioneer.) Within its own restricted framework, then, the Walrasian model *does* solve what for Hayek is the fundamental problem of economics: "how the spontaneous interaction of a number of people, each possessing only bits of knowledge, brings about a state of affairs ... which could be brought about by deliberate action only by somebody who possessed the combined knowledge of all those individuals" (Hayek, 1948, 51).

The Walrasian model is usually set out in terms of individuals with "given" preferences. Thus, there is a sense in which *the economist who sets up the model* pretends to know every individual's preferences. Is this a case of "synoptic delusion," of "the fiction that all the relevant facts are known to one mind" (Hayek, 1973, 14)? I think not. The economist assumes only that each individual's preferences satisfy certain very general properties (such as transitivity and convexity). The theorem then shows that *for any given preferences* (satisfying these general properties), the *tâtonnement* process will lead to a Pareto-efficient outcome. The theoretical move of "taking preferences as given" is merely a step in proving a theorem that applies to any set of preferences. The First Fundamental Theorem of Welfare Economics is an example of the kind of knowledge we can have about the general character of a spontaneous order, without having the knowledge of specific circumstances that would allow us to predict the details of the order that will form in any particular case.

All this can be said without taking any view about how much the Walrasian model tells us about the division of knowledge in real economic systems. Hayek argues that it tells us very little and directs our attention away from the forces which actually drive market economies. He points out that neoclassical economics has little to say about the process by which equilibrium is or is not reached. (The *tâtonnement* process might work in markets where well-defined, homogeneous commodities are traded. Indeed, we can observe auctions that work very much like the Walrasian model. But this process is not remotely satisfactory as a model of how a complex market economy works.) Equilibrium, for Hayek, is a state in which it is possible for each person to carry out his plans without any of his expectations about other people's actions being falsified. In this sense, equilibrium is equivalent to correct foresight. Thus, if there is a tendency for an economy to move towards equilibrium, this tendency must be understood as a process in which individuals acquire new knowledge.

Neoclassical equilibrium analysis (at least as practiced in the 1930s) does not explain how knowledge is acquired (1948, 41–48). Hayek sees profit, and the process of profit seeking, as "the main equilibrating force" in markets. That is why market socialism, which tries to have market equilibrium while dispensing with the profit motive, will not work (1948, especially 170).

We may agree with Hayek about all of this, and still see the Walrasian model as an example of how to theorize about spontaneous order. The basic strategy is to make very general assumptions about the properties of the system being analyzed, leaving open a wide range of particular circumstances which can affect the outcome. Then one shows that, for any given specification of those particular circumstances, the outcome has certain general properties. This may require the theorist to set up her model *as if* she knew the particular circumstances, but this is a legitimate form of reasoning and not a case of synoptic delusion.

For example, consider the following claim by Hayek:

> Liberty is essential to leave room for the unforeseeable and the unpredictable; we want it because we have learned to expect from it the opportunity of realizing many of our aims. It is because every individual knows so little and, in particular, because we rarely know which of us knows best that we trust the independent and competitive efforts of many to induce the emergence of what we shall want when we see it. (1960, 29)

The idea seems to be that there is a body of potential knowledge, as yet undiscovered. Although we cannot describe this potential knowledge in any detail (if we could, it would have been discovered already), we know enough about its general properties to be able to say that some pieces of this body of knowledge would be valuable to some individuals, "value" being understood in terms of each person's own aims. Hayek is advocating a process in which each individual is free to search for new knowledge, and has some property right in what she discovers (so that each person has an incentive to discover what is of value to others). His claim, I take it, is that this process will give each individual the best long-run expectation of achieving her aims — whatever those aims may be.

Analogously with Walrasian theory, we might set up a model based on general assumptions about individuals' preferences and about the nature of the as-yet-undiscovered potential knowledge. Then we might be able to draw general conclusions about the results of different search procedures — conclusions that would be true for any given detailed specification of potential knowledge. In taking this specification as given, the theorist would be setting up her model as if she knew what, by the very nature of the problem, cannot be known. But if the results of the analysis can be shown to be true for any such specification, this method is legitimate.

This commentary has been written to add further support to Hamlin's argument that there is room for an Austrian form of prescriptive economics. If this branch of economics is to be compatible with Hayek's early work, it must be contractarian in character, seeking to recommend general rules which, over the long run, can be expected to work to everyone's advantage. In addition, it must give more emphasis than most welfare economics has done to the limitations of human knowledge. But, like Hamlin, I see no need for a wholesale rejection of the methods currently used in mainstream economics.

Acknowledgments

This commentary was written as part of the Foundations of Rational Choice Theory project, which is supported by the Economic and Social Research Council of the United Kingdom (award number R 000 23 2269). It has benefited from discussions that I have had with Chris Starmer about Austrian Economics.

References

Buchanan, James M. and Tullock, Gordon. 1962. *The Calculus of Consent*. Ann Arbor: University of Michigan Press.

Hayek, Friedrich A. 1944. *The Road to Serfdom*. London: Routledge and Kegan Paul.

———. 1948. *Individualism and Economic Order*. Chicago: University of Chicago Press.

———. 1960. *The Constitution of Liberty*. London: Routledge and Kegan Paul.

———. 1973. *Law, Legislation and Liberty*, vol. 1, "Rules and Order." Chicago: University of Chicago Press.

———. 1976. *Law, Legislation and Liberty*, vol. 2, "The Mirage of Social Justice." Chicago: University of Chicago Press.

Rawls, John. 1971. *A Theory of Justice*. Cambridge, Mass.: Harvard University Press.

Sugden, Robert. 1989. "Maximizing Social Welfare: Is it the Government's Business?" In *The Good Polity*, Hamlin, A. and Pettit, P. (eds.). Oxford: Blackwell.

8 TURNING AUSTRIAN ECONOMICS INTO AN EVOLUTIONARY THEORY

Ulrich Witt

Introduction

Although two of the original protagonists of evolutionary thinking in economics — Schumpeter and Hayek — were born in Austria and educated in Vienna, Austrian economics and the evolutionary approach are usually considered to be two distinct and independent developments. This distinction has something to it and the present chapter will give some hints as to why. However, the two schools also have much in common. It seems worthwhile, therefore, to examine whether matching the two lines of thought could yield a promising research strategy. An exploration of this question is complicated, unfortunately, by the fact that within the Austrian school there is considerable disagreement about various issues (see, Shand, 1981). The same is true with respect to the evolutionary approach that still suffers from a significant lack of coherence (see Witt, 1992a). Before the possible gains from matching ideas from the two camps can be assessed, a thorough review of similarities and differences between, and shortcomings and strengths of, several positions in both schools seems necessary.

The chapter proceeds as follows. Section two briefly summarizes core notions of the two schools and seeks to discover the relationships that exist between them. Core notions of the Austrians, it will be argued, are the subjectivist creed and the predominant interest in the phenomena of process and change in the economy. The evolutionary approach shares the latter, while the problem of subjectivism has until now been grossly

215

ignored. As explained in section three, this attitude, which can be traced back to Schumpeter (1912/1934), is unfortunate. It prevents the evolutionary approach from fully understanding the implications of a crucial feature of evolution, namely, the emergence of novelty. In order to come to grips with novelty, subjectivism must, on the other hand, not be associated with von Mises' (1949) apriorism. Section four shows that apriorism conflicts with basic research interests of the evolutionary approach.

Section five, therefore, advocates a fallibilist methodology that may also help to resolve the epistemological intricacies involved in dealing with novelty. Such a methodology has been worked out by Hayek (1967a). Yet, surprisingly, at the core of his later work — his theory of cultural evolution (Hayek, 1979, epilogue; 1988) briefly reviewed in the section entitled "Hayekian Evolution — a Denial of Individualism?" — the individual and its subjectivity does not seem to play a role anymore. The theory relies on quasi-biological group selection criteria. As explained in section seven, population features — as the one implied in Hayek's criterion — are indeed crucial elements of evolutionary theories. They are not, in principle, incompatible with an individualistic methodology but necessitate some qualifications. Having reached this point, evolutionary theorizing is suggested in the conclusions in section eight as a promising way of developing Austrian economics further.

How Core Notions of the Two Schools Relate

Economic decision makers pursue their aims on the basis of their current views of ends-means relationships. This empirically almost trivial hypothesis can easily be confirmed by introspection. Simple as the hypothesis is, it provides a foundation for subjectivism, a core notion of Austrian economics, once it is recognized that — unlike the neoclassical fiction of uniform, perfect information — the views that the agents hold, and the information they have, may differ. Their understanding of ends-means relationships may, as a result of ignorance and subjective interpretation, be incomplete, biased, and even illusory, in an idiosyncratic way. Accordingly, not only tastes and preferences represent a subjective domain, as generally accepted in economics, but also the current state of perceptions, knowledge, and expectations.[1] All this is not directly observable and may (sometimes) be rather volatile. As economic activities depend on the hidden, inner state of mind, the explanation and prediction of the former requires hypotheses about the latter.

There is a second core notion, which seems generally accepted in

Austrian economics, the idea that individual economic activities may be in — and must potentially be explained as emerging from — permanent flux.[2] It is closely related to, or may even be seen as, an implication of the first core notion, because it is for the imperfections and insufficiencies of the subjective state of knowledge that there is room for discovering and realizing improvements. The agents learn and work out superior possibilities for acting and accordingly readjust their plans. As a consequence, the economy changes continually and, thus, has to be portrayed in terms of a theory of process rather than static theory.

Process and change also represent core notions in the evolutionary approach to economics where evolution has to be understood as more than just dynamics. Evolution is a process in which a system under consideration transforms itself over time. Thus, focus is on endogenously caused change as opposed to change induced by external forces. To use Schumpeter's formulation, the task is to explain "the possibility of development intrinsically generated from within itself.".[3] Given this task, it is natural to ask what counts as the reason for and as the ultimate source of endogenously created change. As a simple consideration shows, the ultimate source of endogenous change is the emergence of novelty. Unless novelty is continually created, change would sooner or later come to an end. The adaptive efforts of the agents would converge simultaneously to an equilibrium state in which everything has been learned and all possible advantageous readjustments have been exploited.[4]

Once novelty has been created somewhere in the economy, the question arises whether and how this novelty diffuses through the economy. As it diffuses, novelty potentially induces adaptive efforts at a growing number of points in the economy and, perhaps, has a self-amplifying effect. The evolutionary approach can therefore be characterized as an attempt to explain the continuing change in, and the transformation of, the economy as a process governed by regularities in the emergence and dissemination of novelty (Witt, 1992b). What seems important here is that a continually ongoing creation of novelty by economic agents does not only explain why change may, for endogenous reasons, never come to an end, it also provides a powerful argument for a subjectivist position in economics (see Witt, 1989a). This connection has already been suggested by Shackle (1959; 1972, ch. 37; 1983) in his work on the imaginative element in decision making and on kaleidic economics.

In the realm of economics, new information emerges from the creative activity of the individual human mind. This information obtains a specific meaning, as new private knowledge, by the particular interpretative framework that has grown out of the individual's experience. Initially, novelty is therefore necessarily subjective. It my be disseminated in communication processes and may then be shared, as a common view, by other agents. Nonetheless, the information sets of the agents in the economy never do completely converge as long as creative activities go on: first, because interpersonal communication is time-consuming, disseminates new information selectively (often even discriminatingly), and is certainly not unambiguous; second, because new information may be interpreted in differing ways and may thus mean different things to different people.

Schumpeterian Evolution—the Denial of Subjectivism

In the previous section the emergence of novelty has been identified as a crucial feature of evolutionary theories. To the extent which novelty, as in the domain of economic theory, originates from the human mind, it has been argued that it is inherently subjective. This seems to suggest a subjectivist perspective in evolutionary economics. However, such a perspective is absent and the subjectivism problem is grossly ignored, notably in the Schumpeterian line of evolutionary economics. This seems remarkable in view of the fact that Schumpeter had Böhm-Bawerk and Wieser among his teachers. It is no secret, of course, that Schumpeter wanted to achieve a standing of his own and thus tended to distance himself from standard Austrian positions from the very beginning (cf. Lachmann, 1982, 34; Boehm, 1987). Thus, the approach he adopted in his first major work, his habilitation thesis (Schumpeter, 1908), was consciously heterodox. The splendid, albeit rather eclectic, discussions of contemporary theoretical problems synthesizes themes, thoughts, and tools from various schools in economics—chiefly, however, ideas from the neoclassical school as represented by Pareto.

In writing his thesis, in particular in the passages where he deals with the restoration of equilibrium after exogenous changes (ibid., part IV), Schumpeter must have noticed that a crucial feature of the historical economic record was missing in the predominant economic theories of his time. There was no explanation for the driving forces of economic change. He sat down to develop the missing—evolutionary—theory in Schumpeter (1910) and (1912/1934). As is well known, this theory portrays economic evolution as a perennial gale of creative restructuring and expansion that is driven by disruptive, innovative activities of pioneering entrepreneurs. The original theory is inspired especially by the attempt to make sense of the cyclical pattern of "prosperity and depression" (Schumpeter, 1910).[5] Nonetheless, Schumpeter takes pains in attempting to explain the development in terms of a self-transformation process, the driving element of which is an innovating "entrepreneur-hero." In no instance, however, does Schumpeter confront the reader with a consideration of the subjectivism problem or with any subjectivist reservation.[6]

The "trick" by which Schumpeter evades such considerations is simple. He contrasts the notion of innovation, "the carrying out of new combinations," which he discusses at length, with the notion of invention. On the basis of this distinction the emergence of novelty can be referred to the domain of inventions. But inventions, Schumpeter postulates, are trivially and abundantly available and known to all sort of people. Their coming into being is declared irrelevant for economic analysis. All that matters in his theory is the pioneering initiative, the "doing it," the carrying out of what is already available but which no one has yet ventured to realize. Consequently, Schumpeter elaborates upon the psychology of his "entrepreneur-hero." He talks about what nowadays is labeled as *achievement motivation* and about the skills needed to attract and command resources into the first ventures. Once these have been performed, an entire wave of imitative enterprises is supposed to follow suit — a metaphor clearly indicating that Schumpeter's theory is all about the dissemination of novelty in the market and the economy as a whole.

The flaw in the construction that was intended to treat the dissemination aspects without going into the problems involved in the emergence of novelty, is easy to identify. The dichotomy of invention and innovation builds on the fiction that the meaning and the relevant implications of new information, once invented or discovered, are instantaneously, exhaustively, and unambiguously revealed to everybody. What actually happens, however, is quite different. First, lack of experience with a newly invented item has to be compensated by imagining what might be attainable with the invention. One and the same invention can mean different things to different people, depending on their subjective, speculative assessments of the implications of the invention. What else but their visionary capacity makes entrepreneurs discern a venture where others see nothing? It is evident that this implies an idiosyncratic, subjective, element in perceptions or expectations. Second, because of lack of experience, the process of innovating is experimental by nature. This means that it is a sequential, and usually highly subjective, revelation process into which further discoveries can intervene so that inventive and innovative activities actually interact recursively. Even if Schumpeter's exclusive focus on entrepreneurial innovations were acceptable, novelty — together with its subjectivist implications — would still be encountered in the diffusion process and would thus need to be taken into account.

It is important to note these flaws because the construction with which Schumpeter tried to circumvent both the problem of emergence of novelty and the related problem of subjective action knowledge has later proved to be the vantage point for neoclassical adaptations of his theory of innovation. Just two decades after the first publication of his evolutionary theory, Schumpeter himself started reinterpreting it, for example, in Schumpeter (1935), probably as a result of the intellectual influences he experienced after moving to Harvard (see Stolper, 1979). Today there is a vast neoclassical literature on industry innovation and R&D. Although it usually relates itself to Schumpeter it has, by completely ignoring the question of how novelty emerges, abandoned even the last traces of his evolutionary elements.[7]

Even if he does not create the new information himself, the "entrepreneur-hero" in Schumpeter's original outline at least had to decide which new information to take up in the attempt to make his way forward. Furthermore, there was room for individuality with respect to willpower and achievement motivation. By contrast, "innovative" activities in the neoclassical literature become competitive races in which everyone chases in the same way after the same success along the same well-known tracks. Correspondingly, "innovation" turns into a particular kind of investment problem under probabilistic perfect information. The problem is portrayed as one of investing in the development of a new product or process where, entirely at odds with the subjective and insecure nature of the tentative knowledge actually involved in pursuing novel ventures, all properties of the new items and even the revenues to be earned are supposed to be common knowledge. What motivates these assumptions is, of course, the attempt to meet the prerequisites for applying neoclassical constrained maximization calculus and equilibrium analysis.

In opposition to such an attempt, increasing efforts have been under-taken to reconstruct, on the basis of loose analogies to natural selection in biology, a theory of Schumpeterian evolution without subscribing to the optimization hypothesis and expectational equilibrium (Winter, 1964; Nelson and Winter, 1982; Day, 1987; Dosi et al., 1988). These contributions provide important new insights into how novelty disseminates (see Witt, 1991). However, the source from which, over and again, new diffusion processes spring — the emergence of novelty — is, here too, left unexplored. As a consequence, the problems resulting from the subjectivity of new knowledge are ignored here as they have been in Schumpeter (1912/34).

What Kind of Subjectivism?

The subjectivism problem, it has been argued above, is at the core of Austrian economics. The evolutionary approach, too, must come to terms with it, if the emergence of novelty is not neglected altogether as in the Schumpeterian tradition. However, the consequences to be drawn from the fact that individual action hinges upon subjective knowledge which, if at all, is only indirectly and partially accessible to the outside observer may differ. The more recent discussion, in particular in the Austro-American school, has been strongly influenced by von Mises' aprioristic methodology, a position difficult to reconcile with the evolutionary approach.[8]

As is well known, von Mises (1949, ch. 2) tries to solve the problem by defining economics as a praxeological science. "Praxeology" is a label for the logic of hypothetical associations of ends and means by which, according to the maxim of "rationality," the most appropriate means is to be derived for the chosen ends. As a mere logical operation, praxeology produces only analytical judgements which, as von Mises rightly points out, cannot be subjected to empirical evaluation. Nonetheless, he claims "Praxeology conveys exact and precise knowledge of real things (namely of action as it appears in life and history, U.W.)" [ibid., 39]. Mises wants to achieve this knowledge not by adding empirical hypotheses, but by deriving from pure ratiocination what he calls the "essence" of an action.[9] How this can work is not clear. In order for the asserted empirical judgement to be feasible to (extended) praxeology, two things would actually have to be added: first, an empirical hypothesis about which ends and means an individual perceives; and second, the — empirical — conjecture that individuals decide in a logically consistent way. If economics were a (faultless) logic of hypothetical ends-means relationships, as defined by von Mises, the second query would be inappropriate. Indeed, von Mises (1949, ch.1) explicitly refers the explanation of behavior deviating from full logical consistency to the domain of psychology.

With this definition of economics as a prerequisite, Mises' solution to the subjectivism problem is almost self-defeating. The fact that decision anomalies have turned out in recent research to be pervasive (see Meyer, 1986) would render economic behavior largely an object of psychology. Even worse, the dynamics of purposive behavior, learning, and creativity can hardly be put in terms of a logic of hypothetical ends-means relationships, a point already made by Lachmann (1951). These aspects, too, would have to be referred to psychology. The narrow definition of the realm of economics, which corresponds to von Mises' aprioristic approach, thus conflicts with basic research interests of the evolutionary approach. Methodological apriorism cannot be expected to provide insights as to how novelty emerges and disseminates in the economy.[10]

A different attitude towards the subjectivism problem has been suggested by Hayek (1952a) in his fallibilistic approach. This attitude is much closer to the empirical orientation prevailing in most of the contributions to evolutionary economics, notably in Schumpeter's work and the Schumpeterian tradition, except that the latter ignores the subjectivism problem. Since one can argue about what other individuals perceive, understand, and conclude, it must be possible to pose empirical conjectures about the subjective state of mind of some individual(s). These conjectures are, in principle, falsifiable, even though they can, at best, be tested indirectly by implications which should be independently observable if the conjectures are correct. Introspection, as well as the (fallibilistic) methodology of *Verstehen*, that is, an attempt to find intelligible elements in observed action, may play a role in deriving such hypotheses (Hayek, 1967b).

In line with this general orientation, Hayek (1952b) develops an empirical theory on how the human mind organizes incoming information. Note that putting forth questions like these requires discarding both aprioristic methodology *and* Mises' restrictive definition of economics. It does not necessarily mean, however, uncritically mimicking the methodology of the empirical sciences, especially physics. In fact, Hayek (1967a) takes pains to draw attention to, and elaborate on, the particular conditions that a fallibilist position meets in the life sciences and social sciences.

While physics faces relatively simple phenomena, economics (for instance) is confronted — not least because of the subjective character of the data — with complex phenomena. Complexity does not allow for all information necessary to completely specify and control the antecedence conditions of the theories to be obtained. Because of the rough and usually incomplete approximation of the preconditions, the explanations or predictions derived this way can only cover certain general features and may be compatible with a great number of circumstances. Such "explanations of the principle" and "pattern predictions" (Hayek, 1967a) reduce the possibilities of falsifying the underlying theory. However, as long as the theory still rules out something, it is testable and thus fallible. Hayek's theory of cultural evolution, to be discussed below, provides an example of such a theory.

How to Deal with Novelty

According to the considerations so far, the Schumpeterian variant of evolutionary economics is (because of its lack of recognition of the role of novelty) as irreconcilable with the subjectivist tenet as Misesian praxeology is (because of its narrow, aprioristic methodology) with the evolutionary approach. A different theory is thus needed as a basis of evolutionary economics, ideally one that discerns both the emergence of novelty and its dissemination as relevant objects of inquiry. The theory should recognize the subjectivism problem, yet be based on a fallibilistic methodology. In fact, as will be explained now, such a methodological orientation is also needed in order to come to grips with the amorphous nature of novelty that poses an intricate problem for evolutionary theories. Although the emergence and dissemination of novelty jointly constitute the evolutionary process, there is a fundamental epistemological difference between the two, and the problems involved here sometimes motivate scientific treatments to neglect the emergence aspects.

The problems can best be approached by noting, first, that novelty may mean different things in the context of emergence on the one hand and in the dissemination context on the other. By definition, the very concept of novelty rules out positive foreknowledge of its informational content. Yet, two cases can be distinguished in terms of who is unable to anticipate the meaning of novelty. Nonanticipatability may be confined to the individual agent who is confronted with something that (s)he does not yet know, but which other agents may very well be familiar with. This may be called the case of "subjective novelty." It is the typical, almost trivial, prevailing case where novelty diffuses in markets or the economy as a whole. New businessmen or consumers continue to "discover" for themselves what others may already be used to.

The characteristic of this case is that the scientific observer can reasonably be assumed to have the same status as those individuals already acquainted with the new item. He can use the existing knowledge to develop and test, according to scientific standards, empirical conjectures about the reactions of those individuals exposed to the new item for the first time (cf. Witt, 1989a). Since the subjective meaning of the new item may differ for each single adopter (or nonadopter) — and, hence, the individual reaction hinges upon the subjective state of mind, the scientific observer is confronted here with the subjectivism problem as explained in the previous section. Thus, within the context of disseminating novelty, evolutionary theory faces no particular new epistemological or methodological problems as long as the diffusion process can, indeed, be explained as a sequence of independent individual adoption or nonadoption decisions (the discussion of the slightly more complicated case where the independency assumption is not valid being deferred to section seven).

The situation changes, however, once the context of emergence is entered. This may happen even within an ongoing diffusion process, if the diffusing item "mutates" significantly in consecutive adoptions. In that case, nonanticipatability is no longer confined only to the individual adopter/nonadopter. The informational content of what newly emerges is unknown in general and thus unknown also to the scientific observer. To distinguish this situation one may thus speak of "objective novelty" here. As a consequence, the methodological strategy developed for explaining what happens in the dissemination context no longer works: hypotheses and predictions contingent on specific knowledge about the informational content of novelty are no longer feasible. It is here that the notions of "explanation of the principle" and "pattern prediction," as developed by Hayek in his fallibilistic methodology, become relevant once more.[11] They suggest the following strategy.

One may easily speculate about the information novelty might reveal. The number of conceivable variants is only constrained by the limitations of imagination, but not all of them will appear equally plausible, given the existing scientific knowledge. Thus, it seems straightforward to develop hypotheses that predict that certain variants of information *not* occur. These "there-will-be-no-such-thing-like" hypotheses clearly have empirical content in the sense that they can be tested and, in principle, be falsified. This means that even though "objective novelty" cannot be positively anticipated, evolutionary theory is capable, in principle, of developing hypotheses which impose limitations on what can be expected to emerge and, presumably, on *how* novelty emerges.

Such hypotheses may be used for explanatory and for predictive purposes. In view of the unlimited number of conceivable realizations not excluded by the hypotheses, the predictive power and the explanatory value of such hypotheses will, of course, be rather weak. It will be confined to elucidating the principles governing the emergence of novelty. Detailed prevision — anything that goes beyond mere "pattern predictions" — cannot be expected. In the case of novelty that is created by the human mind, (the underlying processes seem to be extremely complex) these principles may be even less telling than the principles governing the production of genetic novelty.[12] But, as long as the underlying hypotheses still exclude something they can help to gain insights that would otherwise not be feasible.

Hayekian Evolution — a Denial of Individualism?

While Schumpeterian evolution deals with novelty diffusing, in the form of innovations, through the given institutional framework of the economy,

Hayek goes beyond this to focus on the evolution of the institutional framework itself.[13] The competitive societal evolution on which his theory centers is an instance of "complex phenomena." Accordingly, what Hayek aims for is not to reconstruct or foretell any specific course of events, but an "explanation of the principle" or a "prediction of the pattern" of the evolution of rules of conduct in society and the economy. On a closer look it turns out that the explanations he seeks to give are less concerned with the emergence of new rules than with the various aspects of their competitive dissemination.

Three levels of evolution are distinguished in Hayek (1971; 1979, epilogue): genetic evolution; evolution of rational thought; and cultural evolution, as it operates "between instinct and reason" (Hayek, 1988, ch. 1), that is, between the former two levels. Hayek's major interests lie in cultural evolution. Culture, he submits, "is neither natural nor artificial, neither genetically transmitted nor rationally designed. It is a tradition of learned rules of conduct which have never been 'invented' and whose functions the acting individuals usually do not understand" (Hayek, 1979, 155). Which rules come into play, and how — the context of the emergence of novelty here in the form of new rules — is to Hayek a question of historical accident to which he does not pay much attention. The question his theory is concerned with is: Which of the rules survive? To Hayek, the answer is determined by the outcome of a largely unplanned and not consciously controlled process of selective transmission and replication — a theory that clearly belongs to what has been called above the dissemination context.

In a nutshell, selective cultural transmission is conceived of working as follows. Those groups that succeed in developing and passing on rules better suited to governing their social interactions are supposed to grow and feed a larger number of people. Their relative superiority may enable such groups to conquer and/or absorb less well equipped competing groups and thus, unintentionally, propagate the superior sets of rules. A growing population requires specialization and division of labor that, in turn, presuppose that the spontaneous order governing impersonal interactions is increasingly extended. The rules become ever more differentiated, abstract, and difficult to understand. Over thousands of years, during which human civilization grew, an "extended order" has thus spontaneously evolved. It is assumed to embody superindividual intelligence incorporated into the impersonal rules that have been accumulated during the endless cultural transmission and selection process. The most important achievements according to Hayek (1988, ch. 3) are trade and the emergence of a system of markets.

Thus, Hayek's theory underlies the "twin ideas of spontaneous order and evolution." The backbone of the former is a system of impersonal rules of conduct (cf. Vanberg (1989) for a concise scheme). The backbone of the latter is differential selection of groups with different rules. Taken together, this implies that natural selection not only "chooses" between competing species, but also between competing human subpopulations as the unit to which acquired cultural norms and rules — more or less suited to coordinate social interactions efficiently — are fixed. The group selection hypothesis sounds familiar from sociobiology. Indeed, Hayek (1979, epilogue) refers to, among others, Huxley (1943), Waddington (1960), Dobszhansky (1962) and Campbell (1965) who are inspired by Darwinian concepts of evolution. Hayek (1967c) rightly points out that the very idea of evolution is older than Darwin's theory.[14] Still, his group selection hypothesis comes very close to the theory of natural selection with only two exceptions. First, the traits on which variation and selective replication operate are not genetic but cultural. Second, acquired properties can, therefore, be transmitted directly in a Lamarckian fashion, thus speeding up evolution significantly compared to variation and selection operating only on genetic codes.[15]

The second element in Hayek's theory, the idea of a spontaneous order in social and economic interactions, is to him, in the last resort, the outcome of the cultural transmission and selection processes that generate, and still continue to form, the impersonal rules of conduct. Originally, however, the idea goes back to the Scottish moral philosophers David Hume, Adam Smith, Adam Ferguson, and their forerunner, Bernard Mandeville, who first conceived of the division of labor and a system of multilateral, anonymous markets as a spontaneous order. Spontaneous here refers to something not deliberately planned or only conceived of. Spontaneous order is understood as an unintended side effect of individual actions that, despite their possibly, purely self-seeking motives, work out to the mutual advantage of all. A notion of the process through which spontaneous order comes into being is not provided in the Scottish moral philosophy.

The idea of spontaneously emerging institutions has, in a similar vein (but apparently independently) been advocated by Carl Menger (1883/ 1963) in considerations of his "causal-genetic" method of analysis. Menger submits that regularities in social interactions may be constituted by the individual choices of all participants without anybody having intended or even understood this effect. All individual actions, taken together, spontaneously establish mutually coordinated behavior. Through habit formation, this comes to be taken for granted. Manifest institutional regularities emerge in this way. Already at the rather primitive societal level of self-sufficiency and a household economy one can, for example, observe regularities such as language and common law (examples Hayek often refers to). Menger's conjecture does not encompass, of course, a clear notion of the actual process by which the institutions mentioned emerge.

By synthesizing the spontaneous order conjecture and the theory of the selective cultural transmission (or rule dissemination) process, Hayek achieves an explanation of the principle of cultural evolution that leads to spontaneous order. None of the single components of the synthesis, taken by themselves, is able to provide such an explanation. This is an important achievement, although various facets of the theory still need careful reconstruction, extensions, and improvements.[16] One question arises, however, that seems particularly important for assessing the relevance of evolutionary theorizing in the further development of Austrian economic thought. Is the gist of the quasi-sociobiological, population-oriented selection argument, which figures so prominently in Hayek's explanation of the principle, compatible with methodological individualism as defended, in pursuit of the Austrian tradition, by Hayek (1948) himself? What role is played by the individual in cultural evolution? What relevance can her/his subjective beliefs have at all, if it is an impersonal selection process that determines the regularities in social interactions?

Evolutionary Thought and Methodological Individualism

Methodological individualism is usually taken to mean the attempt to explain social phenomena by reducing them to individual actions from which they are supposed to emerge, where these individual actions are then explained independently (Hayek, 1948). By contrast, the criterion that governs the Hayekian rule selection or dissemination process is "group success"—something that does not seem reconcilable with an individualistic perspective. The contrast has repeatedly been felt as a tension impairing Hayek's theory of cultural evolution (Gray, 1984, 52; Vanberg, 1986). Indeed, a shift in the level of argumentation can hardly be denied.

Suppose an individual comes up with a variation of a hitherto prevailing rule of conduct. An attempt to explain the innovator's motives and expectations would be fully in line with methodological individualism, as would be all efforts to explain the motives and expectations of other individuals who are, or are not, going to imitate the innovator. Yet for the logic of Hayek's cultural selection process, such considerations appear irrelevant. Whatever the underlying beliefs and motives may be, a variation of rules is successful and survives if, and only if, it helps to improve (or is at least not detrimental to) the economic performance of the group. In fact, it does not even matter whether individual action concerning the rules is purposeful or purely random, that is, intelligible or not, for the result of cultural evolution. The competing groups' relative success explains where the entire process ends up and which of the individual innovative rule variations, for whatever reasons they have been undertaken, eventually become socially successful and which are doomed to fail.

Even though Hayek relies on the criterion of group success without even trying to relate it to the level of the individual, this does not necessarily mean, of course, that his theory is incompatible with an individualistic approach. In the domain of the social sciences, novelty emerges from and is disseminated through individual action. Hence, an attempt to explain the evolutionary process by reduction to individual innovative and imitative activities is quite natural, notwithstanding the fact that the very notion of dissemination implies a population as a reference base. One reservation must, however, be made. This reservation reflects a significant feature of evolutionary theories: whenever the individual innovative and imitative activities are not perfectly independent, the evolutionary process cannot entirely be reduced to the level of the individual. Some population-bound criterion or variable remains.

The independency assumption is commonly violated, for instance, in dissemination processes, where it may not be irrelevant for the behavior of some particular individual at which position in the diffusion sequence (s)he is exposed to the new item. Sometimes this kind of dependency is hidden in a self-sorting hypothesis according to which individuals with systematically changing attributes successively act in and, thereby, carry on the diffusion process.[17] More often, however, the dependency effect comes along in evolutionary theories in the form of a frequency dependency hypothesis (see Witt, 1991) that presupposes otherwise identical individuals. The individual choice among a fixed number of reactions is viewed as hinging upon the relative frequency with which the reactions have previously been chosen during the diffusion process by other individuals in the population. Relative frequency is, of course, a population-related variable.[18]

The latter case seems to apply to an individualistic foundation that could be constructed for substituting the group success criterion in Hayek's theory of cultural evolution. A new rule of conduct is retained, it is claimed, if it enhances the success of a subgroup obeying it. The rule tends to propagate in the population, whether for the subgroup's growth or for an imitation of the new rule by other subgroups. If this is interpreted as the outcome of a sequential adoption process, in which each member of the population decides on whether or not to follow the new rule, the explanatory task can be reduced to explaining the individual adoption behavior.

The implications of this individualistic model are consistent with Hayek's conjecture if the "group success" is composed of a positive net advantage that each individual can internalize by adopting, rather than not adopting, the new rule. As has been shown elsewhere (Witt, 1989b), the frequency-dependency effect plays a role here, in so far as the extent to which the new rule disseminates in a given population depends on how the size of the individual advantage varies with the relative frequency of adopters. However, as Vanberg (1986) has rightly pointed out, a problem arises in such an individualistic reconstruction where the adoption of a new rule involves social dilemmas such as, a prisoners' dilemma. Adopters may then find themselves collecting the "sucker's pay-off," if collective adoption would be advantageous, which enhances the group's success, but is vulnerable to individual defection.

In such a case, the individualistic model does not support Hayek's argumentation on the basis of the group success criterion as easily as before. Looked at more closely, it turns out that the frequency-dependency effect is now decisive for whether a positive net advantage from adopting can be internalized by an individual. If a sufficiently large number of members of the population have adopted the collectively advantageous new rule, the individual mean gain from following the rule may outweigh the mean loss caused by the remaining free riders.[19] This means that an individualistic theory of the evolutionary process now necessarily has to account for population aspects in the form of population-bound variables or criteria.

However, notwithstanding this reservation, which may have to be made quite often in evolutionary theorizing, an individualistic perspective is still possible. There is no doubt that, in evolutionary economics, the individual decision maker may be, and should be, chosen as the basic explanatory unit, for this is the level where novelty emerges and is disseminated. The frequency dependency effect does require a consideration beyond the single economic agent. But what provides the key for understanding the ongoing activities is, in last resort, still the situation as the individual perceives it.

Conclusions: What Can Be Gained?

In economics, evolutionary theorizing is often identified with the Schumpeterian tradition. This chapter has argued that such a view is not appropriate. Evolutionary theorizing requires that the emergence of novelty is recognized as a crucial feature. Due to the subjective nature of novelty in the domain of the social sciences, this necessitates, in turn, finding a solution to the subjectivism problem. The Schumpeterian tradition ignores both issues. An evolutionary theory in which the two problems are taken up is congenial in many respects to Austrian economics with its core notions of process and change and its subjectivist creed. An appropriately interpreted evolutionary approach may, therefore, be suggested as a fruitful basis for future research into those issues Austrian economics is traditionally concerned with.

If this suggestion is accepted, sacrifices and adjustments will have to be made. In particular, apriorism will have to be abandoned because evolutionary theorizing presupposes a solution to the subjectivism problem on the basis of a fallibilistic and empirically oriented methodology. This is not only a prerequisite for inquiring more deeply into individual innovative behavior and the particular dynamics it induces in the economy, but also for encountering the epistemological problems involved in the non-anticipatability of novelty. Furthermore, as explained in more detail above, the interpretation of methodological individualism will have to be adapted in order to accommodate population-bound features.

In return, evolutionary theorizing may help by enhancing the understanding of how spontaneous order in economy and society emerges and changes. This encompasses not only the institutional regularities, the rule-governed basis of spontaneous order (on which Hayek's theory of cultural evolution focuses), but also the very process of coordination of the mass of individual economic ventures and activities taking place within the institutional framework and on the basis of established rules. Concerning this process, Austrian economics may also profit from results and insights obtained in the Schumpeterian tradition. What happens here cannot fully be captured by the mere postulates of entrepreneurial alertness and arbitrage in the markets. The reasons for, and the dynamics of, innovative activities and their diffusion through the economy can provide new insights into how an economy works and why the pace and direction of its evolution varies so greatly in history and place.

Acknowledgments

An earlier draft of the chapter has been presented at George Mason University in the Market Process Center, at New York University in the Austrian Colloquium, and in a methodology workshop at the University of Freiburg. I wish to thank all participants, in particular Hans Albert, Howard Baetjer, Peter Boettke, Israel Kirzner, Don Lavoie, Mario Rizzo, and William Tulloh for most valuable discussions. Furthermore, I am grateful to J. Irving-Lessmann and Stephan Boehm for their helpful editorial advice.

Notes

1. See von Mises (1949, 18–21), Hayek (1952, ch. 3) Kirzner (1979, ch. 8 and 9), Boehm (1982), and the thoughtful discussion in O'Driscoll and Rizzo (1985, ch. 2 and 3). There is now also a British subjectivist tradition (cf. Shackle, 1972; Loasby, 1976; Wiseman, 1983) with origins and views related to Austrian economics, see Lachmann (1976) and Wiseman (1985); the connection has recently also been taken up by Loasby (1991, ch. 2).

2. See Kirzner (1973; 1979, ch. 1 and 2), Lachmann (1986), Boettke, Horwitz, and Prychitko (1986); see also Shackle (1943).

3. Schumpeter (1912, 75, my translation according to the second German edition; the appendix to the first chapter in this edition has not been included in the English edition of 1934); cf. also Nelson and Winter (1982, ch. 2), Day (1987), Allen (1988), Faber and Proops (1990, part III), Witt (1991a).

4. Cf. Fehl (1986). If it happens that, because of mutually interfering adjustments of the agents, the adaptive efforts become cyclic, motion would persist but would be confined to a closed set of states. In a broader sense, such equilibrium motions show no change.

5. At a time when ordinary business and routine dominate, that is, in a phase of "circular flow" of the economy, entrepreneurs are assumed to come up with major technical, or organizational innovations, or with creating new markets. The multiplier effects of these path-breaking activities at once attract and support imitative ventures by growing numbers of less and less creative and less skilled entrepreneurs. The economy takes off into a boom phase until, after a while, the wave of innovations and imitations has led to overcapacity. Increasing competitive pressure squeezes prices and profits; the expansion ceases. Credit repayments induce a deflationary tendency and negative multiplier effects. Depression drives inefficient productive capacity out of businesses until eventually, the economy is back in "circular flow," albeit at a higher level of output and welfare.

6. While Schumpeter thus adopted a popular notion as far as the entrepreneur is concerned (see Streissler (1972), (1983), who attributes it to von Wieser), he refrained from taking up the presumably even more prominent discussion on subjectivism, or even pointedly ignored it as Lachmann (1986, 144) argues.

7. See Kamien and Schwartz (1982), Scherer (1984), Baldwin and Scott (1987), Reinganum (1989).

8. There are, of course, considerable differences of opinion in this question, see O'Driscoll and Rizzo (1985, ch. 2), Boettke, Horwitz, and Prychitko (1986), and the recent reflections in Mäki (1990). Although the methodological intricacies of the subjectivism problem seem to have already been recognized by Carl Menger, the founder of the Austrian school did not develop a clear position in this respect, cf. Meyer (1990).

9. He argues that "action" is the result of human reasoning, namely, the logical implication of a hypothetical ends-means calculus; hence, the essential features of action should be reconstructible by analytical reasoning. For a recent reconstruction of essentialism — not apriorism — in terms of realism, see Mäki (1990).

10. Symptomatically, the Austro-American school has not been able to make much out of its early insight that a significant role could be played by novelty. Discovery or creation of novelty is related here to an entrepreneurial human element (Mises, 1949, 252–256), High (1986), Kirzner (1989, ch. 2). But the theoretical underpinnings of this relationships have still not been developed beyond the rather vague concept of alertness, from which the discovery of novelty is somehow believed to spring. For example, Kirzner (1979, 8–9) states: "indeed, we do not clearly understand how entrepreneurs get their flashes of superior foresight. We cannot explain how some men discover what is around the corner before others do. ... As an empirical matter, however, opportunities do tend to be perceived and exploited."

11. In fact, Hayek (1967a) himself explicitly relates them to the emergence of novelty in Darwinian evolutionary theory. In that theory the nonanticipatability condition concretely means that positive predictions of which phenotypic traits will occur, as a result of genetic mutations in a certain species, cannot be made.

12. For the latter cf. Eigen (1988).

13. Hayek came to appreciate the role of evolutionary phenomena only in his later work on what he labeled "social philosophy," cf. Hayek (1973, 5). In his earlier studies of economic theory in the narrower sense, which engaged most of his attention till the end of the forties, no attempt is made to introduce evolutionary theorizing. Symptomatically, there is, to my knowledge, no reference in Hayek's oeuvre in which Schumpeter (1912/34) is recognized as a seminal contribution to evolutionary economics—and not simply as yet another business cycle theory.

14. It can already be found in a line of thought in the arts, social sciences, and law beginning in Germany in the 18th century, and linked to names such as Herder, Savigny, and Wilhelm von Humboldt (see also Bowler, 1989, 104–108).

15. Similar ideas have recently been advocated more rigorously as an extension of sociobiology in the so-called "co-evolutionary view" (Cavalli-Sforza and Feldman, 1981; Lumsden and Wilson, 1981; Boyd and Richerson, 1985).

16. For an excellent appraisal see Vanberg (1986). A discussion of the critical points is beyond the space available here. In generalizing the underlying idea, Lavoie, Baetjer, and Tulloh (1990) have recently attempted an application to the domain of artificial intelligence. An equivalent to cultural evolution has a certain tradition in this field, see Schwefel (1992).

17. An explanation of what is going on here cannot avoid specifying a distribution of attributes over a population and the relative position that has been reached in that distribution. A case in point is Schumpeterian evolution. Even though much emphasis is placed here on the role of the innovative entrepreneurial individual, the actual process can only be understood if the population-bound variable 'relative entrepreneurial skill' is recognized, which ranges from the "promotor" to the "plain business man," cf. Schumpeter (1912/34, 74–94). It is argued there that innovative activities are gradually turning into imitative, and eventually, ordinary, business practices the further the process works its way through each new "swarm of entrepreneurs".

18. Note that the frequency dependency hypothesis describes only a general feature so that it may be taken as a typical example of an "algebraic theory" (Hayek, 1967a) from which only pattern predictions result.

19. Several different hypotheses have been suggested in order to explain the spontaneous solution of the dilemma along these lines (Boorman and Levitt, 1973; Axelrod and Hamilton, 1981; Witt, 1986; Güth and Yaari, 1992). They all share the crucial reliance on the frequency-dependency effect.

References

Allen, P. 1988. "Evolution, Innovation, and Economics." In *Technical Change and Economic Theory*, G. Dosi, C. Freeman, R. Nelson, G. Silverberg, L. Soete (eds.). London: Pinter, 95–119.

Axelrod, R. and Hamilton, D. 1981. "The Evolution of Cooperation," *Science* 212: 1390–1396.

Baldwin, W. L. and Scott, J. T. 1987. *Market Structure and Technological Change*. New York: Harwood.

Boehm, S. 1982. "The Ambiguous Notion of Subjectivism: Comment on Lachmann." In *Method, Process, and Austrian Economics*, I.M. Kirzner (ed.). Lexington: Heath, 41–52.

Boehm, S. 1987. "Einleitung." In *Joseph A. Schumpeter—Beiträge zur Sozialökonomie*, S. Boehm (ed.). Wien: Böhlau, 13–37.

Boettke, P., Horwitz, S., and Prychitko, D. L. 1986. "Beyond Equilibrium Economics: Reflections on the Uniqueness of the Austrian Tradition," *Market Process* 4: 6–25.

Boorman, S. A. and Levitt, P. R. 1973. "A Frequency-dependent Natural Selection Model for the Evolution of Social Cooperation Networks," *Proceedings of the National Academy of Sciences, U.S.A.* 70: 187–89.

Bowler, P. J. 1989. *Evolution—the History of an Idea*, (Rev. Ed.) Berkeley: University of California Press.

Boyd, R. and Richerson, P. J. 1985. *Culture and the Evolutionary Process*. Chicago: University of Chicago Press.

Campbell, D. T. 1965. "Variation and Selective Retention in Socio-Cultural Evolution." In *Social Change in Developing Areas: A Reinterpretation of Evolutionary Theory*, H. R. Barringer, G. I. Blanksten, R. W. Mack (eds.). Cambridge, Mass.: Schenkman.

Cavalli-Sforza, L. and Feldman, M. 1981. *Cultural Transmission and Evolution*, Princeton: Princeton University Press.

Day, R. H. 1987. "The General Theory of Disequilibrium Economics and of Economic Evolution." In *Economic Evolution and Structural Adjustment*, D. Batten, J. Casti, B. Johannson (eds.). Berlin: Springer, 46–63.

Dobzhansky, T. G. 1962. *Mankind Evolving. The Evolution of the Human Species*, New Haven: Yale University Press.

Dosi, G., Freeman, C., Nelson, R., Silverberg, G., Soete, L., (eds.) 1988. *Technical Change and Economic Theory*, London: Pinter Publishers.

Eigen, M. 1988. "Macromolecular Evolution: Dynamical Ordering in Sequence Space" In *Emerging Syntheses in Science*, D. Pines (ed.). Redwood City: Addison-Wesley, 21–42.

Faber, M. and Proops, J. L. R. 1990. *Evolution, Time, Production, and the Environment*. Berlin: Springer.

Fehl, U. 1986. "Spontaneous Order and the Subjectivity of Expectations: A Contribution to the Lachmann-O'Driscoll Problem." In *Subjectivism, Intelligi-*

bility, and Economic Understanding, I.M. Kirzner (ed.). New York: New York University Press, 72–86.

Gray, J. 1984. *Hayek on Liberty*, New York: Basil Blackwell.

Güth, W. and Yaari, M. (1992). "An Evolutionary Approach to Explaining Reciprocal Behavior in a Simple Strategic Game," In *Explaining Process and Change–Approaches to Evolutionary Economics*, U. Witt (ed.) Ann Arbor: Michigan University Press, 23–34.

Hayek, F. A. 1948. "Individualism: True and False." In *Individualism and Economic Order*. London: Routledge & Sons, 1–32.

Hayek, F. A. 1952a. "The Subjective Character of the Data of the Social Sciences." In *The Counter-Revolution of Science*. Glencoe: Free Press, 41–60.

Hayek, F. A. 1952b. *The Sensory Order*, London: Routledge & Kegan Paul.

Hayek, F. A. 1967a. "The Theory of Complex Phenomena." In *Studies in Philosophy, Politics, and Economics*, London: Routledge & Kegan Paul, 22–42.

Hayek, F. A. 1967b. "Rules, Perception and Intelligibility." In *Studies in Philosophy, Politics, and Economics*. London: Routledge & Kegan Paul, 43–65.

Hayek, F. A. 1967c. "Dr. Bernhard Mandeville," *Proceedings of the British Academy*, Vol. 12. London: Oxford University Press.

Hayek, F. A. 1971. "Nature vs. Nurture Once Again," *Encounter* 36: 81–83.

Hayek, F. A. 1973. *Law, Legislation and Liberty*. Vol. 1, *Rules and Order*. London: Routledge & Kegan Paul.

Hayek, F. A. 1979. *Law, Legislation and Liberty*. Vol. 3. *The Political Order of a Free People*. London: Routledge & Kegan Paul.

Hayek, F. A. 1988. *The Fatal Conceit*. London: Routledge.

High, J. 1986. "Equilibration and Disequilibration in the Market Process." In *Subjectivism, Intelligibility, and Economic Understanding*, I. M. Kirzner (ed.). New York: New York University Press, 111–121.

Huxley, J. S. 1943. *Evolutionary Ethics*. Oxford: Oxford University Press.

Kamien, M. I. and Schwartz, N. L. 1982. *Market Structure and Innovation*. Cambridge: Cambridge University Press.

Kirzner, I. M. 1973. *Competition and Entrepreneurship*. Chicago: University of Chicago Press.

Kirzner, I. M. 1979. *Perception, Opportunity, and Profit*. Chicago: University of Chicago Press.

Kirzner, I. M. 1989. *Discovery, Capitalism, and Distributive Justice*. New York: Basil Blackwell.

Lachmann, L. M. 1951. "The Science of Human Action," *Economica* 18: 412–427.

Lachmann, L. M. 1976. "From Mises to Shackle: An Essay on Austrian Economics and the Kaleidic Society," *Journal of Economic Literature* 14: 54–62.

Lachmann, L. M. 1982. "Ludwig von Mises and the Extension of Subjectivism." In *Method, Process, and Austrian Economics*, I. M. Kirzner (ed.). Lexington: Heath, 31–40.

Lachmann, L. M. 1986. *The Market as an Economic Process*. London: Basil Blackwell.

Lavoie, D., Baetjer, H., and Tulloh, W. 1990. "High-Tech Hayekians: Some Possible Research Topics in the Economics of Computation," *Market Process* 8: 120–146.

Loasby, B. 1976. *Choice, Complexity, and Ignorance*. Cambridge: Cambridge University Press.

Loasby, B. 1991. *Equilibrium and Evolution–An Exploration of Connecting Principles in Economics*. Manchester: Manchester University Press.

Lumsden, C. J. and Wilson, E. O. 1981. *Genes, Mind, and Culture: The Co-evolutionary Process*. Cambridge: Harvard University Press.

Mäki, U. 1990. "Scientific Realism and Austrian Explanation," *Review of Political Economy* 2: 310–344.

Menger, C. (1883) 1963. *Untersuchungen über die Methode der Socialwissenschaften*. Leipzig: Duncker & Humblot (English translation: *Problems of Economics and Sociology*, Urbana: University of Illinois Press, 1963).

Meyer, W. 1986. "Beyond Choice." In *Subjectivism, Intelligibility, and Economic Understanding*, I. M. Kirzner (ed.). New York: New York University Press, 221–235.

Meyer, W. 1990. "A Note on Menger's Philosophy of Science," *Methodus* 2: 46–47.

von Mises, L. 1949. *Human Action–A Treatise on Economics*. New Haven: Yale University Press.

Nelson, R. R. and Winter, S. G. 1982. *An Evolutionary Theory of Economic Change*. Cambridge: Harvard University Press.

O'Driscoll, G. P. and Rizzo, M. J. 1985. *The Economics of Time and Ignorance*. Oxford: Basil Blackwell.

Reinganum, J. F. 1989. "The Timing of Innovation: Research, Development, and Diffusion." In *Handbook of Industrial Organization*, R. Schmalensee and R. D. Willig (eds.), vol. I. Amsterdam: North-Holland, 849–908.

Scherer, F. M. 1984. *Innovation and Growth. Schumpeterian Perspectives*. Cambridge, Mass.: MIT Press.

Schumpeter, J. A. 1908. *Das Wesen und der Hauptinhalt der theoretischen Nationalökonomie*. Leipzig: Duncker und Humblot.

Schumpeter, J. A. 1910. "Über das Wesen der Wirtschaftskrisen," *Zeitschrift für Volkswirtschaft, Sozialpolitik und Verwaltung* 19: 271–325.

Schumpeter, J. A. 1912/34. *Theorie der wirtschaftlichen Entwicklung*. Berlin: Duncker & Humblot. (English translation: *Theory of Economic Development*, Cambridge, Mass.: Harvard University Press, 1934).

Schumpeter, J. A. 1935. "The Analysis of Economic Change," *Review of Economic Statistics* 17: 2–10.

Schwefel, H. P. 1992. "Imitating Evolution: Collective Two-Level Learning Processes." In *Explaining Process and Change–Approaches to Evolutionary Economics*, U. Witt (ed.). Ann Arbor: Michigan University Press, 49–63.

Shackle, G. L. S. 1943. "The Expectational Dynamics of the Individual," *Economica* 10: 99–129.

Shackle, G. L. S. 1959. "Time and Thought," *British Journal for the Philosophy of Science* 9: 285–298.

Shackle, G. L. S. 1972. *Epistemics and Economics*. Cambridge: Cambridge University Press.

Shackle, G. L. S. 1983. "The Bounds of Unknowledge." In *Beyond Positive Economics?* J. Wiseman (ed.). London: Macmillan, 28–37.

Shand, A. H. 1981. *Subjectivist Economics – The New Austrian School*. Oxford: Short Run Press.

Stolper, W. F. 1979. "Joseph Alois Schumpeter – A Personal Memoir," *Challenge* 21: 64–69.

Streissler, E. 1972. "To What Extent was the Austrian School Marginalist?" *History of Political Economy* 4: 426–441.

Streissler, E. 1983. "Schumpeter and Hayek: On some Similarities in their Thought." In *Reflections on a Troubled World Economy*, F. Machlup, G. Fels, H. Müller-Groeling (eds.). London: Macmillan, 356–364.

Vanberg, V. 1986. "Spontaneous Market Order and Social Rules," *Economics and Philosophy* 2: 75–100.

Vanberg, V. 1989. "Hayek as a Constitutional Political Economist," *Wirtschaftspolitische Blätter* 36: 170–182.

Waddington, C.H. 1960. *The Ethical Animal*. London: Allen and Unwin.

Winter, S. G. 1964. "Economic 'Natural Selection' and the Theory of the Firm," *Yale Economic Essays* 4: 225–272.

Wiseman, J. (ed.) 1983. *Beyond Positive Economics?* London: Macmillan.

Wiseman, J. 1985. "Lionel Robbins, the Austrian School, and the LSE tradition," *Research in the History of Economic Thought and Methodology* 3: 147–159.

Witt, U. 1986. "Evolution and Stability of Cooperation Without Enforceable Contracts," *Kyklos* 39: 245–266.

Witt, U. 1989a. "Subjectivism in Economics – a Suggested Reorientation." In *Understanding Economic Behavior*, K. G. Grunert, F. Ölander (eds.). Boston: Kluwer, 409–431.

Witt, U. 1989b. "The Evolution of Economic Institutions as a Propagation Process," *Public Choice* 62: 155–172.

Witt, U. 1991. "Reflections on the Present State of Evolutionary Economic Theory." In *Rethinking Economics: Markets, Technology and Economic Evolution*, G. M. Hodgson, E. Screpanti (eds.). Aldershot: Edward Elgar, 83–102.

Witt, U. 1992a. "Evolution as the Theme of a New Heterodoxy in Economics." In *Explaining Process and Change – Approaches to Evolutionary Economics*, U. Witt (ed.). Ann Arbor: Michigan University Press, 3–20.

Witt, U. 1992b. "Emergence and Dissemination of Innovations – Some Problems and Principles of Evolutionary Economics." In *Evolutionary Dynamics and Nonlinear Economics – A Transdisciplinary Dialogue*, R. H. Day, P. Chen (eds.). Oxford: Oxford University Press (forthcoming)

p 215 COMMENTARY
A Non-Austrian Assessment
John Foster

Austrian economics is popularly identified with methodological individual-ism, plus an insistence upon a subjectivist orientation to individual be-havior. Although Ulrich Witt continues to support these basic tenets of Austrianism at the level of motivation, he takes a significant step toward an evolutionary approach which accepts that the group may be a relevant unit of analysis when we are looking at actual behavior. Due cognizance is taken of the fact that "population-bound" features can qualify method-ological individualist explanation in an empirical setting. This concern with the empirical domain is further confirmation that the apriorism of von Mises, with its appeal for only abstract conjectures based upon subjective experience, is disappearing in modern Austrian economics. Witt prefers the methodological stance of von Hayek, with its emphasis upon the evolutionary character of cultural and institutional change.

In all this, the Schumpeterian tradition, which Witt identifies as evol-utionary economics, is taken to task. This, in itself, is fascinating given that Schumpeter also attempted to adapt his own Austrian economics to cope with questions pertaining to historical dynamics. Witt's adverse criticism also extends to the more recent neo-Schumpeterian evolutionary approach. This is understandable from an Austrian perspective since Schumpeter's insights, with their Austrian pedigree, are incorporated in an inspirational, rather than a literal, sense. It is a pragmatic school that, for example, acknowledges contributions to evolutionary economics by institutional economists, who represent a very different intellectual tra-dition from that of the Austrians. In attempting to turn Austrian economics

237

into evolutionary economics, Witt studiously ignores the rather large institutionalist literature on the subject. He has chosen to develop his evolutionary economics by extending Austrianism, in juxtaposition to a rather limited description of non-Austrian evolutionary economics.

In an evolutionary world of process and change, Witt identifies the ultimate source of endogenous change as the "emergence of novelty." Without novelty, it is argued, there would be convergence to an equilibrium state where "everything has been learned and all possible advantageous readjustments have been exploited." Such a conception of "equilibrium" places Witt in the Kirznerian, rather than the Lachmannian, tradition of modern Austrian thought. This starting point is somewhat surprising, given that the intention is to deal with questions of evolutionary change. When we are dealing with structural change in irreversible historical time, no such equilibrium can be possible. As Faber and Proops (1990, 35–36), working in a different Austrian tradition, emphasize, such an equilibrium state assumes no ignorance and, therefore, can be viewed as "an impossible notion." The notion of novelty is inseparable from that of ignorance in historical time. Ignorance precipitates decay in accordance with the entropy law and would seem to be analytically prior to novelty in analyzing the evolutionary process. Decay in systems that already exist is analyzable, but as Faber and Proops (1990, 21) argue, convincingly, "[w]herever an area of study is in an essential way subject to the emergence of novelty an *ex ante* theory cannot be developed."

There is no denial that the emergence of novelty is an important aspect of change in economic processes and that it is a subjective matter at the level of the individual. What is difficult to accept is Witt's assertion that it "provides a powerful argument for a subjectivist position in economics." George Shackle, a writer from the Lachmannian tradition of Austrianism, is cited in support, but a careful reading of Shackle's work suggests a nihilist conclusion with regard to the possibility of a subjectivist economics in any empirical domain. It is because of this that Faber and Proops (1990) avoid subjectivism and prefer to assess the extent to which neo-Austrian capital theory, which focuses on the problem of time rather than novelty, can offer insights in evolutionary economics.

In the last paragraph of section two, Witt explains why there are problems in the diffusion of novelty. Novelty grows from ignorance, but ignorance remains in proportion to the extent and applicability of novelty. Austrians normally accept the theoretical limitations involved in dealing with novelty and assert that "spontaneous order" will emerge with widespread adoption of the "best" novelty. Like the institutionalists, Witt implies that analysis of these evolutionary dynamics is possible. However, he refrains from taking up the kinds of arguments that institutionalists favour. Instead, he goes on to choose a critique of the Schumpeterian tradition as the starting point in applying his subjectivist analysis.

The critique offered of Schumpeter's own work is founded upon the fact that he does not deal with the emergence of novelty but, instead, concentrates upon diffusion. However, this "flaw," pointed to by Witt, could be construed as sensible strategy if we accept Faber and Proops' (1990) position. It is *objectively true*, at higher levels of aggregation than the individual, that a stock of novelties exists. These do emanate from the subjective experience of individuals, but their adoption in behavior is only discernible at the higher level. Schumpeter's "entrepreneur" construct is really a metaphor for the "new firm" and is focused upon the degree to which the institutional environment is favorable to the diffusion of novelty (Heertje, 1988). Particular attention is paid to the availability of credit to firms of various types. Furthermore, although it is true that Schumpeter pioneered the dichotomy between invention and innovation, Witt erects something of a straw man when he infers that this dichotomy involves new information which is "instantaneously, exhaustively and unambiguously revealed to everybody." The dichotomy seemed to be intended to point to a process problem, not an informational one. At least, that is the spirit in which neo-Schumpeterians approach the dichotomy. The practical inseparability of the two, in a knowledge sense (it is better to refer to knowledge rather than information in the context of ignorance), is widely accepted in neo-Schumpeterian circles.

Witt asserts that, as time passed, Schumpeter appeared to become less evolutionary and more neoclassical in his approach. Indeed, given his approval of the achievements of Walras, one could argue, as the institutionalists often do, that he was always neoclassical, after his early Austrian years. Thus, to them, it is highly misleading to use the term neo-Schumpeterian to describe the eclectic evolutionism of, for example, Nelson and Winter (1982). What we must remember is that all of economics was tending towards neoclassical formalism in the later part of Schumpeter's life.

Schumpeter had few mathematical skills, so this tendency in his case manifested itself, instead, in the favourable treatment of neoclassical economics in his *History of Economic Analysis*. However, this does not imply that there was any belated shift in his mixture of evolutionary dynamics and neoclassical statics, as Witt suggests. On the contrary, Schumpeterians tend to argue forcibly that there is little deviation from his early writings, such as the German edition of the *Theory of Economic Development* of 1911, in his later work.

Despite the fact that neo-Schumpeterians offer theoretical advances that are approved of by Witt, the charge stands that the emergence of novelty and the subjectivity of new knowledge are ignored. The mixture of "loose analogies" to biological natural selection, institutionalism and behavioralism is deemed to miss the fundamental subjectivist point concerning the true source of evolutionary change. It is here that the argument takes a surprising turn. Witt rejects the Austrian position, which traditionally separated it from the empirical subject matter of Schumpeterianism, that subjectivism should be concerned primarily with *a priori* conjecture of a nonempirical type. Von Mises's definition of economics as a praxeological science is rejected. Instead, the fallibilistic approach of Hayek is taken. So, in essence, only a particular strand of Austrian economics is accepted as usable in a new evolutionary economics.

Fallibilism, as enunciated in Hayek (1967), is a hypothesis testing methodology whereby conjectures about the subjective "state of mind" of individuals are made. Resultant "pattern predictions" are presumed to be falsifiable in an empirical setting. Witt asserts, contrary to Faber and Proops (1990), that because of logical limitations on the possible range of novelty that can emerge in any given situation, falsifiable hypotheses can be derived. However, it is then asserted that the principles governing the emergence of *genetic* novelty may be more easily isolated. Setting aside a burgeoning, but unacknowledged, literature that deals with problems in applying falsifiability in hypothesis testing, we see the individual disappearing over the horizon, despite all that has been said by Witt concerning a subjectivist approach to novelty. Hayek's (1988) theory of cultural evolution is discussed in fallibilistic terms. As is now well known, Hayek's evolutionary process is sociobiological in spirit with culture in place of genes and, most importantly, with competition between *groups*. Thus, spontaneous order is analyzed in terms of natural selection with some concession to Lamarckianism.

I shall not enter into discussion of the contradictions involved in Hayek's theory but, instead, refer the reader to Hodgson (1991). Witt concedes that Hayek's evolutionary account of the emergence of spontaneous order in the cultural domain relies, in no measure, upon a subjectivist approach to individual behavior. Witt defends Hayek on the grounds that all novelty must originate, as a matter of logic, at the individual level. Irrespective, Hayek's theory is a novelty diffusion one, rather than an emergence one. Thus, it would seem, Hayek must be consigned to the scrap heap along with the Schumpeterians. Curiously, Witt does not choose to press home his subjectivist logic with the same force in Hayek's case. Instead, the ground is shifted to a preoccupation with how individualistic foundations can be retained in a group theory, such as that of Hayek concerning the *adoption* of novelty.

For Witt, this problem can be solved by the application of frequency dependency models, which take explicit account of the fact that an individual's position in the diffusion sequence is important. There is little doubt that because such models take explicit account of historical time, they offer great potential for understanding evolutionary shifts. However, it is difficult to see them as offering a way of bolstering the individualist approach. Witt himself acknowledges the "free-rider" problem and the fact that an individualist theory must, then, account for "population-bound" variables. What Witt calls a mere "reservation" seems to be a more fundamental problem because analysis then must proceed at both the individual *and* the group level.

Frequency dependency models admit historical time, so we cannot pretend in some partial sense that we are looking at a set of independent individuals involved in novelty adoption. They are already bonded by the fact that they share a previous adoption from which they will have to break free. Time irreversibilities, manifested in habits, customs, conventions, etc. are an essential part of the frequency dependency model. The strict dichotomy between the individual and the group, in a behavioral, as opposed to a motivational, sense, breaks down. Schelling (1978) made this point very clear in his argument that frequency dependency models could have application in the social sciences. Witt's final defense returns to the theme that individuals must, logically, be the ultimate decision makers, despite the fact that most of what has gone before in his chapter suggests that, although this is tautologically true in a motivational sense, it does not help us to understand the behavior of organic systems beyond the preliminary phase of introspective speculation which necessarily precedes any serious scientific endeavor.

In this chapter, Witt has struggled to retain a place for subjectivism in an Austrian evolutionary economics. At no point does he succeed in offering a theory of the emergence of novelty that is integrated into an evolutionary approach. Like the Schumpeterians he criticizes, he offers a theory of diffusion. His frequency dependency theory is deeply problematical in the sense that it is difficult to reconcile with his individualist methodology. As Faber and Proops (1990) argue, the way forward for Austrians to develop an evolutionary approach is to build upon their tradition of dealing, explicitly, with processes in historical time. Individual subjectivism is inappropriate as the basis for evolutionary economics but does offer a warning to those who develop aggregate models which are over-mechanical in construction. In this regard, subjectivist critiques of neoclassical economics were entirely appropriate, as were critiques of "hydraulic" versions of Keynesianism. The capacity of individuals to spring novel surprises upon a system should always temper the conclusions we draw from the economic models that we construct on the basis of empirical regularities in time series data.

Unfortunately, Witt ignores the institutionalist literature in his quest for an evolutionary approach. This is understandable, given the battle that has raged in various guises between the Austrians and the German historical school. However, modern institutionalism is more enlightened, and there is much that Witt could have drawn from, for example, Dopfer (1986) or Hodgson (1988) in adapting Austrian economics into an evolutionary context. The latter, in particular, shows a degree of sympathy with the subjectivist position, provided it is set within a wider motivational context. Also, the absorption of the macroscopic approach of Prigogine and Stengers (1985) into modern institutional economics is a development that offers a clear bridge for Austrians to cross. Austrian depictions of the evolution of spontaneous order could be enriched by incorporation of insights from Prigogine's "self organization" approach. However, methodological individualism would have to be sacrificed as the foundation of Austrian evolutionary economics.

Once we accept some degree of time irreversibility in processes, we must also accept that individual commitment to a multiplicity of collective structures, such as households, communities and nations, exists at all points in historical time. This means that economic processes can only be understood at some supra-individual level in any defined historical period. The strict dichotomy between the individual and the group is an unenlightening one in an empirical setting, even though, logically, every aspect of a collective structure can be traced back in history to an individual act stemming from novelty. What Witt says is true tautologically. However, none of these acts occurred in isolation from the collective commitment of surrounding structure and, therefore, none can be viewed as entirely independent of supra-individual structure—in either a cooperative or conflictual sense. If we accept structural irreversibility in historical time, we must also accept that economic science might be able to learn from new approaches to irreversibility in the natural sciences, where behaviour is now being viewed increasingly from a macroscopic, rather than a microscopic, perspective.

In this assessment of Ulrich Witt's chapter, it would be inappropriate to end on too negative a tone. The chapter is evidence of a struggle to escape the limitations of Austrian economics to address evolutionary questions in the empirical domain. It is very likely that some of the most strident critiques of this endeavor will come from other Austrian subjectivists. Ulrich Witt's bravery in entering a zone where he is likely to be criticized from all sides has to be applauded. There is little doubt that in the diffusion process, whereby "evolutionary novelty" alters the discipline of economics, the Austrian emphasis upon the unpredictable and creative dimension of individual behavior will have an important place in the characterization of dynamic processes. However, just as many modern institutionalists accept aspects of subjectivism, when analysing economic motivation, so it is hoped that modern Austrians can accept that a holistic perspective has some merit when economic behavior is dealt with in the empirical domain. Then it would be possible for a shared paradigm, which deals, explicity, with the dynamics of historical processes and evolutionary change, to emerge.

References

Dopfer, Kurt. 1986. "The Histonomic Approach to Economics: Beyond Pure Theory and Pure Experience," *Journal of Economic Issues* 20: 989–1010.

Faber, Malte and Proops, John L. R. 1990. *Evolution, Time, Production and the Environment*. Berlin: Springer-Verlag.

Hayek, Friedrich A. 1967. "The Theory of Complex Phenomenon." In *Studies in Philosophy, Politics and Economics*. London: Routledge.

Hayek, Fredrich A. 1988. *The Fatal Conceit*. London: Routledge.

Heertje, Arnold. 1988. "Schumpeter and Technical Change." In *Evolutionary Economics*, Hanusch, H. (ed.). Cambridge: Cambridge University Press.

Hodgson, Geoffrey. 1988. *Economics and Institutions*. Cambridge: Polity Press.

Hodgson, Geoffrey. 1991. "Hayek's Theory of Cultural Evolution: An Evaluation in the Light of Vanberg's Critique," *Economics and Philosophy* 7: 67–82.

Nelson, Richard R. and Winter, Sidney, G. 1982. *An Evolutionary Theory of Economic Change*, Cambridge, MA: Belknap Press.

Prigogine, Ilya and Stengers, Isabelle. 1985. *Order out of Chaos*. London: Fontana.

Schelling, Thomas. 1978. *Micromotives and Macrobehavior*. New York: Norton.

9 AFTERWORD: AUSTRIAN ECONOMICS FOR THE TWENTY-FIRST CENTURY

Mario J. Rizzo

The editors of this volume have asked the contributors to take a critical look at Austrian economics and ask several questions. What does the future hold for the Austrian tradition? What areas seem particularly promising for future research? What are the weaknesses of Austrian analysis and how important are they in a total assessment of the research program? In this Afterword we shall address ourselves to these questions by taking a very broad look at the prospects for Austrian economics in the fast approaching twenty-first century. We shall address some of the themes in specific contributions to this volume in order to make a general assessment of the overall trends and prospects in the field. In the spirit of critical rationalism we shall venture a bold conjecture: *Without significant changes in its traditional research topics and strategies (as begun here and elsewhere), Austrian economics will become increasingly irrelevant to the major intellectual currents in the next century and will ultimately fail to survive.*

Austrian economics has been pronounced dead many times in this century and, for a while (i.e., the 1950s and 1960s), existed in the minds of only a handful of economists both inside and outside of the academic world. Then, marvelously, a revival occurred, almost exclusively among younger economists, in the mid-1970s. This revival has continued and grown modestly ever since. Although Austrian economics has thus survived, it has not flourished in a really significant way. It still remains largely, though not entirely, confined to the "farther reaches" of the academic world. We do not believe that it can continue this form of existence indefinitely. Austrian economics will either die in the coming century, or it will begin a true flourishing and eventual acceptance at the premier academic institutions.

Our discussion will be centered around three essential questions:

1. What kind of scholarly interaction is required for the flourishing of Austrian economics?
2. What type of research would constitute a fruitful turn in the Austrian research program?
3. What ought to be the connection between Austrian economics and free-market advocacy?

Scholarly Interaction Requirements

The intellectual climate in the mainstream of the profession has become increasingly hostile to Austrian economics. This hostility grows out of the perceived unscientific character of Austrian economics: its refusal to adopt the dogmas of formal method now so pervasive among economic practitioners. Austrian economics is concerned with understanding market and other economic phenomena in terms of causal processes generated by the desires and beliefs of individuals who are constrained by "realistic" informational and computational limits. While the precise meaning of the term "realistic" is subject to some debate (Mäki, this volume), it is clear that neoclassical economics has overstepped, by far, any reasonable imputations of knowledge and ability to deal with complexity to the "human" agents in its models. It has turned economics into a virtual physical science where the conjectural contents of the agents' minds are merely instruments of prediction and postdiction. Accordingly, Austrian economists ought to interact more with the methodologically like-minded in other schools of economics (e.g., Post Keynesianism and New Institutional Economics) and in other disciplines with an interest in economic questions (e.g., law, philosophy, and sociology). In fact, these areas, defined by their methodological commonality, are the incipient new discipline of "interpretive economics" (Lavoie, 1985), or whatever we choose to call it, that may emerge in the next century.[1] After all, the boundaries of disciplines are not fixed. Just as they have changed in the nineteenth and twentieth centuries they will change in the next. Austrians ought to be in the forefront of creating this change.

To better understand the coming transformation of economics, we must understand how economics is currently defined. Today, while there is still some recognition of a special subject-matter ("the economy"), economics has become increasingly identified with its method. In the nineteenth and early twentieth centuries the division between economics and other disciplines was over subject-matter. Economics was the science of wealth or of "man's actions in the ordinary business of life" (Marshall, 1961, 131), that is, of market transactions. By the 1930s, however, a subtle shift occurred. Lionel Robbins (1935, 16−17) argued that economics was not about a compartment of human affairs, but about all of human affairs under a specific aspect — the aspect of economizing behavior. As long as there were different nuances implicit in the idea of "economizing" and, hence, different ways of formalizing it, Robbins' definition still permitted a characterization in terms of subject-matter. But when the profession became fixated, *inter alia*, on the formalization known as Lagrange multipliers, there emerged an unmistakable movement toward defining economics in terms of its method. Gary Becker (1976, 5), for example, claims that "what most distinguishes economics as a discipline from other disciplines in the social sciences is not its subject matter but its approach." This approach has grown to be defined by: 1) maximizing behavior; 2) market equilibrium; and 3) stable preferences.[2] In more recent years the method has expanded still more to include a variety of mathematical techniques designed to implement the basic analytical structure in more sophisticated ways.

Gains from trade, intellectual or otherwise, do not exist when the preferences of the parties are completely unrelated (neither wants what the other possesses). To the extent that Austrians and Neoclassicists operate in significantly different frameworks, gains from trade do not exist because they ask different questions. It is not surprising that the answers they each provide are also different. This is very far from the difference earlier in this century between Austrians and Neoclassicists, wherein they asked similar questions but developed different answers. Our point here will clearly be controversial because it is easy to be deceived by the apparent attention to similar phenomena. However, this is illusory; it is based merely on linguistic similarities. Both schools use terms like *markets, coordination, wealth*, etc. and so it appears that they are addressing the same questions. Neoclassicists will not be satisfied with answers that are not predictive, not based on equilibrium constructs, and not modeled after the physical sciences *because* they do not "see" the same phenomena Austrians do. As both Popper and Lakatos have taught us, observation itself is theory-laden. For example, Austrians see alert entrepreneurs, while neoclassicists see only optimizing agents. Austrians see an economic world in constant flux, while neoclassicists see a world of structurally stable equations. For the former there is true surprise, while for the latter every outcome has been anticipated, if only in a probabilistic sense. Unfortunately, many would characterize these differences as "metaphysical" and, therefore, not subject to productive debate. Yet they have profound implications for the way economics is pursued.[3]

The difference between the Austrian and neoclassical research program is also visible in another way. Normally, we consider the event-to-be-explained ("explanandum-event" or simply "explanandum") as a singular event or a singular complex of events — a rise in the spot price of oil or an upward trend in a statistical time series. This is an oversimplification. Austrians, for example, see the explanandum — event as the connection, if any, between the market phenomenon and the (change in) the real desires and beliefs of individuals.[4] Austrians want to know the outward consequences or manifestations of the internal world of the human mind. How do a myriad of individual minds, acting in the external world, give rise to a spontaneous order? The method of understanding, in terms of desires and beliefs, is thus part of the question.[5]

If Austrians and neoclassicists are so far apart in the questions they ask, then looking for gains-from-trade with mainstream economists may, at the current margin, involve large sacrifices of greater gains achievable by interacting with many nonneoclassical economists. We believe that the gains from interaction with the Post Keynesians,[6] for example, may be quite significant. We have discussed this elsewhere and need not repeat the arguments here (O'Driscoll and Rizzo, 1985, 8–9).

A New Turn in Austrian Economics

Interaction or conversation with other schools of economics is not enough. Austrian economics itself must develop in new ways. As there are many directions in which it may move, by what criterion should Austrians decide to make changes? There appear to be two such criteria. First, Austrians can go along with what is currently fashionable or, better yet, with what is just beginning to excite interest among economists. By demonstrating technical skill at the forefront of the discipline, Austrians might hope to attract "the best and the brightest" to their ranks. Unfortunately, this might very well simply turn Austrians into, for example, game theorists who every now and then include a footnote to Menger or Hayek. More importantly, however, the whole process of expansion would be arbitrary because it is unrelated to the Austrian tradition — it is not an organic growth. This particular turn would only accelerate the demise of Austrian economics. It would ensure that its unique contributions would be masked by "reinterpretation" in an incompatible theoretical framework.

The second criterion for the development of Austrian ideas is Popperian (Popper, 1979, 153–190) and addresses the "problem situation" that the Austrian economist faces. Does the extension, or turn in research, provide solutions to the problems that the current state of research has left us? There are presumably many such problem situations, but our own task here is to outline the central difficulty that has arisen in the Austrian research program and then to point to a path along which a solution may be found. To understand the central difficulty we must remember that Austrians seek to provide explanations in terms of causal processes operating in real time. Thus, the tradition must deal with change and expectations. How can order spontaneously arise in a world of change? Order requires that the expectations of individuals be correct often enough so that plans will change — at least much of the time — in the direction of compatibility and that opportunities will tend not to be missed. All of this requires that individuals learn to cope with the future, or more precisely, develop some means of predicting what others will do. If, for example, an individual is in the business of making home — construction materials, he must have a good idea of how many homes builders wish to construct in the next period. The assumption of perfect foresight will not do, of course, because it violates even the smallest commitment to realism. It also *assumes* the answer to our question: How is the relevant knowledge acquired?

The problem situation of Austrian economics at the end of the twentieth century is usefully addressed by the New Institutional Economics and by Evolutionary Economics. In this volume Richard Langlois has developed themes along lines of the former approach while Ulrich Witt has pursued the latter. If human choice is not a determinate function of the objective circumstances of the previous period, are there no bounds or limits on that choice? If the answer is "no," then prediction of the actions of others is impossible and so is interpersonal order. The challenge for Austrians is to find a middle ground between complete mechanical predictability and totally unbounded freedom of choice.

In his formulation of the research agenda for economists, Carl Menger understood that institutions or regular patterns of individual choice are commonplace among human beings. The task of the social sciences is to explain their undesigned origins in individually purposeful behavior (Menger, 1985, 129–159). Menger did not, however, recognize that his research program faces an ultimate barrier. Unless human choice is determinate, an hypothesis that does not allocate even a small role to the previous institution(s) in the explanation will fail. *Institutionally-unbounded choice alone cannot explain the origins of an institution.*[7] Choice must be bounded by institutional "side constraints" (Langlois, 1989; this volume). Some Austrians have been hesitant to proceed along these lines because they have feared the ghost of the Old Institutionalism. Thorstein Veblen's definition of institutions as "group habits of thought" (Newman et al., 1954, 523) is contrary to methodological individualism and, hence, strikes fear into the Austrian heart. The idea of a living aggregate "entity" capable of thought seems preposterous. On the other hand, defining institutions as "methods of action arrived at by habituation and convention generally agreed upon" [ibid.] is far less threatening and more likely to find acceptance within the Austrian research program. This means, however, that an explanation of an institution cannot proceed in a fully reductionist manner. The economist cannot explain the origin of an institution without making reference to the *previous* institutional setting as one element in the explanation.[8]

Evolutionary economics, on the other hand, sets bounds of a different sort on the individual's freedom of choice. These bounds exclude choices that are detrimental in a significant way to the likelihood of individual or group economic survival. If people who choose according to certain criteria (e.g., those contrary to profit maximization) are selected out of economic existence, then we shall observe constraints on individual choice at the population (group) level. Here, again, Austrians have feared the departure from methodological individualism possibly implied by the idea of "group selection." Despite its name, however, group selection can easily be reformulated in at least quasi-individualist terms (Witt, this volume). For example, in the area of technology adoption, each individual's decision to adopt is dependent on how many have adopted the particular technology *before*. Thus, the size of the individual gain varies with the relative frequency of adoption. Once again, this means that a completely reductionist explanation is impossible. The individual's choice must be constrained by some aggregate data impinging on him from the outside, whether these be the result of an evolutionary process or of the previous institutional setting.

Free Market "Advocacy"

The association of Austrian economics with free-market advocacy has been the source of travail for many Austrians and it has reinforced the assertions that Austrian economics is unscientific. Austrian economics has been called mere ideology, or even worse, an economic apologia for libertarianism. If the consequences of such accusations were not so serious, it would be easy to dismiss the whole matter as absurd because it really does arise out of a negligent misunderstanding of Austrian political economy. Unfortunately, some of those who write on Austrian economics have themselves contributed to this misunderstanding by making incautious claims. Consider the following:

> Praxeology,[9] through its *wertfrei* laws, informs us that the workings of the voluntary principle and of the free market lead inexorably to freedom, prosperity, harmony, efficiency, and order; while coercion and government intervention lead inexorably to hegemony, conflict, exploitation of man by man, inefficiency, poverty and chaos. At this point, praxeology retires from the scene; and it is up to the citizen — the ethicist — to choose his political course according to the values that he hold dear (Rothbard, 1962, 880−881).

Doubtless one could interpret this statement in a way that renders it a more or less accurate representation of Austrian political economy. Nevertheless, it is likely to mislead most readers by painting such extreme alternatives, and by disregarding the quantitative magnitude of adverse effects.

To understand the connection between Austrian economics and the advocacy of free-market policies, we find it useful to state the fundamental Austrian claims in propositional form:

1. The profit and loss system has greater coordinating properties than any other feasible system of allocating resources.
2. Even moderate amounts of intervention produce results that are unsatisfactory from the point of view of the benevolent interventionist.
3. The middle-of-the-road system of intervention is unstable and leads, in the long run, to greater and greater economic control, and, in the limit, to socialism.
4. A system of vast amounts of economic control leads to poverty, that is, a decline in wealth.
5. Socialism results in calculational chaos, that is, inconsistent plans of the interveners. This produces consequences that are unsatisfactory even from their point of view — whatever it may be.[10]

All of these propositions are value-free in the sense that they do not incorporate the values of the economist.[11] Furthermore, some are likely to command assent from those outside of the Austrian School. Many market-oriented economists are likely to agree with an equilibrium version of the first proposition, that is: there will be more coordinated states in a profit and loss economy than in any other feasible system. Propositions two and four would doubtless command widespread agreement among Chicago and Public Choice economists. Furthermore, it is not even clear that these propositions, as stated, are distinctly Austrian in character. On the other hand, the third and fifth claims have a very distinctively Austrian tone, at least in the sense that they have been most developed by economists in the Austrian school. Each of these is clearly a testable proposition and can be decided without recourse to the value judgments of the economist.

The most important proposition in terms of its effect on the nature of Austrian political economy is the third. This is a dynamic claim: The middle-of-the-road system is unstable and leads to greater and greater economic control and, ultimately, to socialism. The reader will see clearly that this does much of the work in conveying an "extremist" or "ideological" impression. The third proposition forces the Austrian to confront a long-run radical institutional alternative: "Either capitalism or socialism: there exists no middle way" (Mises, 1985, 79). Since Austrians are, in their political economy, largely concerned with institutional analysis, acceptance of the dynamic proposition naturally causes them to focus attention on the two ultimate systems. In a comparison of these, most economists would adopt something similar to an Austrian political economy. On the other hand, insofar as the dynamic claim is incorrect, the scope for such global comparisons would be diminished and the nature of political economy would be changed.

Non-Austrians who are attracted to the other features of Austrian economics, but do not like the above claims, must distinguish their "dislike" from scientific disbelief. They can surely work within Austrian economics to show that these claims really do not follow from what is essential in Austrian theory, or more simply, that they are wrong. Austrian economics is, first and foremost, a way of looking at the world and of framing questions. It is only secondarily a system of conclusions about market economies which, when combined with some very commonly held value judgments, produces a free-market "advocacy." The Austrian political-economic propositions stated above are capable of being refuted and ought not to be treated as sacrosanct. In fact, let us here and now welcome interventionists and socialists to join the discussion.

Acknowledgment

I am indebted to Peter Boettke for many helpful conversations on this topic. Responsibility for errors remains mine alone.

Notes

1. Tolerance for non-neoclassical frameworks and methods is much greater in the contiguous disciplines than in what is now economics proper. There are opportunities in the former for the application of Austrian insights to a wide variety of problems. Such application would encourage the growth of "interpretive economics" in these separate fields (and with a little academic entrepreneurship the separate work could be collected into an overall field). The opportunities include, but are not limited to, the nature of entrepreneurial alertness (psychology), the evolution of rules (law), the perception of time (anthropology), the evolution of institutions (sociology), and the impact of ethical rules on the individual's ability to cope with economic change (philosophy).

2. "To many economists (including the author), however, the most striking aspect of economics is not the subject matter itself, but rather the conceptual framework within which the previously mentioned phenomena are analyzed ... What economists have in common with each other is a methodology, or paradigm, in which *all* problems are analyzed. In fact, what most economists would classify as *noneconomic* problems are precisely those problems that are incapable of being analyzed with what has come to be called the *neoclassical* or *marginalist* paradigm" (Silberberg, 1990, 2).

3. These differences cannot be settled by any simple or direct empirical test. Consider, for example, the neoclassical tenet that there are no true surprises and that all is explicable in terms of structurally stable equations. Suppose the economist is unable to find the appropriate set of structurally stable equations in a particular case. Does this "prove" that there is indeed true surprise? Of course not. The economist will just continue to pursue his search until a set is found (and one can always force the past into some structural mold). In fact, we are not here dealing with an hypothesis but with a paradigm or research program.

4. "The object of our study is therefore to establish a degree of correspondence between a phenomenon and an idea" (Lachmann, 1971, 18).

5. Ultimately, method and subject-matter are not easily distinguishable. As Marshall McLuhan said of television, the medium is the message (i.e., the manipulated message). See McLuhan and Fiore (1967).

6. The noted Post Keynesian, Paul Davidson, is excluded by his own choice. See Davidson (1989, 467–87).

7. See O'Driscoll and Rizzo (1985, 6, 32, 39–42) and Boettke (1989).

8. After writing this, the present author learned of two extremely important articles. The first is by Joseph Agassi (1975), in which the middle-ground position adopted above is called "institutional individualism." The second is by Malcolm Rutherford (1989), who demonstrates clearly that the sharp contrast between methodological individualism and institutional economics rests on a superficial understanding of each and cannot be sustained by further analysis.

9. By "praxeology" is meant the broad science of purposeful behavior. Economics is a subdivision of the science that is applied to market exchanges.

10. It should be obvious that this statement excludes interveners whose intention is to create chaos.

11. The first involves the values of those who participate in the economy as manifest in the coordination of their plans. The second and fifth say that the results of government control are contrary to the values (goals) of the intervener. The third involves no value judgments. The fourth defines wealth in terms of the economic agents' preferences.

References

Agassi, Joseph. 1975. "Institutional Individualism," *British Journal of Sociology* 26: 144–55.

Becker, Gary S. 1976. *The Economic Approach to Human Behavior*. Chicago: University of Chicago Press.

Boettke, Peter J. 1989. "Evolution and Economics: Austrians as Institutionalists." In *Research in the History of Economic Thought and Methodology*, Warren J. Samuels (ed.). Vol. VI. Greenwich, CT: JAI Press, 73–89.

Davidson, Paul. 1989. "The Economics of Ignorance or Ignorance of Economics?," *Critical Review* 3: 467–87.

Lachmann, Ludwig M. 1971. *The Legacy of Max Weber*. Berkeley: The Glendessary Press.

Langlois, Richard N. 1989. "What Was Wrong with the Old Institutional Economics (and What Is Still Wrong with the New)?" *Review of Political Economy* 1: 270–98.

Lavoie, Don. 1985. "The Interpretive Dimension of Economics: Science, Hermeneutics and Praxeology." Center for the Study of Market Processes. Working Paper 15. Fairfax, VA: George Mason University.

Marshall, Alfred. [1920] 1961. *Principles of Economics*, I. (Variorum) 9th ed. London: Macmillan and Co.

McLuhan, Marshall and Quentin Fiore. 1967. *The Medium is the Massage*. New York: Random House.

Menger, Carl. [1883] 1985. *Investigations into the Method of the Social Sciences with Special Reference to Economics*. Translated by F. J. Nock. New York: New York University Press.

Mises, Ludwig von. [1962] 1985. *Liberalism — in the Classical Tradition*. Translated by Ralph Raico. Irvington, New York: Foundation for Economic Education, and San Francisco, CA: Cobden Press.

Newman, Philip C., Gayer, Arthur D., and Spencer, Milton H., 1954. *Source Readings in Economic Thought*. New York: W. W. Norton.

O'Driscoll, Gerald P. and Rizzo, Mario J. (1985). *The Economics of Time and Ignorance*. Oxford: Basil Blackwell.

Popper, Karl R. 1979. "On the Theory of the Objective Mind." In *Objective Knowledge*. Oxford: Clarendon Press.

Robbins, Lionel. 1935. *An Essay on the Nature and Significance of Economic Science*, 2nd edn. London: Macmillan and Co.

Rothbard, Murray N. 1962. *Man, Economy and State*, vol. II. Princeton: D. Van
   Nostrand.
Rutherford, Malcolm. 1989. "Some Issues in the Comparison of Austrian and
   Institutional Economics." In *Research in the History of Economic Thought and
   Methodology*, Warren J. Samuels (ed.). Vol. VI. Greenwich, CT: JAI Press,
   159–72.
Silberberg, Eugene. 1990. *The Structure of Economics*. 2nd edn. New York:
   McGraw-Hill.

10 AFTERWORD: APPRAISING AUSTRIAN ECONOMICS: CONTENTIONS AND MISDIRECTIONS

Lawrence H. White

I suppose that the invitations to Mario Rizzo and me to write afterwords to this volume on Austrian economics reflects Bruce Caldwell's and Stephan Boehm's recognition that there are few "practicing Austrians" among the other contributors.[1] In a volume of essays criticizing and calling for new directions in a research program, it is appropriate to provide some space to proponents of the research program being criticized, if only to flag any gross misinterpretations or other errors resulting from insufficient familiarity with the literature. Given that Israel Kirzner is the only practicing Austrian who was assigned to discuss a specific essay, it has been left to the authors of the afterwords to scrutinize the rest of the volume from an Austrian perspective.

This volume as a whole has proven an interesting undertaking, and I commend the editors and contributors for their thoughtful efforts. I find the essays by Uskali Mäki and Martin Ricketts, and the comment by Kirzner, especially enlightening. It goes without saying that such a volume can only be a complement and not a substitute for reading the actual works of Ludwig von Mises, F. A. Hayek, Israel Kirzner and other members of the modern Austrian school. Trying to form one's view of Austrian economics by reading this volume alone would be like trying to evaluate a school of filmmaking by reading various critics' and filmmakers' accounts, never having viewed the films themselves.

The essays are permeated by methodological concerns. It was certainly appropriate to devote one chapter explicitly to methodology, and Mäki's piece is an excellent and constructive contribution. But the benefits from methodology decline rapidly at the margin. The additional chapter on subjectivism, and the attention paid to methodological issues in other chapters, have crowded out a potentially more valuable discussion of the substantive contributions of modern Austrian economics. Fuller treatment of the heuristic explanatory theories and their applications offered by Austrians, following the example of the revealing Ricketts-Kirzner exchange on the theory of entrepreneurship, would have been welcome. There might have been critical appraisals of the modern Austrian work on capital, interest, business cycles, monetary and banking institutions, monopoly and antitrust, law, interventionism, and socialism. These contributions are "the practical consequences of adopting [an Austrian] stance towards economics," to use Peter Earl's words. Important as methodology is for the validation of an approach, surely the flourishing, or otherwise, of the Austrian research program depends on whether it generates interesting empirical "conjectures and refutations." It would be regrettable if this volume were to reinforce the mistaken impression that Austrian economics is "all (methodological) talk and no (explanatory) action."

In the remainder of my remarks I will try to defend some aspects of Austrian economics against apparent misunderstanding (largely due to insufficient familiarity) by several of this volume's contributors. Because of time and space constraints, I will naturally have to neglect many minor problems that might also have been addressed.

Austrian Economics as Such is Nonprescriptive

Ludwig von Mises (1966, 885) firmly maintained that economic analysis is nonprescriptive (or *wertfrei*): "it is perfectly neutral with regard to all judgments of value, as it refers always to means and never to the choice of ultimate ends." To render a positive or negative judgment on a particular government policy *as an economist* was, for Mises, to find it an appropriate or inappropriate *means* to a given end. To judge an end itself as worthy, and on that basis to *prescribe* a certain policy, takes one outside the domain of economics. Israel Kirzner (1976) and Murray N. Rothbard (1976), while placing different "spins" on it, have both endorsed this view — so, too, has Mario Rizzo in his Afterword to the present volume. The contributors to this volume might understandably have wished to criticize the arguments Austrians have advanced on behalf of *Wertfreiheit*, or to appraise the extent to which Austrians themselves have adhered to the doctrine in practice. It is disturbing, though, to find more than one contributor apparently unaware that Austrians claim to be doing *wertfrei* economics.

Alan P. Hamlin's chapter "On the Possibility of Austrian Welfare Economics" proposes that Austrian value theory is "a preference based theory of good," when actually — consistent with the doctrine of *Wertfreiheit* — it is not a theory of good at all. It is a positive theory of relative prices and resource allocation. Hamlin also cites (a secondary account of) Franz Brentano's school as providing, "within the Austrian tradition," a "second theory of value" that "defines value in terms of individuals' *right* preferences." Such a theory is obviously not a positive price theory. But Brentano and his school were philosophers, not economists. Their work is not within the tradition of modern Austrian *economics*. It is perplexing that Hamlin would suggest otherwise. It is perhaps necessary to note explicitly that Austrian economics uses the term "value" in a wholly nonnormative, nonphilosophical way.

The Austrian perspective on value and markets introduced by Carl Menger, as Kirzner (1992, 96) has explained, leads one to see "consumer valuations governing the entire structure of production and rigorously determining the allocation of resources" in a free market system. Such a perspective is analytical rather than normative: it affirms "consumer sovereignty" as a fact rather than as a good thing. Kirzner goes on to note that, when it comes to judging the *desirability* of the market system's results, the analyst remains free to deny that consumers' preferences always deserve complete respect. The analyst is also free to deny that the inherited patterns of property entitlements (providing the various amounts of wealth with which consumers can express their preferences) is ideal.

Menger (1981, 53, 148) himself held that consumers can be mistaken regarding what needs they really have (e.g., some worship false idols), regarding the actual relative importance of their needs (some choose momentary pleasures at the expense of long-term well-being), and regarding which products actually serve to meet their presumed needs (some buy ineffective medicines, cosmetics, and charms). There are certainly contexts in which it makes sense to distinguish, as Menger did, between real and merely imagined needs, between real and merely imagined importance to well-being, and between real and merely imagined properties of goods. But economic theory is not one of those contexts. Whatever explanatory or normative use may be made of these distinctions, Mises (1981a, 170–174) was correct to insist that they have no role to play in the subjective theory of economic value. Economic theory does not incorporate any notion of a "correct" preference ordering among goods. A subjectivist economist does not conflate "what A prefers" with "what is truly good for A," because the subjective theory of value does not claim to deal with the latter.

Nor does economics furnish any notion of a "correct" distribution of (pre-trade) property entitlements. Mises (1981b, 490) pointed out that the incomes and wealth positions of individuals are not completely arbitrary in a free market economy; they reflect the market value of those individuals' contributions toward meeting the wants of other market participants. Kirzner (1989; 1992, ch. 13) adds that entrepreneurial profits are not won at the expense of other market participants; they are (in a relevant sense) created by those who discover them. But neither of these analytical points constitutes an endorsement of the inherited *status quo* distribution of property ownership.

Hamlin also proposes that "moral individualism" is an aspect of the Austrian position. Austrian economics supposedly holds that we must be concerned with the good of individuals, and further holds that there is no sense to the concept of the collective good. I personally find these moral views congenial, but they are no part of Austrian economics. There is no moral component to Austrian economics as such. It is noteworthy that Hamlin fails to cite any Austrians acknowledging that their economics incorporates moral individualism.

When Mises (or Kirzner) criticizes an interventionist policy as inconsistent with the good of individuals, he does so because this norm has been espoused by those who propose the policy (or because it is otherwise thought to be a norm one can properly take for granted). The Misesian strategy is always to seek an immanent critique of an interventionist measure, that is, to attempt to show that it does not attain its own ostensible end, so that arguments over the goodness of ultimate ends remain unnecessary.[2] It is conceivable that one might accept the positive lessons of Austrian economics while rejecting moral individualism, and consequently reject the desirability of free markets. Rather than various theories of good being possible "within" the Austrian tradition, different theories of good are compatible with Austrian economics because they are on a different plane.

The opening paragraph of Robert Sugden's comment on Hamlin begins: "There can be no doubt that much of Austrian economics is prescriptive in character: it is concerned with recommending the institutions of the market." It is true that much of applied Austrian economics is concerned with spelling out the consequences of adopting market or nonmarket institutions. Later in his comment Sugden cites the relevant example of the early Hayek's comparisons between the likely outcomes of market and planned economies. It is also true that Austrian analysis lends itself to finding market institutions comparatively benign (when joined to morally individualistic norms, for example, that the greater provision of the goods and services desired by market participants is a good thing). But Sugden appears, quite inappropriately, to consider Hayek's political philosophy as part of "Austrian economics." The only work he cites in his opening paragraph is Hayek's *The Constitution of Liberty*, which is not primarily a work of economics. Sugden's comment overall cites four of Hayek's works in political philosophy, and only one collection of his economic essays. Hayek's political philosophy obviously contains many noneconomic elements. One should not attribute its undeniably prescriptive character (much less any of Hayek's particular prescriptions) to Austrian economics.

Interpersonal Hedonic Comparisons Cannot Be Derived From Economic Theory

Jeremy Shearmur wonders why economists (both Austrian and neoclassical) hold the view that "we are not able to undertake inter-subjective comparisons of well-being." Shearmur finds such views "grotesquely false" because we can certainly empathize with people who are hungry or thirsty. He is "unmoved" by the economists' reply that such comparisons do not have scientific status, because he considers them open to Popperian criticism. Therefore, economists need not avoid interpersonal comparisons "provided that these are . . . made in ways that are open to intersubjective appraisal and criticism."

Rather than wonder why economists hold that intersubjective hedonic comparisons are illegitimate in economics, Shearmur might have consulted the *locus classicus* of this view, a book reflecting Austrian influences, Lionel Robbins' *An Essay on the Nature and Significance of Economic Science*.[3] Robbins (1984, 140–141) recognized that "of course, in daily life we do continually assume that the comparison can be made," but notes that interpersonal hedonic comparisons rest on merely conventional assumptions that "cannot be justified by appeal to any kind of positive science."

Robbins (1984, 136–39) was particularly concerned to point out that the economic law of diminishing marginal utility does not imply (as had been widely thought) that a rich man receives less satisfaction or pleasure from an additional dollar than does a poor man. Economic value theory (or "consumer theory") has no such implication because "utility" in the theory is only an ordinal index of personal preference (as Hamlin points out in his contribution to this volume). It is not an index of pleasure, or well-being, or of any other hedonic or physiological magnitude that could conceivably (by the methods of *any* science) be measured on an inter-subjective scale.[4] The assumption that behind preference scales lie measurable magnitudes, as Robbins wrote, "is not an assumption which need anywhere be made in modern economic analysis, and it is an assumption which is of an entirely different kind from the assumption of individual scales of relative valuation." Occam's Razor therefore excludes the assumption from economic theory.

As if against Shearmur, Robbins (1984, 139–140) argued further that interpersonal hedonic comparisons are *not*, in fact, open to disciplined appraisal and criticism: "*There is no means of testing the magnitude of A's satisfaction as compared with B's.*" Confronted with a spokesman's claim that "members of his caste (or his race) were capable of experiencing ten times as much satisfaction from given incomes as members of an inferior caste (or an "inferior" race), we could not refute him." We "might poke fun at him" or "flare up with indignation," but "we could not show that he was wrong in any objective sense." Though Shearmur appears to believe otherwise, he does not tell us *how* he believes we could test, criticize, or otherwise appraise such comparisons. Nor does he tell us why doing so should be considered an activity for economists (rather than for social psychologists), given that propositions concerning inter-personal hedonic comparisons cannot be derived from economic theory. Robbins (1984, 140) added that physiological tests could not be used to make hedonic measurements: "If we tested the state of [A's and B's] blood-streams, that would be a test of blood, not satisfaction." Inter-personal physiological or other physical comparisons are certainly open to scientific criticism and appraisal in their own terms, but such endeavors again do not constitute the appraisal of propositions derivable from economic theory.

Robbins (1984, 141) did not claim that policy analysis founded on interpersonal comparisons of satisfaction or "social utility" is necessarily absurd. He argued only that it should be recognized for what it is: "a development of an ethical postulate," namely, that of Benthamite utili-tarianism, which "does not at all follow from the positive assumptions of pure [economic] theory." It does not at all follow, first, because interpersonal comparisons require a "psychological hedonism" (Robbins, 1984, fn. 1, 142) that is extraneous to economic theory, and secondly, because the normative use of interpersonal comparisons additionally requires an extraneous "ethical hedonism" of the sort provided by Benthamite utilitarianism.

Shearmur conjectures that economists swear off interpersonal welfare comparisons out of a concern to avoid making normative judgements, and he correctly observes that such a swearing-off is not sufficient to avoid normative judgements. Naturally, anyone who dispenses economic policy advice must do so against the background of some normative standard. But those who advance non-Benthamite normative standards are free to proceed without the unneccessary baggage of interpersonal hedonic comparisons.[5]

An Austrian Welfare Economics Is More Than Possible; It Exists

Hamlin wants to establish the possibility of an Austrian welfare economics. Astonishingly and regrettably, he takes no notice of the efforts already made in that direction by modern Austrians. The most prominent of these efforts, whose titles alone make their relevance obvious, are Kirzner's recent essay "Welfare Economics: A Modern Austrian Perspective" (Kirzner, 1992, ch. 11); chapter 6 of Kirzner's *Competition and Entrepreneurship*, entitled "Competition, Welfare, and Coordination" (Kirzner, 1973); and Rothbard's "Toward a Reconstruction of Utility and Welfare Economics" (Rothbard, 1956). Having overlooked these works, Hamlin ends up struggling to reinvent the outlines of an Austrian welfare economics that is already largely embodied in Kirzner's work.

The only "representatives" of contemporary Austrian economics Hamlin cites are Ludwig Lachmann and Jack Wiseman, whose views are distinctly more "nihilistic" than those found in the mainstream of modern Austrian economics. Contrary to Hamlin's concerns, which are undoubtedly based on his reading of Lachmann and Wiseman, Austrian economists do not characteristically hold that the future is so unknowable as to make it infeasible for us to identify even the broad patterns of the effects of alternative economic policies.

Shearmur also worries that a serious Austrian subjectivist must concede that individuals may have demonstrably wrong views of the objective world, and that such a concession weakens the political argument for freedom by allowing that state paternalism may be benevolent. Carl Menger, the founder of the Austrian school, himself made such a concession (Kirzner, 1992, 94–95). Lachmannian "nihilism" also provides such an opening. As Brian Loasby notes (with Christopher Torr providing a supporting quotation from Lachmann), a Lachmannian "expects co-ordination failure to be endemic."[6] The mainstream Austrian position, however, recognizes that freedom in a market setting sets in motion a powerful process for discovering and correcting error, while central planning and interventionism do no such thing (Kirzner, 1992, ch. 1). Stephan Boehm in this volume appropriately notes that in Hayek's theoretical vision, a free economy does not tend to get stuck, break down, or destabilize.[7]

Despite his evidently limited acquaintance with Austrian economics, Hamlin, nonetheless, manages to arrive at the key Kirznerian point that the basis for an Austrian welfare economics may be found in a concern for economic processes rather than end-states. He nearly grasps Kirzner's point that the task of such an undertaking is to evaluate institutional structures in terms of their *ability to facilitate coordination*. I say "nearly" because, although Hamlin speaks of "ability to coordinate" as a norm for institutions, he appears to mean by that their ability to resolve conflicts of interest, rather than (with Kirzner) their conduciveness to processes that will swiftly and surely discover and eliminate unexploited gains from production and trade.

Austrians who accept Kirzner's coordination norm endorse the market not just because it is feasible (doesn't make impossible demands), as Hamlin proposes, but because their positive theory tells them that the market does coordinate plans. They do not "lack the basis for any judgment of 'betterness'" in addressing policy alternatives. Such a normative basis comes from outside *wertfrei* economic analysis, of course, but there is a sense in which the coordination norm is more "Austrian" than other norms. Consistent with Hamlin's vision of an Austrian welfare economics, a welfare economics using the Kirznerian coordination norm is indeed less ambitious than a neoclassical welfare economics of the sort that goes beyond the Pareto criterion to use an interpersonally aggregative Social Welfare Function.[8]

Austrians Are Not Blind to the Theory of the Firm

Peter Earl suggests that their focus on *market* processes seems to have "blinded" most Austrians to the ways in which firms use internal planning systems, as explained by Ronald Coase (1937) or Oliver Williamson (1975). Earl even speculates that the insight of the transaction-cost literature — that internal planning takes place within firms because markets are imperfect in some sense — discomforts Austrians because it "may be too much like the thin edge of a wedge towards recognizing possible merits of a mixed economy." In fact there is no incompatibility of either sort between Austrian economics and the Coasean theory of the firm.[9] Kirzner (1992, 161–162) has shown that the Coasean view of the firm as "an island of planning in the sea of the market economy" can be treated as complementary to the Austrian view of the knowledge problems inherent in economy-wide planning. Richard Langlois emphasizes in this volume that recent developments in the theory of the firm are congenial to Austrian economics, and offer a fertile field for the application of Austrian insights.

Langlois himself, however, finds that "Austrians have paid comparatively little attention [to] the business firm," and speaks of "the reluctance of Austrians as a group to take Hayekian insights into the theory of the firm." These statements (and *a fortiori* Earl's remarks) might appropriately have been tempered by taking notice of published work by Donald Boudreaux and his coauthors that applies Austrian insights to the theory of the firm (Boudreaux and Ekelund 1987; Boudreaux and Holcombe 1989).

Concluding Remarks

It would be unfair for me to criticize Mario Rizzo's Afterword here, given that he has not had the opportunity to criticize mine. But largely to provide a counterweight to his remarks, I would like to make here the following three related declarations: (1) The main playing fields of the economics profession have not become increasingly tilted against Austrian economics in recent years (neither have they become significantly less tilted); (2) Greater gains are to be expected from interacting with neoclassical economists than with Post Keynesians and old-style Institutionalists; (3) I do not find the modern Austrian School's association with free-market advocacy a "source of travail," nor do I believe that many Austrians do.

The crucial fact of the matter, as Israel Kirzner (1992, 10) has recently emphasized, is that despite their methodological differences both Austrian and neoclassical (equilibrium-centered) economics contribute to our understanding of "the co-ordinative properties of the market." In the present volume, Kirzner rightly describes Austrian economics as "sharing with mainstream neoclassical economics an appreciation for the systematic outcomes of markets, but differing from it in the understanding of how these outcomes are in fact achieved." The contributions of Post Keynesian and old-style Institutionalist economics are almost entirely of another sort. (Rizzo recognizes this contrast, but does not draw from it what seems to me the obvious conclusion as to where lie the greater gains from intellectual interaction.) It would be a mistake to reason in this regard that "my (methodological) enemy's enemy is my friend."

Austrians should of course be ready to acknowledge valid economic insights arrived at by members of any school, should conduct their own research with strict objectivity, and should be careful not to make incautious claims that would play into the hands of those who are eager to dismiss them as promarket apologists with foregone conclusions. But Austrians need not play down the fact, again in Kirzner's (1992, 10−11) words, that "it has been the mid-century extension, by Mises and by Hayek, of the Austrian understanding of the entrepreneurial-competitive market process which has supported the most consistent and profound appreciation for the benign consequences of market co-ordination." On the contrary: with events in Central and Eastern Europe having dramatically widened the credibility of "the Mises-Hayek demonstration of the fallacy of seeking social efficiency *without* the market" (Kirzner, 1992, 36), Austrian economists should be able to make profitable use of their intellectual capital by stepping up their applied research into the dynamic problems of the mixed economy.[10]

Acknowledgment

I thank George Selgin for comments.

Notes

1. Of the contributors to Richard Ebeling's (1991) recent conference volume of Austrian work, only Israel Kirzner and I are also contributors to the present volume.

2. As Rothbard (1976) indicates, this strategy has its limitations. It has little or nothing to say about deliberately acquisitive interventionism (rent-seeking).

3. He might also have consulted Cooter and Rappoport (1984). Their account is sympathetic to Robbins' opponents who wished economists to make interpersonal comparisons of material welfare.

4. It is for this reason that I speak of "interpersonal *hedonic* comparisons." When "utility" is interpreted as an ordinal index of personal preference, "interpersonal *utility* comparisons" are simply an absurdity.

5. I have in mind such alternative ethical standards as Millian utilitarianism (Mises, 1978), the coordination norm (Kirzner, 1992, ch. 11), and libertarian natural rights (Rothbard, 1982).

6. Peter Earl suggests, perhaps facetiously, that no Austrian could really think this

way, because it would run counter to "the typical anti-interventionist stance of Austrians." But Lachmann never subscribed to such a stance.

7. Peter Earl should, therefore, not be suprised that Austrians have not been keen to embrace Hyman Minsky's view that financial market institutions are inherently unstable. For an Austrian critique of Minsky's and similar views see Selgin (forthcoming).

8. Kirzner (1985, ch. 6) applies the coordination norm to government economic regulation in a rather general way.

9. This speculation is puzzling given that Coase and Demsetz, two pioneers of transaction-cost economics, are generally considered staunch defenders of free markets rather than the mixed economy.

10. Jeffrey Friedman (1991, 156) has recently called for Austrians to undertake research of just this sort (in the course of his larger plea for scholars to examine whether minimal statism can be given a stronger consequentialist grounding). Unfortunately, he is (by his own admission) unaware of any efforts that have been made to apply the Mises-Hayek analysis to contemporary mixed-economy problems. At a minimum he should consult Kirzner (1985, ch. 6), Lavoie (1985), Selgin (1988, ch. 7) and, taking a somewhat different tack, Grinder and Hagel (1977).

References

Boudreaux, Don, and Ekelund, Robert B., Jr. 1987. "Regulation as an Exogenous Response to Market Failure: A Neo-Schumpeterian Response," *Journal of Institutional and Theoretical Economics* 143 (December): 537−54.

Boudreaux, Donald J., and Holcombe, Randall G. 1989. "The Coasian and Knightian Theories of the Firm," *Managerial and Decision Economics* 10 (June): 147−54.

Cooter, Robert, and Rappoport, Peter. 1984. "Were the Ordinalists Wrong About Welfare Economics?", *Journal of Economic Literature* 22 (June): 507−30.

Coase, R. H. 1937. "The Nature of the Firm," *Economica* n.s. 4 (November): 386−405.

Ebeling, Richard M. (ed.) 1991. *Austrian Economics: Perspectives on the Past and Prospects for the Future* (vol. 17 of the "Champions of Freedom" series). Hillsdale, MI: Hillsdale College Press.

Friedman, Jeffrey. 1991. "Postmodernism vs. Postlibertarianism," *Critical Review* 5 (Spring): 145−58.

Grinder, Walter E. and Hagel, John, III. 1977. "Toward a Theory of State Capitalism: Ultimate Decision-making and Class Structure," *Journal of Libertarian Studies* 1 (Winter): 59−79.

Kirzner, Israel. 1973. *Competition and Entrepreneurship*. Chicago: University of Chicago Press.

———. 1976. "Philosophical and Ethical Implications of Austrian Economics." In *The Foundations of Modern Austrian Economics*, Edwin G. Dolan, (ed.). Kansas City: Sheed & Ward, 75−88.

————. 1985. *Discovery and the Capitalist Process*. Chicago: University of Chicago Press.

————. 1989. *Discovery, Capitalism, and Distributive Justice*. Oxford: Basil Blackwell.

————. 1992. *The Meaning of Market Process: Essays in the Development of Modern Austrian Economics*. London: Routledge.

Lavoie, Don. 1985. *National Economic Planning: What is Left?* Cambridge, MA: Ballinger.

Menger, Carl. 1981. *Principles of Economics*. New York: New York University Press.

Mises, Ludwig von. 1966. *Human Action: A Treatise on Economics*, 3rd ed. Chicago: Henry Regnery.

————. 1978. *Liberalism: A Socio-Economic Exposition*. Kansas City: Sheed Andrews and McMeel.

————. 1981a. *Epistemological Problems of Economics*. New York: New York University Press.

————. 1981b. *Socialism: An Economic and Sociological Analysis*. Indianapolis: Liberty Classics.

Robbins, Lionel. 1984. *An Essay on the Nature and Significance of Economic Science*, 3rd ed. New York: New York University Press.

Rothbard, Murray N. 1956. "Toward a Reconstruction of Utility and Welfare Economics." In *On Freedom and Free Enterprise*, Mary Sennholz, (ed.). Princeton: Van Nostrand, 224–262.

————. 1976. "Praxeology, Value Judgments, and Public Policy." In *The Foundations of Modern Austrian Economics*, Edwin G. Dolan, (ed.) Kansas City: Sheed & Ward, 89–111.

————. 1982. *The Ethics of Liberty*. Atlantic Highlands, NJ: Humanities Press.

Selgin, George. 1988. *The Theory of Free Banking*. Totowa, NJ: Rowman and Littlefield.

————. (Forthcoming). "Banking 'Manias' in Theory and History," *Journal of Financial Services Research*.

Williamson, Oliver E. 1975. *The Economic Institutions of Capitalism*. New York: The Free Press.

Name Index

Abele, H., 15, 23 n. 1
Agassi, J., 253 n. 8
Albert, H., 231
Alchian, A. A., 77, 175
Allen, P., 231 n. 3
Allen, R. G. D., 24 n. 10
Alter, M., 23 n. 1
Arrow, K. J., 20
Axelrod, R., 173, 232 n. 19

Baetjer, H., 231, 232 n. 16
Baldwin, W. L., 231 n. 7
Barro, R. J., 139
Bartley, W. W. III, 122
Barzel, Y., 175
Becker, G. S., 247
Bentham, J., 110
Black, R. D. C., 2
Blaug, M., 2, 13, 17–18, 56
Bliss, C. J., 24 n. 17
Boadway, R., 205 n. 1
Boehm, S. B., 57, 160, 163, 189, 218, 231, 231 n. 1, 264
Boettke, P. J., 165, 190 n. 2, 231, 231 n. 2, 231 n. 8, 253, 253 n. 7
Böhm-Bawerk, E. von, 10, 22, 31–32, 218
Boland, L. A., 139
Bonar, J., 4
Boorman, S. A., 232 n. 19
Boudreaux, D. J., 265
Bowler, P. J., 232 n. 14
Boyd, R., 232 n. 15
Brentano, F., 259

Broome, J., 205 n. 2, 206 n. 4
Browne, M. S., 23 n. 8
Bruce, N., 205 n. 1
Buchanan, J. M., 83 n. 2, 104, 114–116, 118, 169, 174, 193, 203, 211

Caldwell, B. J., 2, 23, 23 n. 6, 57, 125
Campbell, D. T., 226
Cantillon, R., 143
Cartwright, N., 58
Cassel, G., 22
Casson, M., 143–145, 147, 153–154
Cavalli-Sforza, L. L., 232 n. 15
Chamberlin, E. H., 8
Cheung, S. N. S., 175, 179 n. 10
Chipman, J. S., 24 n. 20
Chisholm, R., 206 n. 6
Clower, R. W., 161
Coase, R. H., 138–140, 153, 175, 176, 178, 179 nn. 10–11, 184, 264, 267 n. 9
Coats, A. W., 2
Commons, J. R., 165
Cooter, R. D., 266 n. 3
Cosgel, M. M., 179 n. 9
Cournot, A. A., 21
Cowling, K., 76
Craver, E., 6, 23 n. 7
Crawford, R. G., 175
Csontos, L., 179 n. 4
Currie, M., 10

Darwin, C., 170, 186, 188, 226

Subject Index